T0132665

# The Debugger's Handbook

# The Debugger's Handbook

J. F. DiMarzio

Auerbach Publications is an imprint of the
Taylor & Francis Group, an informa business

Auerbach Publications
Taylor & Francis Group
6000 Broken Sound Parkway NW, Suite 300
Boca Raton, FL 33487-2742


Printed in the United States of America on acid-free paper
10 9 8 7 6 5 4 3 2 1

International Standard Book Number-10: 0-8493-8034-0 (Hardcover)
International Standard Book Number-13: 978-0-8493-8034-1 (Hardcover)



**Library of Congress Cataloging-in-Publication Data**

DiMarzio, J.F.
The debugger's handbook / Jerome F. DiMarzio.,
p. cm.
Includes bibliographical references and index.
ISBN 0-8493-8034-0 (alk. paper)
1.Debugging in computer science. 2. Computer software--Quality control. I. Title.

QA76.9.D43D56 2006
004.2'4--dc22 2006044272

**Visit the Taylor & Francis Web site at**
**http://www.taylorandfrancis.com**

**and the Auerbach Web site at**
**http://www.auerbach-publications.com**

# Dedication

This book is dedicated first and foremost to my family — to my loving wife, Suzannah, for her love, dedication, and work, and to our children, without whom it would be meaningless.

# Contents

# About the Author

**J.F. DiMarzio** is an IT manager with 14 years of experience in the technology industry. His other books have been translated into five languages and sold worldwide. He currently works as a management consultant in the southeastern United States.

# Acknowledgments

I would also like to thank a number of friends, family, and other important people who each made this possible in their own way — Mom, Dad, Matt, Diana, Laura Lewin and the team at Studio B, John Wyzalek, Kimberly Hackett and the team at Taylor & Francis ... Go Red Sox!

# Preface

## About This Title

*The Debugger's Handbook* teaches software programmers and testers how to prevent, identify, and remove everyday bugs from applications. It provides a guide to good code-writing habits and common testing and logical debugging techniques. Written from a language-independent perspective, the book provides code samples in VB.NET, C#, C++, and Java. By using this style the book can focus on general programming concepts that are intended to provide programmers with a mental debugging toolbox no matter what language they use. Following the complete process of writing, testing, and debugging an application from beginning to end, the book begins with an exploration of computer bugs and defines exactly what they are. It then teaches programmers different techniques for identifying and avoiding bugs within their code and producing bug-free code. The book concludes with a number or common real-world scenarios. After working through this practical guide and reference, programmers will be able to think in a way that helps them to catch more bugs before any code is compiled. The book also accomplishes the following:

- Teaches programmers how to recognize, identify, and remove bugs from a language-independent perspective
- Covers topics such as coding habits, the design process, design time debugging, and testing
- Provides simple tips and techniques for avoiding common coding mistakes and making code easier to debug
- Includes exercises at the end of each chapter to test your new debugging skills
- Provides code examples in VB, VB.NET, C++, and Java

# Introduction

Welcome to *The Debugger's Handbook*. The goals of this book are to give you a better understanding of what makes a computer bug, teach you how to avoid bugs in your own applications, and show you the tools and skills needed in removing common bugs once you find them. To achieve these goals you will be introduced to a broad range of knowledge, designed to expose you to as many aspects of the debugging process as possible. In doing so you will have the greatest technical tools set at your disposal, and your applications will be better for it.

There are a myriad of debugging methods and methodologies taught in school. The problem with many of these textbook approaches to debugging is that they treat debugging the same way doctors treat illnesses. A human walks into a hospital and based on a list of symptoms the doctor determines what is wrong with the patient and treats him or her accordingly. However, if there is a set of symptoms that is sporadic or hard to define, the doctor's job is infinitely harder and may even be impossible.

Debugging should not be treated this way. Because of the nature of application development, not every bug or type of bug is going to present itself the same way every single time. Therefore, the best way to debug an application is to avoid bugs in the first place. That is where this book sets itself apart. We will not be subscribing to any of the textbook methods for debugging. Rather, we will focus on making you a natural debugger by broadening your knowledge base and forcing you to think about bugs at all stages of application development.

Hopefully by gaining a greater knowledge of applications, systems, and application structures you can learn to identify and avoid situations where bugs can manifest. By avoiding bugs you can create code that will test better, cost less in revisions, and allow you to focus your energies on other tasks. As technically minded individuals, though, we all know that it is nearly impossible to avoid every bug; therefore, you will also be exposed to a number of bug-finding skills and techniques. Finding and eliminating bugs is not hard as long as you have the right information.

Much has been written on the subject of application debugging; however, we will take a slightly different approach to the subject than most. Unlike almost any other book written on the subject, we will take a multifaceted approach to the topic of application debugging. Many people consider a bug to be something that exists in a finished application; therefore, application debugging is an action performed on a completed piece of software. In this book, although we will cover traditional application debugging from the point of view of completed applications, we will also take a step back. We will spend a good part of the book looking at ways to avoid bugs when writing code. This will introduce you to the concept of bug avoidance as a form of application debugging.

The first subject we will tackle in this book is defining exactly what a bug is. The definition of a bug has certainly changed over the years, and before we can become tried-and-true bug hunters, we need to know exactly what we are hunting. There is no doubt that you should already have a preconceived notion of what a bug is, and although your interpretation of a bug is most likely 100% correct, the terms of that definition may differ when compared to a colleague's definition of a bug. Therefore, Chapter 1, "Bugs: Fact or Fiction?," will ensure that we are all on the same page when it comes to identifying system anomalies that turn otherwise good code into a system-destroying mess. We will operationalize our definition of a bug and explore the history of bugs to learn where they are most likely to manifest.

> Operationalization is that concept whereby a definition contains within itself enough objective critical criteria so that an uninformed observer can determine if a thing is the thing defined. In other words, we want to make sure that when we flag something as a bug, we all know what that means.

Once we have defined bugs and learned how to identify them, we will begin tackling the complex subject of avoiding them. Through different techniques and actions we will create programs that are as bug-free as can be expected. By writing the most bug-free code possible, you will save time and money in future tech support costs and you will save on development of code revisions. Admittedly the best form of debugging is to not have bugs in your code to begin with. Therefore, although it may be considered more of an antibug measure rather than a debug measure, we will spend considerable time looking at how to keep bugs out of our code.

However, not every bug can be foreseen or avoided. Do not get a false sense of security thinking that this book will help you create completely bulletproof code. In fact, it would be nearly impossible to anticipate every bug and malicious interaction that could possibly arise. This book will give you the best toolbox you could have in an effort to protect yourself against a lot of bugs, but you need to be able to write code that will adapt to situations and not crumble when presented with a problem. Success will be measured by helping you achieve a level of programming where bug anticipation, identification, and removal become an extension of your daily work flow.

The remainder of the book will serve more as a debugger's reference guide. The last few chapters will give you many common error codes, descriptions, and code solutions for use in your everyday programming. That is, multiple error codes from the larger software manufacturers will be listed by number and description, accompanied by possible solutions and code samples for those solutions.

## Who This Book Is For

*The Debugger's Handbook* is geared toward programmers and project managers. That is, if your job involves coding, either directly or indirectly, then you stand to gain from this book. Programmers should gain a greater direct knowledge of debugging, techniques for avoiding bugs, and techniques to get the most out of testing. Similarly, project managers should, by getting a look into the processes needed to thoroughly produce bug-free software, be able to strengthen their skills as managers in that they can more accurately account for the time needed to complete a project.

If you are a programmer, you should have at least basic, or entry-level, knowledge of one of the following programming languages:

- Visual Basic®
- Visual Basic .NET
- C#
- Java™

This book tends to teach by example, and in doing so, these languages are featured prominently (some more than others because of their prevalence in the market). However, the topics covered are introduced in a way that any knowledge of basic programming concepts and practices will help you tremendously in understanding and achieving the goals set herein.

Although more experienced programmers, and those who are actively involved in coding projects on a daily basis, can more easily put into practice what they learn from this book, any level of programmer will be able to strengthen his or her abilities. However, as previously stated, programmers are not the only people who will learn valuable lessons from reading *The Debugger's Handbook*.

Project managers, too, should have some experience in programming to fully understand the concepts contained within. By following along with the examples and taking the time to understand the outlines given in the first three chapters, a project manager will be better prepared to anticipate the needs of the programmers they are working with. Although the more technical aspects of the book are geared toward programmers, the topics are presented and ordered in a way that project managers can easily see how a coding project should be organized.

## What This Book Will Not Do

This book is not intended to teach you a specific programming language or operating system programming technique. Rather, this book will cover general programming concepts meant to help you no matter what language you use. As a general rule, most code samples will be provided in four common programming languages: VB, VB.NET, C#, and Java. This will give you a broader understanding of solving general bug problems in most of the popular programming languages.

## Getting the Most from This Book

You will get the most from this book if you read it while in a place or situation where you can try the provided code samples on your own. This book is packed with code samples and examples that can be used to further drive home the lessons of each chapter. Code samples are given in VB6, VB.NET, C#, or Java for some of the examples in the book. This will help you understand the concepts we are covering no matter what language you are most comfortable with.

Whether you are directly involved in the programming process as a programmer, tester, or debugger, or you are indirectly involved in the process as a project manager or lead, you will be able to extrapolate from this book a broad range of knowledge. This knowledge will help you in the day-to-day activities of fighting and preventing bugs in applications.

However, to get the most from this situation you should be actively involved in a project or scenario that will allow you to use the skills you are gaining as you progress through the chapters.

Also, to get the greatest impact from the lessons, it is best to fully understand each example and each chapter before moving on to the next. Each chapter builds on the knowledge gained from the last; therefore, if you do not fully comprehend a given chapter, the book will become harder to follow as you go on. The later chapters will make more sense if you have mastered the earlier material. Take all the time needed to review the given material before moving on — it will prove to be beneficial in the end.

One tool provided to help you understand this material is a set of exercises at the end of each chapter. These exercises include questions on the previous chapter, code samples to debug, and descriptions of programs to test your new skills. The answers to all of the exercises will be at the end of the book. It is suggested that you read each chapter, then attempt the exercises at the conclusion of the chapter; check your progress with the provided answer key.

Another tool provided within this book to help you understand the provided lessons is the numerous code samples. Because these code samples could be presented in one or more programming languages, they will be formatted in a very specific way. The following is a code sample from Chapter 1:

**Listing 1.1: VB6/VB.NET**

```
Private Function AddMe(number1 AS Integer, number2
AS Integer) AS Integer
'**************************************************
'Function used to add two numbers and return the sum
'jfd
'05/05/2005
'**************************************************
'Variable Definitions
'**************************************************
Dim number1 as Integer
Dim number2 as Integer
'************************
'Add number1 and number2
'************************
```

```
AddMe = number1 + number2
End Function
```

The first thing you should notice about the example is that the language it is written in is always listed at the top of the sample. In cases where multiple examples are presented in multiple languages, each sample will be separated by this header, which denotes what language the sample represents.

Finally, each chapter will contain a section entitled "Looking Ahead." This section will provide an overview of the concepts discussed in the following chapter. Having a brief overview will facilitate thought about the coming material, familiarize you with the concepts being covered, and provide an element of preparation for each new stage of the book.

One axiom of teaching stresses that any acquired knowledge will quickly be lost if it is not put to use. The more a new skill is used in the student's daily life, the longer it will be retained. This is also true in computers and computer programming. If you do not use the skills and techniques taught in this book, you will not retain them very long.

The importance of carefully following the chapters and performing all of the exercises contained within cannot be stressed enough. Although this book will explain to you the core knowledge behind application debugging, that knowledge will not sink in as deep if you do not use it. By taking part in the post-chapter exercises, you have a chance to use and gain a better understanding of that chapter's material.

## How the Book Is Organized

*The Debugger's Handbook* is organized in a very deliberate way. From the order of the chapters to the layout of the material within the chapters, I have taken every precaution to ensure that you get the highest impact from the logical progression of the information.

The first chapter of this book provides for you all of the information needed to understand the remainder of the book. The first chapter can be thought of as the prerequisite for the information covered throughout the final chapters.

After you have been given the prerequisite knowledge, the book will progress. The next series of chapters deal with the pre-compile activities of bug avoidance. That is, topics including project organization, coding, and design time debugging will be discussed. These are activities that will take place before the application is compiled.

Once the program has been compiled, the book will move through a series of chapters that include discussions of applications testing and post-compile debugging. The specific order of the chapters is deliberate in that they follow the natural project progression. The order in which you would need or use the knowledge in the book is the order in which it is presented.

Finally, the last chapters contain a number of the most common real-world application bugs. These bugs are presented by topic, discussed, and corrected by example to show you how each was located and removed.

The layout within each chapter is also very deliberate. Each chapter will contain two major parts. The first, as with most books, will be the presentation of the information. All of the information needed to understand the topics will be presented and discussed in a clear and easy-to-read manner. This will include multiple examples and code samples to help bolster the lesson.

After the information of the chapter has been presented and discussed, review questions will be presented. These questions are designed to help you think about the material in the chapters and use it in a real-world sense. The combination of the two major chapter parts will give you the greatest opportunity to learn the information provided in *The Debugger's Handbook*.

# Chapter 1

# Bugs: Fact or Fiction?

Know your enemy.

**—Sun Tzu, from *The Art of War***

It is fitting that a quote from *The Art of War* starts off this book. At times it can seem that we, as application programmers, truly are at war with elements of design, bugs, and even deadlines. However, the enemy we fight has no face, has no form, and is born of our own doing. The ongoing struggle of every programmer is in keeping bugs out of our systems. Bugs are an enemy of our own creation that we must be ever vigilant of, yet many of us do not do enough during the programming process to keep them at bay.

Thousands of hours of university courses have been devised to teach young programmers the textbook methods for debugging code. However, bugs are not always textbook. With rapid advancements in technology, code is always changing and so are bugs. Although they do a good job of teaching a programmer the basics, the textbook methods of debugging do not fit every situation. Therefore, the purpose of this book is to teach you the skills needed to debug code in a natural way, akin to how you program.

How often is a programming planning session held where one of the objectives is minimizing bugs? Admittedly, it does not happen nearly as often as it should. Most people do not consciously think about writing bug-free code as much as we think about the overall objective of the project at hand.

One of the reasons why we do not think about writing bug-free code is because a common (possibly mistaken) comparison is made between bugs and bad code. That is, many people, both technical and nontechnical, see bugs as being spawned by poorly written, bad code. This comparison, for many people of both technical and nontechnical backgrounds, can be easy to understand. The comparison being that bugs are in applications, applications are written in code, bugs are bad, good applications have no bugs, and so bad code must produce bugs. Therefore, it is believed that if you write syntactically correct code, you will write bug-free code. As solid as that comparison may seem on the surface, it is inherently incorrect. This common misconception is what will be addressed in this chapter.

The problem in thinking that poorly written code is at the root of bug creation, for average business-level programmers, is flawed in that the compiler guards against this very problem. The compiler, or the portion of the programming tool that takes code and converts it to machine language, will identify and alert the programmer to syntactical and structural errors in blocks of code. The compiler, then, is safeguarding the user against poorly written code.

It is true, however, that the compiler may not catch every problem in every line of code. Rare coding errors that may slip through the compiler could create bugs within the application. However, these instances are very uncommon, especially given the accuracy of many modern compilers, making it more likely that the bugs in today's applications are from unanticipated interactions rather than bad code. Given the role of the compiler, we must now look deeper to find the root of a bug.

Not all bugs — in fact very few — are from bad code. The code that generates bugs is actually good code. The code is syntactically correct, and in other scenarios may run correctly, but for reasons to be discovered throughout this chapter, in certain instances, it causes bugs. Therefore, to say that bugs are born of bad code is a generalization that does not correctly sum up the situation.

In fact, bugs can be generated from otherwise good code. The role of the programmer is to recognize and anticipate what code is going to execute in a way that is harmful to the systems under certain conditions. Most programmers, even those with basic experience, have a general idea of the proper execution of code. The more you look at code in its context, the more you will learn to identify the locations and functions of certain objects within an application. Unfortunately, this knowledge alone will only help you to a point. Programmers need to be able to see the oftentimes subtle indications of a bug and quickly identify the block or code that generated it. This can prove to be tricky at times, and it is when this objective is overlooked that bugs manifest themselves in our applications.

It can be easily argued that bugs are indeed the product of poorly written code in that optimally written code would anticipate any problem and react accordingly. However, a growing school of thought is that not every programmer or program can, in good faith, foresee every problem that may exist or arise in a system. Some processes are better left to the operating system, such as monitoring application interactions, threads, and memory usage. By this, bugs are not necessarily the product of poorly written code so much as a breakdown in the chain of management between the application and the operating system that could not be planned.

At one point, the operating system of a PC was considered to be a simple host. It would reside on the PC and act as a delivery device for applications. However, as the application market exploded, applications began to clash with each other in attempts to access resources such as volatile memory, video memory, and disk space. Because there was no feasible way for one application developer to alert every other application developer as to what its particular application would do on a system, applications would commonly conflict with each other.

It soon became apparent that one of two things needed to happen: either the operating system developers needed to publish detailed descriptions of how their systems functioned, in an attempt to help application developers better understand the platforms their programs would run on, or the operating systems themselves needed to become more like a referee and less like a toll booth. Therefore, to this point operating systems have become a strong element in ensuring applications work well with each other.

The purpose of this chapter is to help you understand exactly what an application bug is. We all know a bug when we see or experience one, but like most intangibles, it can be very hard to define. The goal of this book is not to teach you the textbook definitions or methods of debugging code. Rather, this book will help you formulate your own methods and best practices that work in your specific situations. Think of defining a bug as trying to define an emotion such as happiness or anger. We can all list examples of things that exude happiness, but how do you define the feeling of happiness? While if multiple people listed the items that make them happy there may be some common items between them, what those items mean to each of those people may be different.

The same is true of an application bug. We have all experienced at least one bug, and we can all give examples of common application bugs, but do we each have the same definition of what a bug is? That is, if you had to explain what a bug is without using an example, would your definition match that of anyone else's? Chances are it would not. Without having a working definition to use in our daily programming, finding bugs before they externalize themselves can be extremely difficult. It is a common definition that will give us all a step onto equal footing. Therefore, no matter your experience or background, we will all be starting at the same place with a shared common idea of what we are looking for, and from this point we will better be able to identify and remove bugs.

To achieve this unified definition of what a bug is, we will be looking at the history of bugs and following how they have changed and manifested over the years. We will trace the roots of the modern bug to see how it evolved into the system-crashing menace it is today. This definition will give us something tangible to look for when producing our own code. Having a working definition of what constitutes a bug and where they are most likely to exist will help you spot them as you read through your code, and even prevent them in your writing. That is, even years after you have finished this book, you will be able to examine practices, error messages, and even blocks of code and determine if they are prone to bugs by comparing them with our definition.

Having an operationalized definition of a bug is important because you need to know exactly what you are trying to prevent before you can attempt preventing it. Admittedly, attempting to find something without knowing exactly what it is you are looking for would not be productive. Let us look at this as a scenario. For example, if you were asked to go through all of your code and pull out all of the operators, chances are you would know exactly what you were looking for. As programmers, we know that operators are generally characters such as <, >, or =. It is easy for you to separate these characters when asked, because everyone knows the definition of an operator, regardless of the language. Therefore, extracting the operators from the following block of VB6 code would not be a very laborious task.

**VB6/VB.NET**

```
Private Function AddMe(number1 AS Integer, number2
AS Integer) AS Integer
'****************************************************
'Function used to add two numbers and return the sum
'jfd
'05/05/2005
'****************************************************
```

```
'Variable Definitions
'*****************************************************
Dim number1 as Integer
Dim number2 as Integer
'************************
'Add number1 and number2
'************************
AddMe = number1 + number2
End Function
```

Look through the code sample provided and identify the operators. Obviously, the operators appear in the line

```
AddMe = number1 + number2
```

This scenario was easy to complete because we all know what an operator is. Programmers already have a common, unified definition of what an operator is. Therefore, as soon as we see one, we can immediately identify it as an operator.

When we are talking about bugs however, the task is a bit harder. To this point we still have not defined what a bug is; this fact makes finding one quite difficult. There is no character or object identifier to look for when going through code looking for bugs. Anyone can say, "Go through that code and remove all the bugs," but if it were that easy, there would be no bugs in the code to begin with.

Let us look at a new example. For the purposes of the scenario, this example will have to be a bit hypothetical. In this scenario, you are asked to look through a block code and pull out all the bugs. What do you look for? There is no common object or delimiter to identify bugs by, as in this fictitious block of C++ code.

### C++

```
//this is my sample program, it contains a bug
//jfd
//05/05/2005
int main()
{
 cout<<"Hello World"<<endl;
return 0;
//insert bug here
//******************************
```

```
(This is a bug) //if it were this easy, all bugs
would be in parentheses
//*****************************
}
//end sample program
```

Most of the time, bugs do not present themselves in such an obvious manner; they are often more abstract and can span multiple lines of code. For this reason, we must know exactly what we are looking for when we start to debug code, or else we could be on a wild goose chase.

Here is a block of code that actually contains a bug. Can you find it? It definitely does not present itself in the way our fictitious bug did.

## VB.NET

```
Public Function LogErrors(ByRef colProcessErrors As
Collection, fileName as Variant) As Boolean
'*******************************************
'Function for logging error
'jfd
'05/05/2005
'*******************************************
     Dim objFso As Scripting.FileSystemObject
     Dim ts As Scripting.TextStream
     Dim strFileName As Integer
     Dim objProcessError As ProcessError
     Dim strLogLine As String
     Dim hshParams As Hashtable
     Dim strKey As String
     Dim strLogDir As String
     Dim objCommonMethod As New CommonLib.Method()
     Dim strIniDir As String
'*******************************************
     strIniDir = objCommonMethod.AppPath
     Dim objTextIniReader As New
CommonLib.TextIniReader(strIniDir & "\Enviroment.ini")
     objFso = New Scripting.FileSystemObject()
     strLogDir = strIniDir & "\ERRORS\"
```

```
    If Not Directory.Exists(strLogDir) Then
        Directory.CreateDirectory(strLogDir)
    End If
    'Only one log file exists for each month
    'Set file name to the beginning of the month
    strFileName = fileName

    If File.Exists(strLogDir & strFileName) Then
        'If file exists, append
        ts = objFso.OpenTextFile(strLogDir &
strFileName, Scripting.IOMode.ForAppending)
    Else
        'If file does not exists, create it
        ts = objFso.OpenTextFile(strLogDir &
strFileName, Scripting.IOMode.ForWriting, True)

ts.WriteLine("Date|Number|Location|Description|
Parameters")
    End If
    'Loop for each error
    For Each objProcessError In colProcessErrors
        strLogLine = ""
        strLogLine += objProcessError.ErrorDate & "|"
        strLogLine += objProcessError.Number & "|"
        strLogLine += Chr(34) &
objProcessError.Location & Chr(34) & "|"
        strLogLine += Chr(34) &
objProcessError.Description & Chr(34) & "|"

        'Add the being " for the params field
        strLogLine += Chr(34)

        'Add all the params to the LogLine string
        For Each strKey In objProcessError.Data.Keys
            strLogLine += strKey & "~" &
objProcessError.Data.Item(strKey) & "^"
        Next
        'Remove the extra ^ in the params field
```

```
        If objProcessError.Data.Count > 0 Then
            strLogLine = Left(strLogLine,
Len(strLogLine) - 1)
        End If
        'Add the ending " for the params field
        strLogLine += Chr(34)
        ts.WriteLine(strLogLine)
    Next
    LogErrors = True
GarbageDump:
    objCommonMethod = Nothing
    ts.Close()
    ts = Nothing
    objFso = Nothing
End Function
```

The bug in this function appears in one of the opening lines:

```
Dim strFileName As Integer
```

Here the variable `strFileName` is being fed by a `Variant` parameter to the function. Therefore, the code will compile correctly, and in case where an integer value is being passed to the function, it will execute properly as well. The problem occurs as soon as an alpha value is passed to the function. The function will return an error when it attempts to assign this alpha value to the variable `strFileName`.

This scenario gives you a good example of what debugging involves. The VB.NET code involved is somewhat long, and the bug only involved one line that would otherwise be fine. In fact, this particular code VB.NET function should compile without issue and should work under certain situations. The only time this function would throw an error is if you attempted to pass an alpha filename to it. If you only pass integer-based filenames, that function will not throw an error.

Did you recognize the bug? Would you have recognized the error as a bug? Let us now take a look at the history of bugs so we can begin to understand and begin to form our definition of a bug.

## The History of Bugs

When most of us think of bugs, we think more of glitches in software and rarely hardware. However, bugs are found in hardware-based systems as well, though admittedly not as much now as perhaps 20 to 30 years ago. Although the focus of this book is in fact software bugs, the genesis of the bug is actually found in hardware. Therefore, it is in the foundations of hardware that we must look first if we are to trace the history of and define bugs.

In the beginning, the focus of all computing systems was hardware. And although hardware is still very important today, we as programmers would not have a job, nor would there be a reason for this book, if applications were not the foundation of the modern computing platform. Whether you took computing classes in school or have just researched the subject of computer history on your own, you no doubt have heard of the early relay calculators, vacuum tubes, and punch cards. These old hardware systems are where we will begin our search for the origin of the computer bug.

Some of the earliest computers ever built were the Harvard Mark series of relay calculators created by Howard Aiken and IBM. These hulking masses of metal and early electronics were mechanical marvels. Basically a giant math processor, the Mark I was over 50 feet long, weighed 5 tons, and cost over $300,000 to produce. According to About.com and the University of Limerick Computer Society, the early Mark I consisted of 78 individual adding machines sequenced together by a rotating shaft, over 700,000 moving parts, and could perform an addition of a 23-digit integer in 1/3 second. Although by today's standards this is unbelievably slow and large, for its time, it was truly a wonder of modern science.

---

## *Mark I vs. Today's PCs*

For comparison, the current Pentium 4-based hyper-threading processors measure but a few inches long, weigh ounces, and can perform upward of 3 billion additions per second, as opposed to the Mark I's three per second. Proving that the progression of technology over the past 60 years has been truly amazing, computing hardware has grown in speed by a power of nearly 20 and are about 1/3000th the size.

It is amazing to look at how far we have come in the first half century of computing. At its current pace, how far will we go in the last half century? Computing hardware has been evolving at an astronomical pace; there is really no telling how far we will go, but it is sure to be an amazing ride.

In the 1940s a young female Navy officer stood on the verge of making history with the fledgling successor to the Mark I, the Mark II. Grace Hopper, one of the country's first computer programmers, joined the naval reserves in 1944. In 1945 she was assigned to work with Howard Aiken at Harvard University. With Aiken, she began testing the Mark II relay calculator. According to the Naval Surface Warfare Center Computer Museum in Dahlgren, Virginia, at 3:45 P.M. on September 9, 1945, Grace Hopper made a historic entry in her manual log-book. (Courtesy of the Naval Surface Warfare Center, Dahlgren, VA, 1988.)

---

## *Relay Calculators*

The relay was first invented to help extend the distance Morse code signals could be transmitted. We have all seen a Morse code tapper; they are basically two pieces of metal that complete an electric circuit when they are touched together. A relay was very similar in that two pieces of metal were separated by a third piece of metal attached to a magnet. This relay was then placed between two distant Morse points. When the magnet intercepted the weakened electric signal, it would pull one side of the relay toward it, thus recreating the signal and sending the now recreated strengthened signal to the distant point.

It did not take very long for people to realize that this type of relay signified something that is still used in computing to this day, the binary system. A relay is inherently in one of two states, open or closed. These two states could then be used to represent the binary digits of 0 and 1. Therefore, connecting enough relays could allow for the computation of large numbers.

Early computers or relay calculators leveraged exactly this kind of hardware. They were series of relays connected in a way that they could be continually switched on and off, representing the addition, subtraction, division, and multiplication of large numbers.

---

While testing the Mark II, a problem had been recorded with some of the values produced by the giant calculator. Something did not look correct with the output, and Grace Hopper decided to investigate. The input, which consisted of a combination of hard switch settings and punch tape, seemed to be correct; however, the output was still puzzling. In looking through the giant apparatus, it was discovered that a moth had become lodged in the computer and was blocking one of the relays, keeping it in the open position. The offending moth was removed from the machine and taped to the logbook adjacent to the following message:

**First actual case of bug being found.**

(http://www.history.navy. mil/photos/pers-us/uspers-h/g-hoppr. htm; Photo NH 96566-KN)

With these seven words Grace Hopper landed herself a place in computer history as the first debugger, literally. Thus, on the surface, we have our first example of a computer bug, albeit primitive. However, a close observer would notice something about the implied syntax of her message. She mentions the problem as being the first *actual* case of a bug being found. This implies that the term *bug* existed before Grace Hopper used it to describe the problem between the moth and the relay. We now must look further into the history of computing and electronics to find the basis for using the term *bug* in describing the problem Grace Hopper experienced.

The term *bug* itself had been used to describe problems in electrical equipment long before computers. In 1896, the Hawkins' *New Catechism of Electricity* described a bug as follows:

> To a limited extent to designate any fault or trouble in the connections or working of electric apparatus.

Now we have two pieces of our puzzle: we have found where the term *bug* was coined, and we have found our first written case of it being used to describe a computing problem. Now we can relate the two and somehow develop our definition of a bug, because as simplistic as it would be, we cannot define a bug as a moth the gets lodged within a relay.

So the term *bug* precedes the first computer by almost 50 years and the modern computer by almost 80. Therefore, for the first years of computing a bug was only something that affected hardware; at some point this had to change. Our view of the process had to be altered by some event to move the focus of what a bug was from something that affected hardware to something that resided with our software.

This is important to understand because although the term *bug* itself is meant to describe any fault in a piece of electrical equipment, admittedly this is not the best definition for our purposes. We need to come up with a more specific definition for applications and application programming. We must now take what we have learned about the origin of the bug and apply it to modern programming. Let us now investigate how the current computing environment has changed both how we look at programming and how we describe bugs.

## The Rise of the Modern Programmer

Computers, although driven by software, were seen as a dominant piece of hardware through the 1970s. That is, like their relay calculator predecessors, the mainframes of the 1960s and 1970s were still considered to be primarily ruled by hardware. When you think back to the computing environment of the 1970s, the first thought is large clunky boxes, reel-to-reel tapes, and monochromatic screens. As evidenced by the Mark II, and those that followed it, hardware was king and it drove the computer industry. The software was seen as portable programs that could be run on anything; it was the hardware that was going to make the real difference in the quality and speed of the output.

> The modern computer age began in the late 1970s with the advent of the personal computer, the refinement of the silicon chip, and the greater acceptance of computer science as a legitimate field of study. Before that time, the costs of training, hardware, and support, kept the computing field in the dark ages. It was viewed as a great unknown that only a select few people understood.

Companies like IBM made their fortunes in selling hardware. As with all emerging technologies (even today), new, cutting-edge products are exponentially more expensive when they are first released. In the 1970s, computers were still extremely expensive, so much so that unless you were a big business, owning one was very much cost-prohibitive. Given the expense involved in owning an early computer, training programmers was not an everyday occurrence. Not only could very few people afford to be trained on real equipment, but very few people could understand the complex languages and methods used at the time. All of these factors combined to create an environment where hardware was at the forefront of the computing market and applications were but an afterthought. The applications were seen as something that could be used anywhere, and your big choice was which hardware platform you thought would give you the best results.

This changed when the computing environment was turned on its head with the release of the first mass-marketed personal computers. While some lesser known personal computing devices came and went over the years, the PC market exploded in 1981 with the releases of both the IBM PC and Apple II. All of a sudden anyone could own a computer, and garage development projects sprang up all over the country. Using languages such as BASIC, everyone could develop their own software.

For the first time, computers were being marketed as educational tools, personal and small business management tools, and to a minor extent entertainment devices. It did not take long for the general public to see the new, smaller, personal computers as more than a business machine and as something that could positively impact their lives.

Though still expensive, more people could now own, and better yet experiment on, computers. This put the tools for developing and implementing all kinds of software into the hands of the average person. The development of homegrown applications flourished as more people began to try coding with the more user-friendly programming languages that were introduced with the personal computers. Through the 1980s and 1990s the world experienced an unprecedented rate of new developments, and before long software was the new king of the computer industry.

The hardware of a computer was still important, but users now looked for specific applications to help them with their everyday lives. It would not be long before the forward progress and trends in computing were governed by the development of software and not the capacity of hardware. By the late 1990s users would buy hardware based on its ability to run specific hardware, which is a complete turnaround from how computing started.

In the early 1980s, almost any preteen Generation X (Atari age) individual could make a decent argument for needing a home computer; more, though admittedly not many, schools accepted printed homework rather than handwritten, educational software promised to teach us the mysteries of the world, and computers were just supposed to make you smarter (all according to the media at the time). Therefore, more computers kept popping up in homes across the country. These early home computers really did not do very much on their own, and software support was fairly limited. However, one thing most new personal computers had was a built-in development environment.

The early PCs could be thought of more as application development kits than modern computers. My first computer, a Tandy TRS-80 Color Computer II, did little more than run a few cartridge-based games, but it did come with its own small version of BASIC to program with. Given the small amount of memory registers, the nongraphic environment, and the storage media (at the time the most common was a standard audiocassette), the average homegrown application was not very large. However, they represented the earliest forms of an industry that was about to explode. The following is an example of a 14-line program written in 1982 on the TRS-80 CCII.

## BASIC

```
10 Print "Welcome to the ninja battle."
20 Print "You are fighting 3 ninjas."
30 Let a = RND(10)
40 Input "Please select a number from 1 to 10" b
50 If a > b then Print "The red ninja won with a ", a
60 Print "You are fighting the black ninja."
70 Let a = RND(15)
80 Input "Please select a number from 1 to 15" b
90 If a > b then Print "The black ninja won with a ", a
100 Print "You are fighting the white ninja."
110 Let a = RND(20)
120 Input "Please select a number from 1 to 20" b
130 If a > b then Print "The red ninja won with a ", a
140 Run
```

This program, however simplistic, was written by a nine-year-old in 1982. A generation before, something on this level would have been unheard of. However, here we are on the verge of an application revolution. Children are controlling the computers, and software is about to become king.

Anyone with a PC and a desire to be creative could now be a programmer. By today's standards very little could be done on these machines programmatically. There were a few registers that could be written to and read from, and if you were lucky you had a cassette drive or tape-style printer to interact with. The really brave programmers attempted plotting pixels and crude geometric shapes on the screen. However, from early games to business applications, mom-and-pop software development houses were rising up all over the country. The average citizen now had the tools needed to turn the hulking Mark II's of the world into the sleek necessities we are used to now.

Today software is the core of the computing world. There are more software developers now than ever before, and our job could not be more complicated. Many of the world's programmers use one of three popular platforms for their applications: Microsoft® Windows®, UNIX, or Linux. In an effort to keep up with the growing needs and demands of programmers, operating system developers have had to increase efforts in producing more robust systems and platforms for running applications.

Whereas the hardware industry once dictated the direction of the computing market as a whole, the hardware vendors now find themselves keeping up with the demands of the software developers. As soon as new hardware can be developed, software developers will already have applications that will take advantage of its power. This leads to rapid development of hardware and the development of software on fledgling systems that may or may not be fully tested.

The combination of these factors may be the leading cause in the development of bugs, the main cause being the speed at which new advancements in technology are made, and a lesser factor being the "every man" aspect to the programming community. Examining how the two have combined to produce modern bugs will give us the definition we are looking for.

## Killing Bugs Is Just a Game

Since the advent of the personal computer, advances in software development have been quick and consistent. That is, as the hobbyist programmers of the 1980s became the computer professionals of the late 1990s they realized how much more these machines were capable of and pushed them to their limits. However, this quest to push the limits of the current computing environment may have been what led to the modern bug. Let us examine how these factors came together to create the bug.

> The following generalization does not apply to any one software developer, but rather the overall climate in the software industry in the late 1980s and early 1990s.

In an effort to be the first out with a revolutionary new product, some software development houses may not thoroughly check every aspect of every program for potential conflicts with other products. The fact is that to check every product against every other product would take too much time and require too many man-hours. The added cost in testing new software against all existing applications on the market would leave the price of most new products out of the budget of consumers. Yet, this was almost the situation the software industry was in as the early 1990s rolled around.

With most consumer operating systems only treating applications as items to be served up when called and not mitigating communications between them, applications commonly stepped on each other within the operating environment. Developers did not know who else was programming for the environment, or how many other applications might be fighting for the same resources, nor should they.

The smaller software developers were left to fend for themselves when testing their applications for conflict problems between their products and those of other. Many products were released that, when installed in conjunction with other applications, would cause crashes, corruptions in data, and other unanticipated behaviors.

As consumers we came to expect a certain level of "bugginess" in the applications released at the time. It was known, and sometimes expressed directly in the manuals, that software product A could not be used with software product Z. Nowhere was this more evident than in the world of PC gaming.

PC games had been around since the advent of the PC. From simple text-based games to the earliest crude graphics, people have always enjoyed a little entertainment with their business or education. However, when PCs were first released, they were not initially meant solely for gaming. Therefore, the types of games that could be run on a PC were primitive at best, and nothing near in quality of that which could be seen in the now thriving arcades. At this time, PC game developers (what few existed) were not considered legitimate PC developers in the application inner circles. This viewpoint would quickly change.

In the early 1990s PC gaming was just coming out of its infancy. By this time people had been playing games on PCs for a few years, and game makers were now legitimate PC application developers. However, the platform that PC game makers had to work with was not stable. The operating system at the time was MS-DOS (Microsoft's disk operating system — also referred to simply as DOS), and a major software package was on the market that wanted to use all of DOS's available resources, Microsoft Windows. At this time Windows was not yet an operating system unto itself; it still ran on top of DOS. This situation created havoc in the world of game design. Games had to be designed within a DOS environment, but must work with Windows. Many times the solution was to shut down Windows and run the game in DOS.

Games, which even today test the limits of desktop computing, historically require nearly every resource a PC can offer up. It was not uncommon to have bugs in games that would cause memory leaks, graphics problems, and sound issues when used with Windows. Because debugging Windows was almost unheard of at the time, the fix offered by many developers was to create a customized boot disk that would load the user's PC clean of Windows, thus eliminating most of the bugs.

> Although Windows itself could just be shut down, leaving you in the DOS operating environment, this would not solve the problems or bug. Windows would often use resources and not release them, even upon its closure. Therefore, a disk that would allow you to boot clean of Windows was often the only choice.
>
> Telling consumers that to use an application bug-free they need to create a boot disk with custom memory settings, and leave behind Windows, would spell doom for a developer in today's market. Modern consumers do not accept products unless they work perfectly out of the box. Software programmers began to develop a better sense of what to look for when creating applications. Several characteristics of buggy software were assembled and used as a guide of what to avoid when developing.

The most common bugs found at the time were:

- Memory bugs
- Graphic errors
- System crashes
- Resource locking

From this list we can now define what a bug is, then look at how one company has worked to eliminate them (or at least make the task of finding them easier).

Reading through the last few sections, one theme should be clear: many bugs are created by adverse reactions or conflicts with other software products. That is to say that when two or more products fight over resources, the resulting conflict can be called a bug. A resource can be memory, a particular function, a printer, or anything that can be accessed by more than one object.

In a broad sense this will be our working definition of a bug. Analyzing this definition, it is visible that one common element blamed for creating bugs may seem to be absent — bad code (going back to our discussion for earlier in this book about the fact that bad code does not necessarily equal bad code, and vice versa).

Most common compilers do a better job than ever before of finding and labeling bad code. Bad code, as in code with major syntactical errors, accounts for very few of the bugs in today's software. However, even the best programmers in the world still miss a variable call or a parameter in a function. Therefore, our definition of bug is really twofold.

We can start our definition of a bug by describing what we now know about bugs. Looking back over the last section, we can start our definition as follows: A bug is an unanticipated error or reaction created by application-level conflicts with other objects in the process of gaining, releasing, or locking resources. Bugs are also evident in code that has not been fully realized, traced, or is syntactically incorrect.

This definition states that a bug is any part of an application that causes a conflict when attempting to use any of the computer's resources. We go on to add that bugs can also be found in code that has not been fully realized, traced, or is syntactically incorrect. Together these represent parts 1 and 2 of our bug definition.

Having the definition is really only half the battle; we must now interpret what this definition means and how it affects us as programmers in our daily lives. We need to answer the following questions:

- What does this definition mean?
- How does it affect our attitude toward debugging?

Now that we have our definition, let us discuss what it means to today's programmers.

## Dissecting a Bug: Definition

Let us take a look at the first half of our definition of a bug:

> An unanticipated error or reaction created by conflicts with other objects in the process of gaining, releasing, or locking resources.

If you have been programming for any amount of time, especially with an object-oriented language such as C++, the first thought that might have come to your mind here may have been memory conflicts. One of the most common bug conditions is in fact some form of memory conflict. Memory conflicts or bugs can be caused by either of the following:

- Not allocating enough memory for a given object
- Not releasing memory when it is no longer needed

Let us discuss the first point: not allocating enough memory for a given object.

> In some languages such as VB, memory allocation and de-allocation problems are mostly handled by the runtime environment. VB programmers have very little control over how or when memory is allocated for specific objects. However, this has changed in VB.NET. The user now has more say over processes such as garbage collection and memory de-allocation.

When a programmer does not allocate enough memory for a given variable or object, it can easily cause an application crash. A simple example of this would be if a programmer creates a 16-bit integer variable and then, during runtime, attempts to place a 32-bit value into the variable. This situation would cause the application to immediately halt or throw an error to the operating system. Such situations are more localized examples of memory bugs because they are contained to, and generally affect only, the application to which they are confined.

This is true for most object-oriented languages, such as Java and C++. Memory allocation bugs can also be found in smaller support languages, such as T-SQL. That is, especially in some languages such as T-SQL, the amount of memory to be used by each parameter, column, and various other objects must be specified with the object's definition. Subsequently, any further calls to that object must be prepared to handle the correct amount of data.

These kinds of local memory bugs can be fairly easy to find. While the compiler may or may not pick up on such a situation as that previously described, a programmer would definitely see it upon running the applications, either for the first time or in debug mode. However, given the ease of detecting such a local memory bug, they are also fairly common.

> Debug mode and other debugging environments and techniques will be discussed later in this book.
>
> Conversely, the second type of memory bug — not releasing memory when it is no longer needed — can be harder to find and more destructive. Knowing when to release resources is a bit trickier than creating the object in the first place. Every programmer can easily find the point at which memory should be allocated to an object: the first time the object is defined, called, or otherwise used. However, tracking the last time an object is needed, so that its memory can be released, can be a bit harder, especially if the object is shared across multiple blocks of code.

As in the previous example, a programmer should allocate memory for the objects needed throughout the application. This memory must also be de-allocated when it is no longer needed. By de-allocating the once used portions of memory, you are telling the operating system it is okay to use that memory for other functions. When this memory does not get de-allocated, the operating system never realizes those segments can be reused. Thus, the memory is dead and cannot be accessed. Such dead memory segments can be very harmful to a system if not monitored.

This kind of memory bug, also known as a memory leak, can manifest itself in a few different ways. First, the overall performance of the PC will begin to slow. This is due to the fact that the PC now has less memory to run on. The operating system may now have to juggle segments of data to work around the dead memory that was not de-allocated by the application. Over time, and possibly after several uses of the offending application, the memory leak may build to a point that the PC has no operating memory and crashes.

Think of the results this way. Run an application that uses a lot of memory at one time without releasing it, such as a small game. Now attempt to run another application; you should notice that there is a little bit of lag, but nothing that is unbearable. Close the application but leave the game open. If you can, open a second instance of that game. Now reopen the application you opened before. Does it open slower? Does it open at all? Chances are that the system is running pretty slow at this point. This is the same effect that memory leaks have on a system.

However, system freezing and crashes are not the only hazard of memory leaks. Another symptom of memory leaks, and the one that makes them fairly difficult to find and diagnose, is that in a weakened state these bugs may affect applications other than those creating them. That is, one program may cause the memory leak, and although this leak may not be large enough to crash the system, another program could attempt accessing the dead memory and fail. This failure could cause the second application to crash or become corrupt. The slowness caused by the buildup of dead memory can also make it difficult, if not impossible, to open diagnostic tools, making troubleshooting such problems a hard project.

Over the years, the major operating system manufacturers have made great strides in creating programmer-friendly environments. Windows in particular has changed greatly over the past 15 years. Where once programmers shuddered at the thought of producing code on Windows, opting to shut Windows down and run application in DOS, they now flock to Windows, making it one of the most dominant programming platforms.

After the release of Windows 95, when Windows moved from a DOS application to a full-fledged operating system, Microsoft began to realize that it needed to create an environment that would not only be easier to program on, but also allow multiple developers' products to work together without fear of adverse interactions.

Consequently, with the release of Visual Studio .NET, Microsoft has made even more strides and taken even greater precautions in avoiding exactly these kind of memory errors. Features such as dynamic memory allocation and garbage removal will help programmers avoid some memory bugs; however, you must still be aware of their existence and the steps needed to find and eliminate them.

So, we have concluded that the first part of our definition of a bug (an unanticipated error or reaction created by conflicts with other objects in the process of gaining, releasing, or locking resources) not only is the most common type of bug you will experience, but also can be the most destructive. Throughout this book we will focus on comparing this definition against our code to help find and eliminate bugs. Let us now look at the second half of our bug definition:

> Bugs are also evident in code that has not been fully realized, followed through, or is syntactically incorrect.

This, the second part of our definition, is by far the more complex of the two halves of the bug definition, and it covers much more ground. Where the first part of our definition focused on one specific type of bug, a memory bug, the second half of the definition covers the more general bugs you are likely to come across.

Whereas memory bugs are quite specific in their symptoms, yet can be hard to track down, these more general code bugs can have symptoms that are best described as quirky in nature but are relatively easy to fix. The majority of the bugs that fall under the second half of our definition are also considered bad code or sloppy work by some, but for our purposes they will be called code bugs, as opposed to memory bugs.

> Through the remainder of this book bugs will be referred to in one of two ways, memory bugs or code bugs. Although memory bugs are ultimately caused by an error in coding, for the purposes of separating the bugs' techniques and symptoms, they will be referred to thusly.

According to the definition of a bug, code bugs can be separated into three different categories:

1. Code that has not been fully realized
2. Code that has not been followed through
3. Code that is syntactically incorrect

Let us briefly look at how each of these can materialize in your code.

## Fully Realized Code

Most projects begin on a white board, or in some other type of planning session. Here, all of the different components are laid out and connected in a way that makes the target application seem more achievable. Different ideas are put down, everyone's input is gathered, and eventually a working model is created that can be used as a reference during the programming stage of the project.

However, many things can change when it comes to the actual coding of the application. Some features may turn out to be a little ambitious for the level of coding being done, the timeline may not be realistic, or the fact that everyone has his or her own way of interpreting ideas and writing code may turn the earlier plans on their side. These situations are a sample of what may lead to code not being fully realized.

Fully realized code is code that is complete in every aspect. That is, everything that was set to be done has been done. For example, a basic representation of this concept would be the omnipresent "Hello World" application. Our goal is to create a VB6 application that will display a dialog box with the phrase "Hello World!"

### VB6

```
Private Sub Form_Load()
***********************
'Hello World
'5/1/2005
'-jfd
'***********************
msgbox "Hello World!" 'Displays -Hello World dialog box
'***********************
End Sub
```

However simple it is, this small VB6 application is fully realized. Everything that we set out to do has been done. Although this may seem to state to obvious — finish what you set out to do when you are dealing with multiple programmers and thousands of lines of code — things can get overlooked. Whether it is an error handler in an obscure function or a modal Windows form in place of a nonmodal one, code that is not fully realized can cause bugs.

The problem with bugs that are caused from code that is not fully realized is that they may only materialize in very specific conditions. That is, the use of the region of code that has not been fully realized will generate the bug. The following VB6 function accepts two numeric input values, adds them, and returns the sum; however, the code is not fully realized and contains a bug.

**VB6**

```
Public Function AddMe(iVal1 as Variant, iVal2 as
Variant) as Integer
'****************************************
'AddME
'function to add values and return sum
'5/1/2005
'-jfd
'****************************************
AddMe = iVal1 + iVal2
'****************************************
End Function
```

> Even if you are not proficient in Visual Basic 6 code, just follow along. As we move through the book, all examples will be in VB6, VB.NET, C++, or Java. However, where these are very basic samples to further the discussion, they are just in VB6.

If you execute this code with parameters of 2 and 3, the function will return 5, and supplying values of 130 and 6 will yield 136. This function, as written, definitely does do what we wanted it to do; we feed it two numbers and it will add them and supply us a sum. Look at the code again and see if you can spot where this code has not been fully realized; where is the bug?

What if the user supplies an A and a 4, what will the function yield? An error. The parameters `iVal1` and `iVal2` are dimensioned as variants. However, the function is fully expecting to add two integers. This is a bug that will materialize in a fairly specific situation, but it is a bug nonetheless. To be fully realized, this VB6 function needs some form of error trapping or integer validating. There are a few ways to fully realize this code. One would be to use the internal VB6 function `IsNumeric` to test the parameters before adding them.

**VB6**

```
Public Function AddMe(iVal1 as Variant, iVal2 as
Variant) as Integer
'******************************************
'AddME v.2 - using IsNumeric
'function to add values and return sum
'5/1/2005
'-jfd
'*******************************************
'*******************************************
'if the supplied parameters are numeric, add them
'*******************************************
If IsNumeric(iVal1) and IsNumeric(iVal2) Then
AddMe = iVal1 + iVal2
End If
'*******************************************
End Function
```

Another way to fully realize this code would be to throw in an error handler. Just to be safe, we will use both the numeric test and the error handler; this will give us a good, fully realized VB6 function.

**VB6**

```
Public Function AddMe(iVal1 as Variant, iVal2 as
Variant) as Integer
'*******************************************
'AddMe v.3 using an error handler
'function to add values and return sum
'5/1/2005
'-jfd
'*******************************************
```

```
'New error handler code - redirect
'*******************************************
On Error GoTo AddMeErrorHandler
'*******************************************
'if the supplied parameters are numeric, add them
'*******************************************
If IsNumeric(iVal1) and IsNumeric(iVal2) Then
AddMe = iVal1 + iVal2
End If
'*******************************************
Exit Function'function exits on completion
'*******************************************
AddMeErrorHandler:'error handler
'code for trapping and/or displaying error goes here
'I like to display the error, unless I have reason
not to
msgbox Err.Description
'*******************************************
End Function
```

The previous segment of code would be considered a fully realized function. It meets the goal it was designed to fill, accepting two numeric inputs and returning a sum. The function goes further in that it also validates (to a degree) the parameters passed to it and it contains basic error handling.

## *Code Follow-Through: Tracing*

Sometimes, especially when working on large projects or with multiple programmers, it can become hard to avoid kangaroo code, that is, code that jumps from function to function and even jumps around within the same class. Code writing in this way can be difficult to follow visually and can even harbor bugs.

This is not to say that writing applications that utilize functions, calls, and other subroutines is bad; in fact, the opposite is true. However, making too many leaps from code segment to code segment, if not closely monitored, can help create bugs. Therefore, when I say bugs are also evident in code that has not been followed through, what I am referring to are the jumps between code that, when not followed closely, lead to dead ends or unfinished thoughts.

The following C++ code demonstrates how not following through on your code can cause bugs.

**C++**

```
//Sample C++ code which has not been followed through
//***********************************
#include "stdafx.h"
#using <mscorlib.dll>
using namespace System;
//***********************************
int addMe(int iVal1, int iVal2);
void displayResults(int iResults);
//***********************************
int _tmain()
{
     int iVal1, iVal2;
    // The following lines ask the user for 2 values.
     Console::WriteLine(S"What is the first value
like to add?");
     iVal1 = Convert::ToInt16(Console::ReadLine()) ;
     Console::WriteLine(S"What is the second value
like to add?");
     iVal2 = Convert::ToInt16(Console::ReadLine()) ;
//the values obtained from the user are now added
together
     addMe(iVal1,iVal2);
     return 0;
}
//***********************************
int addMe(int iVal1, int iVal2)
{
//***********************************
//Function to add values
//5/1/2005
// -jfd
```

```
//***********************************
     int iResults;
     iResults = iVal1 + iVal2;
     //Sum is displayed to screen
     displayResults(iResults);
     return iResults;
}
//***********************************
void displayResults(int iResults)
{
     if (iResults != 753)
     {
         Console::WriteLine(iResults);
     };//To be finished after lunch
}
//***********************************
```

If you follow along with the code, you will see that the user is expected to supply two numbers. Those numbers are then passed to a function that adds them together; the sum is displayed to the screen. However, if the sum of the two numbers equals 753, a second function was to take over and do something with the values. You can see that if the sum of the two numbers supplied does equal 753, nothing happens; it gets lost in code and dies. This is a case when the code was not followed through and a bug was created.

## Syntactically Incorrect Code

Most modern compilers guard against, or at least alert the user to, code that is syntactically incorrect. For example, if the following function declaration was passed to a C++ compiler, an error would be immediately generated.

### C++

```
//***********************************
Void addME(int iVal1, int iVal2);
//***********************************
Void addMe(int iVal1, int iVal2)
```

```
{
     //rest of function follows
}
//***********************************
```

Because C++, unlike VB, is a case-sensitive programming language, the spelling of "addMe" vs. "addME" will cause the C++ compiler to generate a build error. Although the fact that the compiler caught this error is a good thing, not all compilers will catch all syntax errors. Throughout the remainder of this book we will find and discuss more syntax errors and examine how they create bugs.

## Review Questions

The answers to the review questions at the end of each chapter can be found at the end of the book.

1. Who discovered the first computer bug?
2. In what year was the term *bug* first used to describe an electrical fault?
3. What is the definition of a bug?
4. How did the advent of the personal computer help create the modern bug?
5. What was a common way for game developers to avoid Windows bugs when running their games?
6. Name the two causes of memory bugs.
7. How has Microsoft helped in the fight against memory bugs?
8. Name the three different types of code bugs.
9. Why is it important to follow through on your code?

## Looking Ahead

### *Avoiding Bugs*

Now that we know what bugs are, we can focus on two things: getting rid of them and avoiding them altogether. The next chapter discusses the latter. Using our definition of a bug, it should be easy to come up with several points for avoiding bugs.

To avoid writing buggy code, we must:

- Have a clearly defined set of goals
- Fully realize our goals through our code

- Follow through on every aspect of our code
- Write code that is syntactically correct

In Chapter 2 we will explore several skills and techniques for putting these concepts into action.

# Chapter 2

# Writing Bug-Free Code Part I: The Design Process

Now that we have defined what a bug is and have a general idea of what we are looking for, we can start discussing tools and techniques for debugging. The remainder of this book is going to explain debugging while following a natural progression. The flow of the book from this point out will be close to that you would follow if you were designing an application.

> The reason for this book being set up to follow the same progression any project leader would take through an application production project is twofold. First, the tips and techniques will make much more sense if we discuss them in the same context that you would be using them in. Second, the book as a whole will be easier to retain if it is presented to you in an order that you may already be familiar with.
>
> The ordering that we will use, beginning with this chapter, will move from planning, through production, and into testing and rollout. The current chapter will look at preplanning and bug avoidance issues, while the remaining chapters will look at bug detection, information gathering, and error codes. Following this natural progression will give you a well-rounded education in debugging.

This chapter is going to focus on reinforcing the habits that make good programmers into even better debuggers. We will cover several techniques and skills that you can apply to your everyday work habits that will help you eliminate many bugs within your code and find others more easily. Many of these techniques are language independent, so you can apply them using whatever programming language you are most comfortable with.

Throughout Chapter 1 we defined what a bug is. This definition provides us with a blueprint of what we need to be looking for in our own code. Our goal is to use this definition in conjunction with the techniques and skills discovered in this chapter to avoid a greater percent of bugs. Although there will always be a chance of discovering a bug in code regardless of how diligently you program, our goal is to drastically reduce that chance.

This chapter will help you learn how to prevent bugs in your code by anticipating where they will appear in the planning process. These early stages of project development are crucial for debuggers. The difference between a good and bad application is made when the application is in planning. An application's health can hinge on the amount of true careful planning that is performed before any coding even begins.

In this chapter we will cover the importance of good planning. It can easily be argued that the most important part to any application project is the planning and design of the project. Good planning leads to good code writing (covered in Chapter 3) and thus successful, bug-free programs. Chapters 2 and 3 will fit together in that this chapter will cover the planning stages of the project, and Chapter 3 will cover the knowledge you should have as you are coding.

## Planning Your Bug-Free Project

As stated earlier, the first step, and arguably the most important, is planning. In the planning stages, all of the objectives pertaining to the project at hand are discussed and agreed upon. The way these items are agreed upon can vary from environment to environment. In some situations there may be multiteam brainstorming sessions, and in other situations you may be the only person charged with planning and designing. Whether you are working alone or in a team, the main objective will stay the same: design a feasible application that meets the requirements set forth in planning.

If we are to have a successful development project, we must first have a goal to accomplish; otherwise, how would we know when the application was finished. Although this may sound basic or elementary, too many people rush into projects with either only the most rudimentary understanding of the goal or no clear goal at all. Therefore, the first step to having a successful project, and one that can be easily debugged, is to have a clearly defined, obtainable goal.

One of the key words in defining the goal of a project is *obtainable*. The goal must be within the reach of the programmers and other teams involved in the project. A good project team will know the strengths and limitations of everyone involved in the project and plan accordingly.

At this point the project is still a blank page and can literally go anywhere. Nothing is set in stone and nothing has been set forth that cannot be changed with relative ease. This is the time when details are hashed out and every aspect of a project is drawn out and discussed. The preplanning stages of application development set the overall tone for the remainder of the project.

In the same way we spent the first chapter of this book researching what constitutes a bug and creating a definition that encapsulates that research, so too must you put time and effort into planning and defining your project. Although the coding of an application is the bulk of the labor involved in program development, the planning stages should take up the lion's share of the brain power. If the planning is complete, detailed, and well done, the actual coding should flow quite smoothly.

Keep in mind too during this process to watch for areas where bugs can develop, hence the reason we are discussing the process in this book. At this point you may not be looking at too many specific bugs, i.e., "We cannot use ADO in this situation because X, Y, and Z." Although you may have a few of those situations occur in planning, the majority of the bugs you can avoid are those that are generalized. For example, if you know that a single .dll dealing with database processing would be more likely to have a bug in it if two different teams were to share the load of coding it, then this would be the time to set the schedule so that a single cohesive unit was responsible for its production.

The antithesis of proper planning is improvisation. That is, when proceeding without a clear, well-defined plan, the temptation to make things up as you go along is much greater. Thus, there is more of a chance, especially in larger teams, to create disconnects and bugs in your applications. Improvising your code as you write it can lead to not following through on your code. Therefore, without having a well-defined plan, you will not know when your code is fully realized.

This is where we tie in proper planning with debugging. The second part of our bug definition states that bugs can arise from code that is not (among other things) followed though or fully realized. Good, careful work during the planning and development stages can greatly reduce the risk of this happening. Having a clear plan available to all of your programmers will serve two purposes in debugging. First, it will give you and your team members a visual representation of what needs to be done. More importantly, it will provide a resource for deciding who needs to code certain pieces of the project. The latter is more important in that in larger teams, there needs to be communication concerning who is responsible for coding particular areas of an application, thus ensuring that nothing is left behind.

Whether you are one person working on a small project or a team of programmers on a large application, proper planning is important. When working with a larger group of programmers, it is more likely that each person will be working on a separate group of functions, classes, or other pieces of code. Therefore, being able to quickly point to a plan and tell what each programmer's responsibilities are will help reduce redundancy and ensure each piece of the project is completed.

Several key tasks need to be accomplished during the planning stages of a project. The results of these tasks will shape the remainder of the project and decide how we approach the development of the application. More importantly, we will now have a template that we can apply to our definition of a bug to ensure that the code we are writing will not produce any bugs, or at least produce as few bugs as possible. The tasks needing to be accomplished during planning are as follows:

- Define the purpose or goal of the application
- Identify the flow of the application
- Identify the key internal components
- Identify all external application components
- Create a realistic timeline

Let us discuss these points one at a time.

## Define the Purpose

Again, although it might seem that having to define the purpose of a project is elementary and should go without saying, it is often either overlooked or rushed through. Being first and foremost programmers, it is our natural tendency to want to jump right into the programming aspect of a project. If ever there was a programmer's motto, it might be "Code first, ask questions later."

However, it is the questions themselves that are the focus of this section of the chapter. We need to ask those questions and adhere to the answers.

All applications are created for a reason, and you need to find out what that reason is before you can begin. Sometimes getting to the purpose of an application can be as easy as doing your research or asking some basic questions. Try asking these questions, or questions similar in nature, to dig into the reasons behind a potential application project:

- What need is this application intended to fill?
- What could possibly be impacted by the presence of this application?
- Are there any other needs (not directly related to the core need) that can be met by this application?

Finding out what needs are being filled by the application will give you a better understanding of where you need to go in your planning. Make it a point to communicate with the client and ask as many questions as it takes to get a clear and concise picture of what the client is expecting from you and the project. The more questions you ask now, the more you can reduce the amount of confusion later in the project.

When you finish gathering your information, and feel you have a grasp of the client's goals and expectations, take a step back and examine the needs. A client's need can be as specific as "a module needs to be updated to cope with an environmental change" or as general as "the accounting department needs a new application for tracking payroll." Either way, even if just to yourself, you should ask the questions listed to ensure everything is being covered.

If you feel comfortable in the fact that you have all the information needed to move on, you may have a clearly defined goal. This is the first step in preventing serious bugs in the final product. Try to be cognizant, based on your own experience, about what conflicts can arise based on the client's target goal.

> Throughout the remaining portion of this book, you will see reference to the "client." We will be using this more as a general term to describe the person or people you are creating an application for than in reference to a literal client.

Basically, your reason for defining the purpose is to eliminate the chance of surprises further into the development process. Keep in mind that this is the easiest place in the application's development process to make changes. The further into the job you go, the harder it becomes to make changes cleanly to the overall project. Also, when concerning the purpose of a project, the more you know about your target goal, the easier it will be to plan for the avoidance of bugs. This is the reason why we are taking time out to fully prepare and discuss this subject here.

A well-formed, written purpose should include in it all of the expectations of the client. For example, using a general client need of "the accounting department needs a new application for tracking payroll," we will hypothesize how the purpose could be more clearly defined.

> It may seem like that what we have discussed so far in this book has little to do with programming. In fact, programming is more than the physical act of writing code. Couple that with the fact that debugging is a larger process than the act of removing bad code from a block of application instructions. Although so far we have not yet delved into the process of physically write code, the skills we are discussing are important to programmers and have a lot of bearing on debugging as a whole.

The first task should be to ask more questions and really get at the heart of what the client needs. Try not to leave the goal as a broad statement that is open to interpretation. Different people could interpret the same thing different ways. This too can lead to miscommunications and possibly bugs. After asking questions and exploring the client's expectations, a finished purpose of the application may, hypothetically, look like this:

> Create a VB.NET application for the tracking of payroll. The application will interface with an existing SQL database containing the employee data, pay schedules, and pay rates. The application should use Windows authentication for security and only allow access to members of the "Accounting Supervisors" active directory group. Three reports should be built for the application: "Employees by Salary," "Month-to-Date Payroll," and "Year-to-Date Payroll." The application should also allow for the editing of employee and salary data, and should export that data to a file that can be transmitted to the company that will issue checks once a week.

After reading the new purpose of the application, it is very clear what the expectations of the programmers are. This more concise project goal can now be used to test the project's status, and it can be used when determining the completeness of the applications. This is not to imply that goals and directives never change, but at least we now have a solid foundation to build this project. The project now has a base on which the remainder of the planning can be built.

Although planning is arguably the most important part of the programming process, there is one thing you should keep in mind: no purpose statement, no matter how clearly defined, is written in stone. For the most part, these are living documents that are subject to change at almost any time. The more well defined your purpose is from the start will determine how well your purpose adapts to the changes that are almost inevitable.

Once you have your purpose defined and you are confident in the goal of the project, it is time to move on. The next step in bug-proofing your applications during the planning stage is to identify the flow of the application. That is, how the application communicates within itself and with systems external to its structure needs to be identified. Let us now discuss the process behind identifying an application's flow.

## *Identify the Flow of the Application*

Now that you have a well-defined purpose for your application, it is time to identify the application's flow. This refers to a more physical concept in comparison to the logical concept that is defining an application's purpose. It stands to reason that the larger the project, the more complex the flow will be. However, that is not to say that complexity is in any way equal to importance. No matter how large or small, complex or not, it is always important to identify an application's flow.

Let us quickly define what the flow of an application is. The flow visually plots the way an application's functions are tied to each other. That is, a representation is made of how the internal components of the application and the system it runs on are interconnected.

Identifying the flow of an application will give you a visual representation of that application's components. This is important because it allows you to anticipate the communication needs both within your application and external to it. In essence, the flow will let you plot out all of the application's interactions because a single line of code is written. This visualization will let you see some conflicts before they happen.

All of these factors help you avoid the criteria outlined in the definition of a bug. The flow will also let you assign resources in a logical manner and more easily track the progress of your work. After we discuss the process of creating the flow, we will examine how to use that flow to help avoid bugs.

If you have worked on any programming projects before, or even read a book about programming, you have most likely seen an application flowchart. These charts, using a series of shapes, arrows, and captions, show the logical progression an application will follow during its execution — from mapping the user interface to detailing what functions and classes will serve what areas of the application. They show what external systems will be affected by the program; a well-done application flowchart will show it all when it comes to application execution.

Because flowcharts can contain so much information, they can take a while to build. So why go through the trouble of building something so complex? Let us think of it this way: the purpose or goal we defined in the previous section can be thought of as the destination on a long journey. Just because we know where we are going does not necessarily mean we know how to get there. To that effect, knowing the destination and having a general idea of the path to take in getting there does not mean we know the best way to go. The flowchart (or diagram) will let us see the best way to get to our goal, and help us visualize any roadblocks that may stand in the way.

Application flowcharts provide a road map to help us get to our goal. By following this road map, we are ensured that not only are we going to get where we need to go, but we will not miss anything on the way. Our application will do everything it is supposed to do, and contain all of the elements needed to be fully realized. This is a major step in preventing bugs.

Let us now look at some ways we can create application flowcharts. Depending on the corporate culture, or lack thereof, within your environment, you may follow different specifications in your flowcharts. However, for the generalized process we will follow should get you through most situations.

> In many business environments, especially those with larger programming and business teams, an application flowchart may not only be a required part of the planning process, but also be just a smaller part of a larger process. Many companies will include application flowcharts, sample screens, impact statements, and other pieces of paperwork in a single planning session. Many times the application itself is more or less written before the programmers get physically involved. The more due diligence that is done here, the easier everyone else's job can be later.

Before creating a flowchart it may be necessary to really dissect your project. This will help you uncover what components will be involved in the flow of the application. Because the program is not actually written yet, you will need to brainstorm some ideas to get at the underlying structure.

Let us now go back to our hypothetical accounting example. We have a clearly defined purpose and goal. It is now time to dissect this application and see if we can create an application flowchart. Using the accounting application example from the previous section, the following could be the result of a quick brainstorm.

## Accounting Application: Component Brainstorm

- Connect to database.
- Obtain database connection settings.
- Get user information from Windows.
- Display reports with data from database.
- Allow for input to database.
- Allow for recall of previous records.
- Print current record.
- Process for exporting database to flat file.
- Process for transmitting flat file to third party.

We were able to brainstorm nine major components for an accounting application. In most cases, your projects will have many more components than we have here; however, we will try to keep things somewhat simple here. Now that we have these different pieces we can begin to think about putting them in order and assigning them to a flow.

> There are different ways to produce a flowchart or diagram. Although you can hand-draw them just as you would with your brainstorming, most people choose to use a specialized application. The application used to produce the application flowcharts in this book is Microsoft Visio.

Looking at the list of application components we can almost get a feel for how the application should flow before we even create the diagram. It should be clear what components need to go together and which need to interact with which. From this information we can begin to draw relationships between the elements that make up the application and its components. The first step in doing this is to now look through the list you have created and group the elements in a logical manner.

For example, the process that inputs user data into the database and the process that retrieves user data from the database can interact and likely be part of the same process. Likewise, the process that creates the flat file and the process that transmits the flat file both need to communicate with, among other things, the flat file. Therefore, in the application flow these items will be shown interacting with the flat file. Do not overlook the obvious, and try not to overcomplicate things when designing your flow. The following illustration shows an application flowchart based on the accounting brainstorming session. Figure 2.1 illustrates a simple flowchart based on our accounting application.

Now that the flow is created, it is easy to see how the application is expected to work. More importantly, we can see exactly what needs to be done, what components rely on others, and we can have a better chance at fully realizing this project. Examine the application flow carefully; it provides a greater overall picture of how you will need to proceed with your application's development.

In examining the application flowchart, it may become obvious that you have missed something. Luckily, this is the point in the process where such realization can be easy to deal with. In the event that components need to be added to the application, this is the point in the process to do it with the greatest ease. At this point, we can see exactly what will be affected by any changes. Admittedly, it is much easier to work such changes into the project here than during later phases of the project.

To add, remove, or modify a component of the application, simply make the appropriate change and rework your flowchart. Admittedly, redrawing a schematic is a lot easier than recoding hundreds or thousands of lines of code. For this reason, you should spend an extra amount of time on this stage to ensure that you have thought of everything and have planned thoroughly for all possible scenarios.

With the flowchart complete, we can now identify the key internal and external components of the application. The reason we need to identify these components is to be able to create a cohesive project plan. Once we know what all of the internal and external components are, we will then, with greater ease, be able to accurately say which elements should be grouped together, thus combining our programming efforts. This increases our chances of fully realizing this project.

## Identify Internal and External Components

The flow is now complete and it is time to identify how the application is to be divided before we proceed. That is, the key internal and external pieces of the application need to be defined. Defining and categorizing

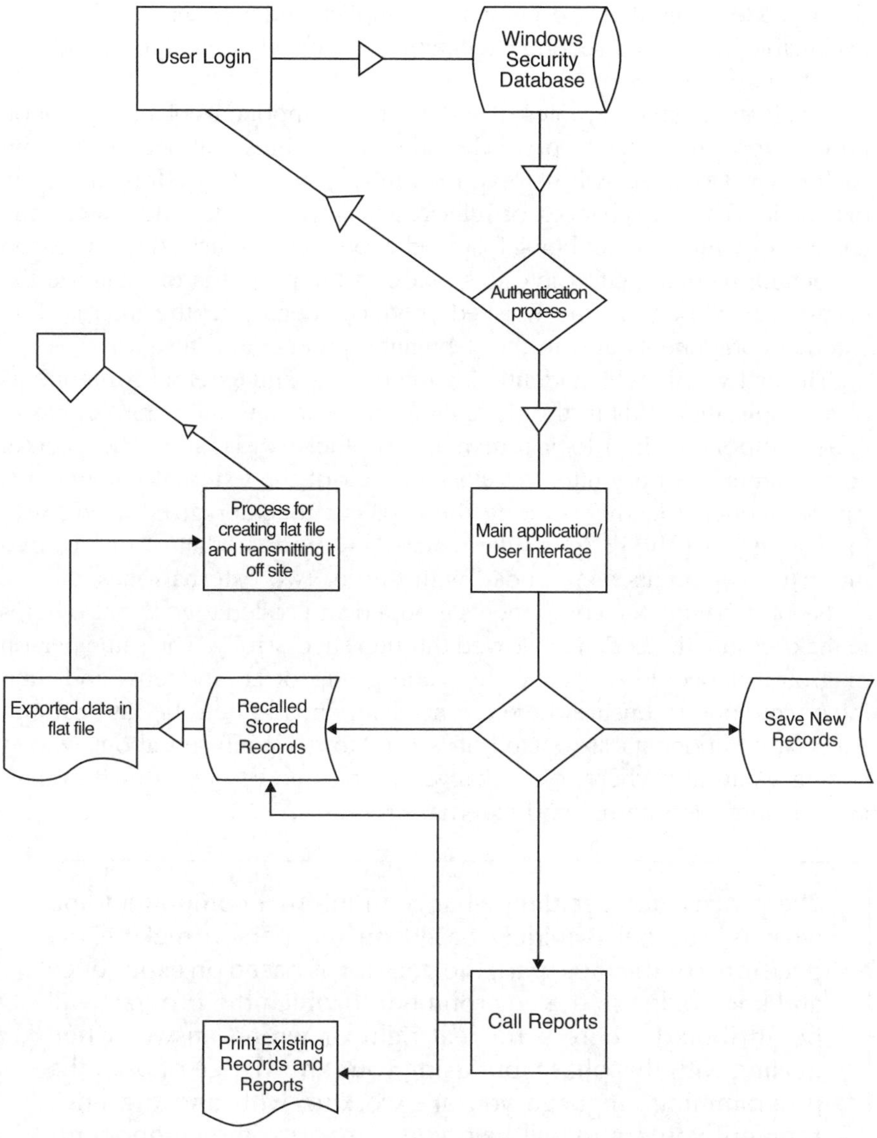


**Figure 2.1 Accounting application flowchart.**

the components of an application as either external or internal will greatly affect how the project is coded.

The internal components of an application are those pieces of code that are generally contained within the compiled executable. All of the classes, functions, modules, and other code that are compiled into the final executable can be considered internal components. Conversely, all of the code items that are generally compiled independent of the main executable, in either a second executable, .dll, or other file, are considered an external component.

By identifying the key internal and external components of an application project, you can better map which code architectures will need to rely on each other. Doing so will help you organize your coding efforts in a way that optimizes your chances of fully realizing your code, and lessens the chances of your code not being followed through. Obviously, the key reason for putting so much effort into this phase of the project is to minimize the occurrence of bugs in the finished product. Identifying the internal and external components aids in the debugging process in a few ways.

The first way in which identifying the internal and external components of an application aids in the debugging process is by allowing people to code components in a logical manner. In other words, all of the internal components can be written together and all of the external components can be written together. Coding these pieces together goes a long way in ensuring that the code is fully realized — more so than if one or two internal components were coded with one or two external ones.

Second, having the components grouped and coded together also helps in making sure the code is followed through successfully. The same person or group of people can code the same group of components and then trace that code to ensure there are no dead ends. When the internal and external components are mixed, it is easy to get confused about who is coding what and where. With that said, let us go through our flowchart and identify the internal and external processes.

> The process for deciding what is an internal component and what is external is widely based on the person making the decision. For the most part, the decision is based on experience and knowledge of the environment to which the program will be attributed. There is no real right or wrong answer when dealing with this phase, but using your knowledge of both the programming language you are working with and the environment you are in will help you categorize the components in the way that is best for your needs.

### *Account Application: Internal and External Components*

#### Internal Components

- Connect to database.
- Get user information from windows.

- Allow for input to database.
- Allow for recall of previous records.
- Print current record.

### External Components

- Display reports with data from database.
- Connect to database.
- Create flat file from saved data.
- Export flat file to third party.

With all of the components identified, you can move on to creating a working timeline for the project.

## *Create a Realistic Timeline*

When planning an application development project, time is everything. It can be construed that if time were not an issue, programmers would be able to fully optimize their code and all applications would be tested for adverse interactions with other systems, nearly eliminating bugs and the need for books like this. However, time is an issue, and you must make the best of it.

Often there are two opposing forces at work in determining the timeline with which an application should be written. There is the time of expectancy on behalf of the client, and there is the time within which the application developers want to finish the project. These two timelines can differ greatly from project to project, and you must be able to objectively determine exactly how much time you will need to complete your task.

> Although this part of the process is geared to people in roles where assigning timelines to projects is key, anyone can benefit from it. Even in the toughest corporate environments you as a programmer may have some say as to how long you will need to develop a given piece of code.

In dealing with creating a timeline within which to complete the project, there are multiple factors to consider. On one hand, there is always the temptation to complete the project as quick as possible and impress the client with a snappy turnaround. On the other hand, there is the view that the more time to develop and test, the better, and a project can never have too much of either. The skill here is knowing how to take a little bit from both hands to create a realistic timeline.

When I plan projects, I try to do it in two distinct phases. The first phase includes everything we have discussed to this point in the book, naming the goal, creating the flow, identifying the internal and external components, and then creating what I think is a realistic timeline. Then, because the programmer's and client's expectations tend to differ, in the second phase I go back to the client with the flow and the preliminary timeline and we can work from there.

Again, because there is no clear right or wrong when making a timeline, you just have to go on instinct and experience. However, try not to rush yourself when possible. If you have the time to follow through and fully test everything, use it; the finished product will be that much better.

## Review Questions

1. What are the hazards of improvising or not planning your coding projects?
2. What is the main reason for defining the purpose of a project?
3. What should a well-formed purpose include?
4. What questions should you ask when defining the purpose of an application?
5. True or false? The more complex an application is, the more important it is to identify its flow.
6. If defining the purpose is an intellectual process, what is identifying the flow?
7. Why is it easier to add components to the project after the flow is complete?
8. Describe an internal application component.
9. Describe an external application component.
10. What are the two (common) opposing forces in determining a project timeline?

## Looking Ahead

In Chapter 3 we will look at the habits of good debugging programmers. That is, we will examine what habits, skills, and techniques you can use in your programming (now that the planning is complete) to create a successful bug-free application.

# Chapter 3

# Bug-Free Code Part II: The Coding Process

This chapter will pick up where Chapter 2 left off, in that we will discuss what happens after project planning. We will be examining more habits, skills, and techniques that can make you an effective debugger by preventing bugs in the first place. Where the last chapter focused on the design process and the concepts of aiding code follow-through and code realization through planning, this chapter will look further into the coding process.

Now that our sample accounting program has been thoroughly planned out, and you have a realistic timeline for completing the job, you can shift your focus to the heart of your project: the coding. This chapter will cover some simple techniques that can be applied in code to prevent or aid in the removal of bugs.

The concepts covered in the chapter will include:

- Commenting
- Coding standards
- Functions and subroutines
- Reusable code

First we will discuss one of the strongest tools a programmer has in the fight against bugs: comments.

## It Is All in the Comments

One of the worst feelings in a programmer's career is opening a program written months, possibly years before, only to find that it was not commented thoroughly, if at all. Given that there are often multiple ways to achieve the same end result in programming, it can be difficult to figure out what is going on in even the easiest of programs if there is no guide to help you find what you are looking for. This scenario can be made even more complicated with the added pressure of trying to track down a bug in a jungle of uncommented code.

The easiest way to ensure quick bug tracking in your programs is to comment your work thoroughly and completely. The comments you add will help you read through your code and find the possibly affected sections of code with ease. Because comments are written in plain English, they can be read more quickly than code and can be more verbose and descriptive.

Many programmers say that the process of commenting is too time-consuming, distracting, or simply not worth the trouble. Others simply believe that they will remember everything, and therefore have no need to comment their work. The facts are that the short amount of time it takes to comment a block of code is not nearly equal to the amount of time that would be needed when hunting through the unfamiliar code; after you become used to the process, the act of commenting is not distracting, and they really are worth whatever trouble they may seem to cause.

When forming your comments, you should try to gear them as though they were for someone completely unrelated to the project and unfamiliar with the code. That is, picture someone who has no prior knowledge of your code attempting to locate a specific line or function. This is a good way to justify how and where to comment.

Comments should give enough information so that someone completely unfamiliar with the program or project can easily find a specific area of the code. How much information is enough? This is completely objective; however, there is a fine line between enough information and too much. Take the following VB.NET subroutine, Listing 3.1.

### Listing 3.1: HelloWorld VB.NET Subroutine

```
Public Sub HelloWorld(txtBox as TextBox)
txtBox.Text = "Hello World!"
End Sub
```

An overzealous coder might comment this as seen in Listing 3.2:

**Listing 3.2: HelloWorld with Too Many Comments**

```
Public Sub HelloWorld(txtBox as TextBox)
'This is the beginning of the HelloWorld SubRoutine
'This subroutine is public
'This subroutine was written on May 5th 2005 by
J.F.DiMarzio
'so far there have been no revisions to this
subroutine
'The following line of the subroutine accepts a text
box object and writes "Hello World!" to it
txtBox.Text = "Hello World!" ' see, it says "Hello
World!"
'That is the end of this subroutine
End Sub
```

Although his or her heart may be in the right place, this is clearly too much information to describe the subroutine. Not only is there too much information, the information that is there is fairly hard to read. Take a look at Listing 3.3, a more concise version of the same subroutine with comments.

**Listing 3.3: HelloWorld with Good Comments**

```
Public Sub HelloWorld(txtBox as TextBox)
'***************************
'Write "Hello World!" to text box
'j.f.d
'5/5/05
'****************************
'revisions:
'****************************
'****************************
'Begin
'****************************
txtBox.Text = "Hello World"
'****************************
'End
'****************************
End Sub
```

The latter version of the subroutine, although not much shorter in length, contains less extraneous information and more valuable information. The comments are also organized in a way that makes them easier to read and easier to apply to multiple projects. We can clearly see the start and end of the code block, the purpose stands out at the top, and the revision section is nicely separated. Even if we were just scanning through this subroutine, we could quickly identify the different components of the code as they passed by.

> One concept you will surely pick up on throughout this book is that of standardization. Creating standards and being consistent with following those standards is key in many areas of programming, but more so in debugging. Whether dealing with comments or code, when you work according to standards your eyes will become trained to look for certain elements in certain places. By following the same standards over and over, you will quickly pick up the ability to scan through your code and find problem areas.

Looking at the two commenting examples, one may ask, "What information should be put into comments, or what is extraneous when it comes to commenting?" Although the answer will depend partly on what information you think will be important to people looking at your code, there are some general guidelines that we can follow:

- Identify the purpose of the segment of code; this can include names, return types, and dependencies (introductory comments).
- Mark the beginning and end of key sections of code to make them more visible.
- Clearly label all revisions (including reviser and revision date).
- Explain more complicated lines of code with in-code comments.

Before we take a look at these different kinds of comments and the information that should go in each, let us examine the comment characters for different languages. The next section explains how to comment code in VB.NET, C++, C, C#, and Java.

## Comment Characters of Multiple Languages

Consider this section a refresher in commenting. It makes sense to ensure that everyone is on the same page before continuing to the next sections.

Where the next sections deal with what information should be put into comments, this one will quickly explain how to comment.

Let us start with the Visual Basic series of languages, and then we will look at C, C++, and Java.

Although there are a host of differences between Visual Basic 6 and Visual Basic .NET, one thing that they still share is their commenting character. The apostrophe, also referred to as the tick, is used to separate commented text from the surrounding code. Listing 3.4 shows the VB comment marker.

**Listing 3.4: VB.NET Comment Maker**

```
Dim string1 as String'Variable Declaration
'This is a VB / VB.NET comment line
```

C++ and Java share a common comment character (or set of characters). Both languages use a double forward slash, //, to mark comments, as seen in Listing 3.5.

**Listing 3.5: C++ Comment Maker**

```
//This is a C++ comment line
int myNum = 3; //Integer variable
```

C++ and Java also share a second set of comment characters with another language, C. The opening comment marker, /*, can be used with the closing */ to comment off blocks of code, as in Listing 3.6.

**Listing 3.6: C Comment Marker**

```
/* The
Following lines of code
Are all comments
*/
```

## Introductory Comments

During your testing of a new application, you discover that there is a memory bug. The bug manifests itself when the application opens an external file. Now you must scan through the 30 modules of the program looking for the one that contains the function that in turn opens the file. However, you did not comment your code; therefore, the search could take hours.

Many programmers do look down on commenting because it arguably distracts from their thought process and takes too much time to type out. With the right information, comments can become a time-saving tool. If there were a proper commenting structure that told you exactly where to look, the aforementioned scenario would take only a minute rather than hours.

Introductory comments are placed at the top of classes, modules, functions, and subroutines. In the case of classes and modules, introductory comments explain and outline what can be found within. They would normally outline the general purpose of the enclosed functions, subroutines, and classes. Other information can include the author or authors of the enclosed code, the date it was written, and the dates and purposes of any revisions.

When writing introductory comments it is important not to include too much information, yet put in enough detail that anyone not related to the project can still find a specific piece of code with relative ease. Commenting in such a way will make debugging your application code exponentially easier. Remember, debugging applications at the code level is very different than debugging at the runtime level. When you are performing code-level debugging, it may not be immediately discernable exactly what you are looking for. For this reason, a good comment structure is needed to lead you quickly to the points you need to go in your code.

Let us assume a bug has been reported in our accounting application. The finished application consists of multiple classes, functions, and subroutines. Now we may have a rough idea, based on the description of the bug, what module or class may be generating the bug. However, by scanning through the introductory comments, we can easily find the description of the code block that will lead us right to the offending code.

Now that we know the purpose behind introductory comments, let us look at what information should be included and how you can format it.

> Keep in mind, there really is no right or wrong way to do this, and no one is going to sneak up on you, fan through your code, and grade you in your comments, but there is a better way to do it for better results when it counts.

As we have discussed, introductory comments are meant for one purpose, introducing you, or any other coder, to the section of code to which the comments are attached. Where in-code comments serve to explain specific lines of code, introductory comments simply outline and summarize the accompanying code. There are several key pieces of information that should be included in your introductory comment structure, depending on your needs and environment. These pieces of information are:

- Purpose of class, module, function, or subroutine
- Identity of programmer who created the code
- Date the code was created
- Revision history
- Optional information
- Return type
- Dependencies
- Applications used in

The purpose of the class, module, function, or subroutine explains exactly that, the purpose of the code block. For example, our accounting application may have a module containing functions and subroutines dedicated to performing different pay rate calculations. The purpose section of the introductory comments may look something like this:

**Listing 3.7: VB6/VB.NET Purpose**

```
'***********************************
'Contains functions for pay rate calculations
'***********************************
```

**Listing 3.8: C Purpose Comments**

```
/*
Contains functions for pay rate calculations
*/
```

**Listing 3.9: C++/Java Purpose Comments**

```
//***********************************
//Contains functions for pay rate calculations
//***********************************
```

***Insert NOTE icon here***

Notice the lines of asterisks (or in the case of the C comments, the blank line) both proceeding and anteceding the body of the comments. This gives the comments better readability and a more organized look within your code. The neater your comments look, the easier it will be to read through them quickly. Offset lines like these are generally used to mark large sections of comments and not for in-code comments.

The identity of the programmer is important to have within your introductory comments to allow people reading the code to direct additional questions to someone. I hesitate to say that such information be used for accountability, but in fact, knowing the identity of someone who may be causing you exponentially more time in bug fixes than in the initial development may also be helpful. I generally identify my code by initials, followed by the date the code was started.

#### Listing 3.10: VB6/VB.NET Identity Comments

```
'**********************************
'jfd
'5-5-2005
'**********************************
```

#### Listing 3.11: C Identity Comments

```
/*
Jfd
5-5-2005
*/
```

#### Listing 3.12: C++/Java Identity Comments

```
//**********************************
//jfd
//5-5-2005
//**********************************
```

Finally, the revision history tacks the important information, including version numbers, related to any changes made to the enclosed code. This information is important in understanding when and why changes were made to the code. You may be hunting down a bug that was already thought to have been fixed, or even a bug that was caused by a fix you did not know had been made. The revision section should look like this:

#### Listing 3.13: VB6/VB.NET Revision

```
'**********************************
'revisions:
'    Change made to tax calculation.
'    MA tax corrected from 4% to 5%
'    jfd
```

```
'    5-10-2005
'    version 1.1
'*********************************
```

**Listing 3.14: C Revision**

```
/*
revisions:
     Change made to tax calculation.
     MA tax corrected from 4% to 5%
     jfd
     5-10-2005
     version 1.1
*/
```

**Listing 3.15: C++/Java Revision**

```
//*********************************
//revisions:
//   Change made to tax calculation.
//   MA tax corrected from 4% to 5%
//   jfd
//   5-10-2005
//   version 1.1
//*********************************
```

Depending on your environment or the type of business you are in, you may want to include additional information in your introductory comment structure. This information includes the return types of your functions, dependency information for your code, or, in the event of reuse, a list of the applications that this code appears in. The information you include really depends on what you find as important within your corporate structure. Some of the optional information is shown as follows:

**Listing 3.16: VB6/VB.NET Optional Comments**

```
'*********************************
'Return Type:
'    Boolean
```

```
 '**********************************
'*********************************
'dependencies:
'    requires criticalDll.dll to run
'This code also appears in:
'    calcRate.dll
 '**********************************
```

**Listing 3.17: C Optional Comments**

```
/*
Return Type:
    Boolean
*/
/*
dependencies:
    requires criticalDll.dll to run
This code also appears in:
    calcRate.dll
*/
```

**Listing 3.18: C++/Java Optional Comments**

```
//*********************************
//Return Type:
//   Boolean
//*********************************
//*********************************
//dependencies:
//   requires criticalDll.dll to run
//This code also appears in:
//   calcRate.dll
//*********************************
```

Assembling the information we discussed in this section, a typical introductory comment structure is as follows:

**Listing 3.19: VB6/VB.NET Full Comments**

```
'*********************************
'Contains functions for pay rate calculations
'jfd
'5-5-2005
'*********************************
'*********************************
'revisions:
'    Change made to tax calculation.
'    MA tax corrected from 4% to 5%
'    jfd
'    5-10-2005
'    version 1.1
'*********************************
```

**Listing 3.20: C Full Comments**

```
/*
Contains functions for pay rate calculations
jfd
5-5-2005
*/
/*
revisions:
     Change made to tax calculation.
     MA tax corrected from 4% to 5%
     jfd
     5-10-2005
     version 1.1
*/
```

**Listing 3.21: C++/Java Full Comments**

```
//*********************************
//Contains functions for pay rate calculations
//jfd
```

```
//5-5-2005
//**********************************
//**********************************
//revisions:
//   Change made to tax calculation.
//   MA tax corrected from 4% to 5%
//   jfd
//   5-10-2005
//   version 1.1
//**********************************
```

With an understanding of basic introductory comment structure, let us now examine in-code comments.

## *In-Code Comments*

Comments that run through your code blocks, explaining lines of code as they are written, are known as in-code comments. In-code comments are the comments that most of us are familiar with, and the comments that most programmers find time-consuming and unnecessary.

One misconception that many programmers have, and the one that leads many of them to not like the act of commenting, is that to truly comment your code correctly you must explain every line. This simply is not true, and in fact, if every line had to be commented, no one would do it.

Rather, as with the introductory comments, there is a fine line between good in-code comments and too much information. When writing in-code comments, try to limit your comment descriptions to the important facts about those lines of code that other programmers may have trouble interpreting. In other words, try not to write a book about every line of code in your program. Rather, write a short description about the lines that someone with a basic knowledge of programming may not recognize. For example, look at the following block of VB code:

### Listing 3.22: Easy VB Code

```
Public Function AddMe(val1 as Integer, val2 as
Integer) as Integer
AddMe = val1 + val2
End Function
```

Admittedly, you do not need to be a VB expert to understand what this function is doing. Now add some extraneous comments and this rather simple example of a small VB function becomes messy and difficult to read.

### Listing 3.23: More Complex VB Code

```
Public Function AddMe(val1 as Integer, val2 as
Integer) as Integer
'This is a function for returning the sum of two
values
'written by j.f. dimarzio on May 5th 2005
'there have been no revisions and this function
returns an integer
'The following line of code accepts two integer
values assigned
'    to the variables val1 and val2, then adds them
together
'Begin code now
AddMe = val1 + val2   'adding values val1 and val2
'End code now
'The sum of val1 and val2 is returned to the user
through AddMe
End Function
```

As you can see, this very simple function has become a mess of unnecessary comments and is fairly hard to read. A function this simplistic would almost require no comment structure at all. However, for the sake of keeping your code standardized, we should still include some basic introductory comments.

### Listing 3.24: VB Code with Introductory Comments

```
Public Function AddMe(val1 as Integer, val2 as
Integer) as Integer
'***********************************************
*
'Function for returning sum of two integers
'    jfd
'    5/5/2005
```

```
'*************************************************
*
addMe = val1 + val2
'*************************************************
*
End Function
```

Let us look at a more complicated block of code, one that requires some in-code comments. This block is provided in VB6 only, so as to give you a sense of the comment structure itself (the actual code is irrelevant).

**Listing 3.25: More Complex VB Code without Comments**

```
Public Function GetValues() As Values
queryString = "Select values from valTbl where
closureCode = NULL"
rs.Open queryString, connection
If rs.BOF = False Then
     getValues.openCode = rs.Fields("openCode")
     getValues.userName = rs.Fields("nameFirst") &
" " & rs.Fields("nameLast")
     rs.MoveFirst
End If
Do Until rs.EOF
rs.Close
End Function
```

Examining this code block, it might be slightly more difficult for someone with limited programming experience to scan the code and know exactly what is happening. Even with introductory comments added, the task is not mush easier.

**Listing 3.26: Commented Complex VB Code**

```
Public Function GetValues() As Values
'******************************
'Function issues query to valTbl, retrieves
'    the open code and user name
'    jfd
```

```
'    5/5/2005
'******************************
'Revisions:
'******************************
'Begin
'******************************
Dim queryString as String
Dim connection As Object
Dim connectionString As String
Dim rs As Object
Set connection = CreateObject("adodb.connection")
Set rs = CreateObject("adodb.recordset")
szConnect = "DSN=" & Trim(frmConfigure.txtDSN.Text)
& ";UID=" &_ Trim(frmConfigure.txtUserName.Text) & ";
PWD=" & Trim(frmConfigure.txtPassword.Text)
conn.Open szConnect
queryString = "Select values from valTbl where
closureCode = NULL"
rs.Open queryString, connection
If rs.BOF = False Then
     getValues.openCode = rs.Fields("openCode")
     getValues.userName = rs.Fields("nameFirst") &
" " & rs.Fields("nameLast")
     rs.MoveFirst
End If
rs.Close
'******************************
'End
'******************************
End Function
```

Even with our introductory comments in place, reading the code block is not very easy. The introductory comments are doing their job by providing us with an introduction to the purpose of the function. However, if we needed to track down a bug that was generating a Structure Query Language (SQL) database error, we still might not know where to look. Some in-code comments are needed to help guide the debugger through the code.

Keep in mind that we do not want to comment every line of code (unless it is absolutely necessary).

Therefore, we can quickly look through the function and identify those lines that possibly may not need to be commented. That is, any lines that are simplistic and universal in their meaning — enough so that even someone with basic programming knowledge may understand their meaning.

Here is a list of the code from our function. The lines have been numbered to make them easier to discuss.

```
 1. Dim queryString as String
 2. Dim connection As Object
 3. Dim connectionString As String
 4. Dim rs As Object
 5. Set connection = CreateObject("adodb.connection")
 6. Set rs = CreateObject("adodb.recordset")
 7. szConnect = "DSN=" & Trim(frmConfigure.txtDSN.Text)
    & ";UID=" &_ Trim(frmConfigure.txtUserName.Text)
    & ";PWD=" & Trim(frmConfigure.txtPassword.Text)
 8. conn.Open szConnect
 9. queryString = "Select values from valTbl where
    closureCode = NULL"
10. rs.Open queryString, connection
11. If rs.BOF = False Then
12. getValues.openCode = rs.Fields(“openCode”)
13. getValues.userName = rs.Fields(“nameFirst”) & “ “
    & rs.Fields(“nameLast”)
14. rs.MoveFirst
15. End If
16. rs.Close
```

Lines 1 through 4 represent dimensioning statements; this is Visual Basic's tool for declaring variables. These lines generally do not need to be individually commented. Everyone should be able to recognize a variable declaration; therefore, to comment them would be redundant. However, in an effort to make the code look more organized, it is advised to use comments in marking off the variable declarations from the body of the code.

Lines 5 through 7, on the other hand, represent some database-building functions, and unless you have worked with database before, you may not know the direct meaning of every line. These lines should be commented to some degree. (After we examine all of the lines we will discuss the actual comments that should be included.)

Line 8 is fairly obvious in its language, as is line 9. A value is being assigned to a variable named `queryString`. This line may not need to be commented as it is easy to see that `queryString` equals the quoted text. Regardless of the language that you are accustomed to programming in, and most likely regardless of your skill level, you can identify what is happening in line 9.

Lines 10 through 14 do deserve some explanation through comments. These lines are somewhat more complicated in nature, and it may not be immediately clear what their function is.

Finally, lines 15 and 16 are also very self-explanatory. Line 15 marks the end of an `IF` statement, while line 16 closes an object that was opened in line 10. These two lines generally should not need to be commented. If you feel you want to comment them to bring a sense of closure to your code you can mark them using an `End`, as was done in the previous example.

Let us look at how this code block could be commented to help in the debugging process.

**Listing 3.27: Possible VB Comments**

```
Public Function GetValues() As Values
'*******************************
'Function issues query to valTbl, retrieves
'    the open code and user name
'    jfd
'    5/5/2005
'********************************
'Revisions:
'********************************
'Variable Declarations
'********************************
Dim queryString as String
Dim connection As Object
Dim connectionString As String
Dim rs As Object
'********************************
'Begin
'********************************
```

```
Set connection = CreateObject("adodb.connection")
'Set active connection
Set rs = CreateObject("adodb.recordset")  'Set rs as
current recordset
'Build Connection String
szConnect = "DSN=" & Trim(frmConfigure.txtDSN.Text)
& ";UID=" &_ Trim(frmConfigure.txtUserName.Text) & ";
PWD=" & Trim(frmConfigure.txtPassword.Text)
'

conn.Open szConnect
queryString = "Select values from valTbl where
closureCode = NULL"
rs.Open queryString, connection     'Populate rs with
data from query
If rs.BOF = False Then              'Loop through
current record set
     getValues.openCode = rs.Fields("openCode")
' assign values to getValues
     getValues.userName = rs.Fields("nameFirst") &
" " & rs.Fields("nameLast")
     rs.MoveFirst
End If
rs.Close
'*******************************
'End
'*******************************
End Function
```

Now if we knew there was a bug in the SQL connection string for this function, using the comments we could quickly find the line that builds the connection string and fix it. In this way, comments can be one of the most important tools in finding existing bugs in application code.

With the advent of Microsoft's .NET programming suite, programmers have a pair of tools at their disposal for commenting code. The use of eXtensible Markup Language (XML) comment tags and .NET regions can boost the effect of commenting for more readable code. XML comment tags will be covered in greater detail in Chapter 7, and the next section of this chapter will focus on .NET regions.

## Using .NET Regions

A .NET region is a block of code that is visually set apart from the surrounding code elements. Regions allow programmers to group similar code in a way that makes it easier to parse through, for both the programmer and testers/debuggers. One great feature of regions is that they are language independent; you can use them in any .NET language (VB.NET, C++.NET, C#, J#).

Within the .NET Integrated Design Environment (IDE), regions appear as collapsible objects identified by a common English name. That is, when looking through your code, you may see a collapsed object named "My Variable Declarations." Expanding this region would then show all of the code contained within "My Variable Declarations."

> You are not forced to name a region in a way that describes its contents. For example, you can name a region "My Dog Spot" if you wanted to. However, seeing that this is a tool to be used for making code scanning easier, it would be better to let the name of the region describe its contents. The name "My Dog Spot" really does not help to identify the contents of the code block.

A region, or block of code, can be visually set apart from the surrounding code using a region directive. The directive you use is dependent on the language you are using. In VB.NET the `#Region` directive is used to open a region and the `#End Region` directive is used to close it, as seen in the following example.

### Listing 3.28: VB.NET Region

```
#Region "<NAME OF REGION>"
     <.NET code>
#End Region
```

However, in C# and in J# the directive is slightly different; `#region` is followed by `#endregion`. C++, as of Visual Studio 2005, will support the use of `#pragma region` and `#pragma endregion`.

Previous versions of Visual Studio .NET support the use of `#pragma region` and `#pragma endregion` in C++, but they do not have the same visual impact that `#region` and `#end region` do in other languages. In VS 2005 the `#pragma region` directive creates collapsible regions in C++.

The name you apply to the region will be used to identify the block of code when the region itself is collapsed. Figure 3.1 shows a standard region from a VB.NET application.

Every VB.NET application has this region in it at creation. That is, it is automatically inserted by Microsoft when the project is started, and contains initialization code. Microsoft hides this code in the region to keep it out of the programmer's way, yet allows it to be accessible when needed. Figure 3.2 shows what this region looks like when it is expanded.

As you can see, this generic region contains information required by the VB.NET form to run. The region is used to keep the code neatly packed away. This makes the code visually more pleasing and much easier to work with.

For example, if there were a problem with the generic Microsoft code, you would know exactly where to look. You could move straight to the region and expand it. This would display for you all of the code contained within the region, allowing you to edit what you need. When you are finished, simply collapse the region and move on.

One common use for regions is to separate out logically distinct blocks of code. The following example shows how you would set your variable declarations apart from the surrounding code using regions.

**Listing 3.29: VB.NET Region with Variables**

```
#Region " Variables "
Dim myString as String
Dim myInteger as Integer
Dim myBool as Boolean
#End Region
```

**Listing 3.30: C# Region with Variables**

```
#region Variables
int myInteger;
string myString;
#endregion
```

Another difference is in the way the directives can be used. Although this is not a major issue, there is a slight difference in how and where VB.NET and C# allow you to use `#Region` and `#region`, respectively. VB.NET will not let you use the `#Region` directive within a contained block of code. That is, a region must fully contain one or many code blocks;

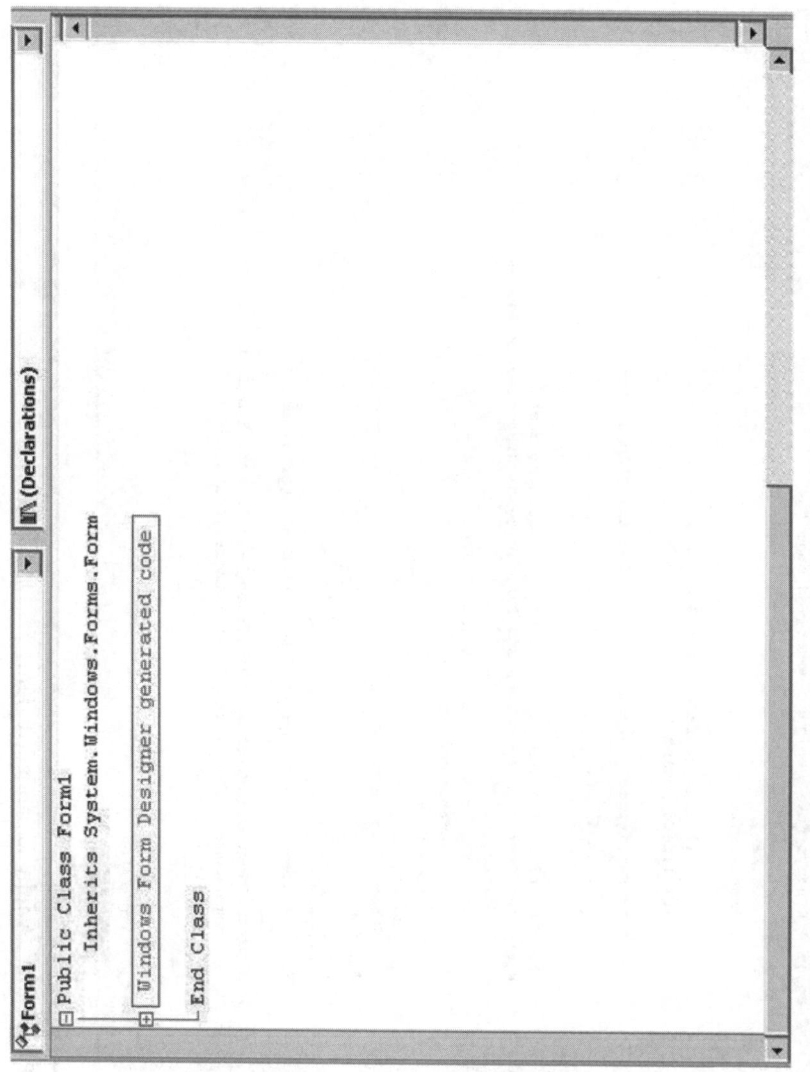


**Figure 3.1 A collapsed .NET region.**

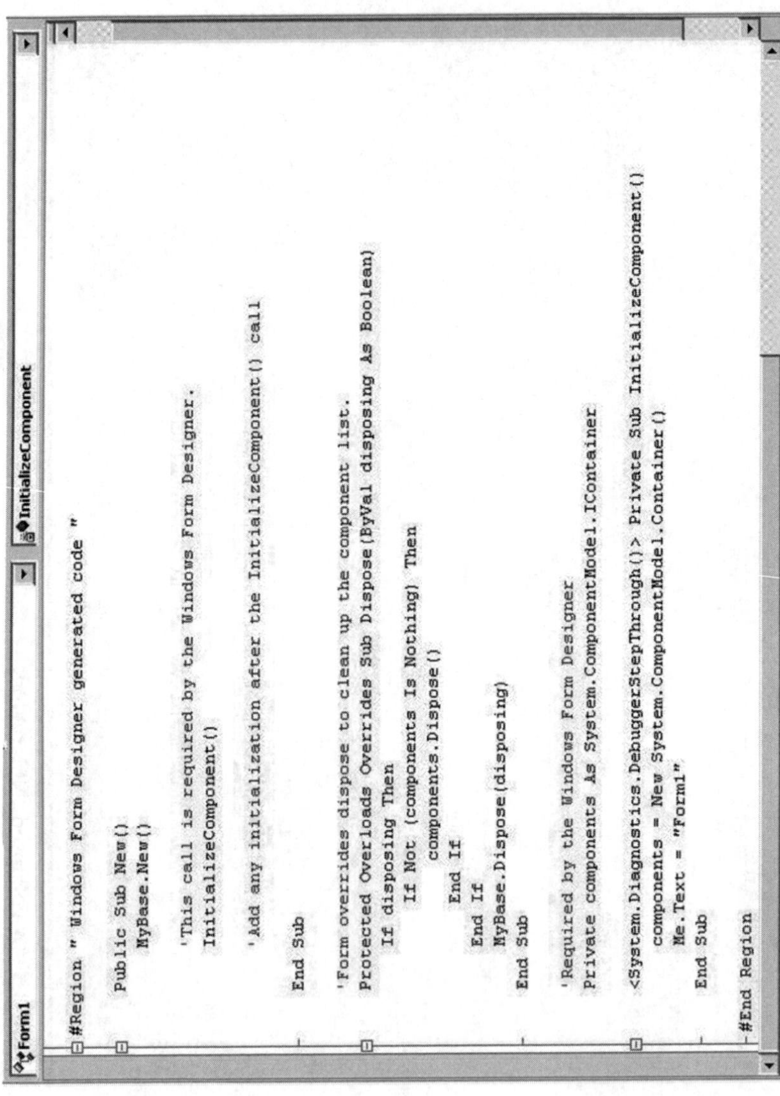


**Figure 3.2 A fully expanded region.**

> Notice also a subtle difference in the way the two languages accept a naming parameter for the region being created. In VB the name of the region must appear in quotes, i.e., "Variables", but in C# and J# the region name should not be quoted.

however, a code block cannot contain a region. For example, a VB.NET region can contain a VB function, as illustrated in the following code:

**Listing 3.31: VB Function within a Region**

```
#Region "TestFunction"
Public Function TestFunction as Boolean
'All of my test code
End Function
#End Region
```

What VB.NET does not allow you to do is more like what we find in the following code:

**Listing 3.32: Invalid Use of VB Regions**

```
Public Function testFunction as Boolean
#Region "Variables"
Dim myString as string
#End Region
'The rest of my test code
End Function
```

C#, on the other hand, does allow you to use `#region` wherever you need to. For example:

**Listing 3.33: C# Use of Regions**

```
#region MainEntryPoint
     static void Main()
  {
     #region RunAppCode
     Application.Run(new Form1());
     #endregion
  }
#endregion
```

Notice in the C# example we used the `#region` directive both in and around the block of code.

Regions can also be nested, as shown in the C# example. That is, one or several regions can appear within another region, in both VB.NET and C#. Regions are extremely flexible and allow for a great level of scalability. Figure 3.3 illustrates a fully collapsed nested region.

Examining Figure 3.3, a group of nested regions (here labeled "This is a Parent region") appears as any other region within your code. Expanding this parent region will show the internal, nested regions. Figure 3.4 show this parent region expanded, exposing its nested child regions.

The parent region, when expanded, shows all of the code and any child regions contained within. After expanding the parent region of a nested region group, the child regions will still appear collapsed, as seen in Figure 3.4. These regions are easily expanded to display the code contained within. Figure 3.5 illustrates all of the regions of the region group expanded.

Now that we have talked about the syntax behind regions and quickly looked at how to form them, let us discover their usefulness. The following code is a module taken from a fictitious VB.NET application. Looking at the module, even though it is quite simplistic, the code is mixed together and uneasy to decipher at first.

#### Listing 3.34: A VB Module without Regions

```
Module modFunctions
     Public intAge As Integer
     Public stringName As String
     Public boolRespond As Boolean
     Public Function GetName(ByVal txtName As
TextBox) As Boolean
         On Error GoTo getNameErrorHandler
         If txtName.Text.ToString <> "" Then
             stringName = txtName.Text.ToString
             getName = True
         Else
             getName = False
         End If
         Exit Function
getnameerrorhandler:
         Debug.WriteLine(Err.Description)
```

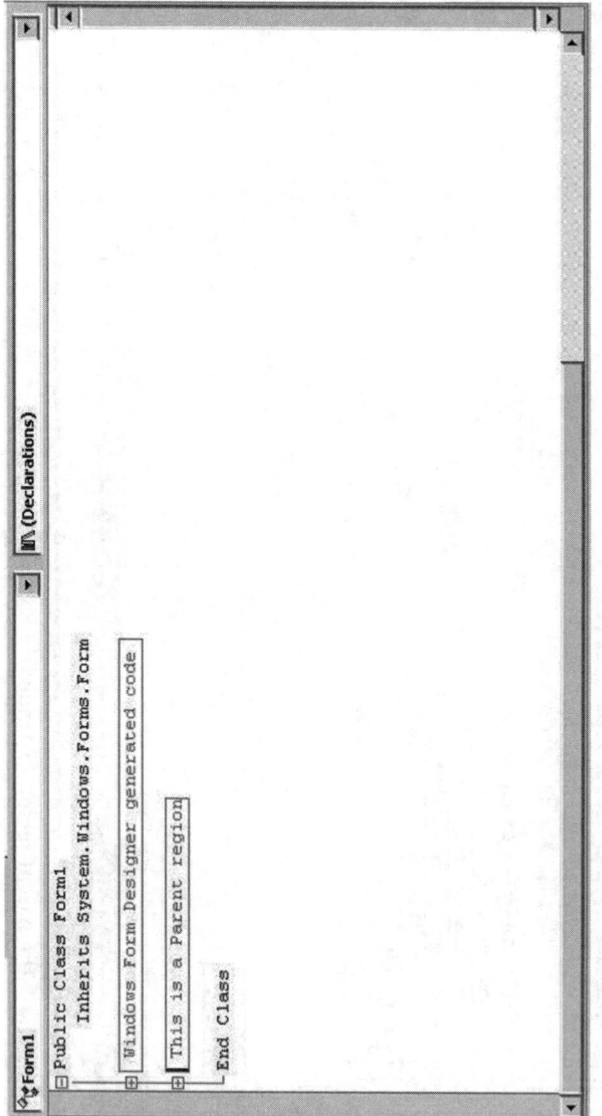


**Figure 3.3 A fully collapsed nested region.**

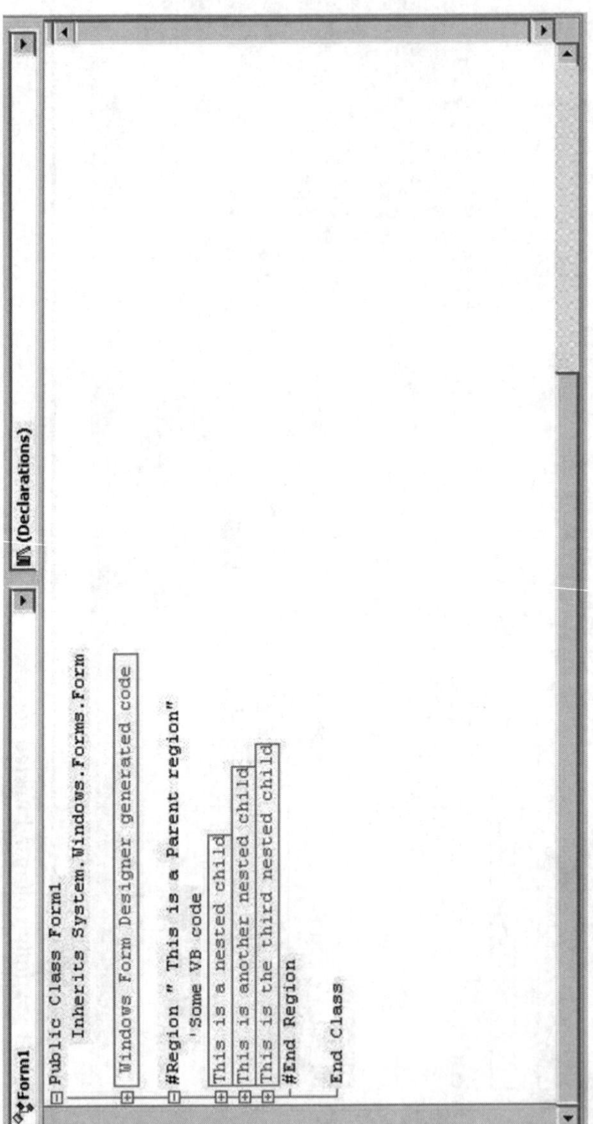


**Figure 3.4 The parent region expanded.**

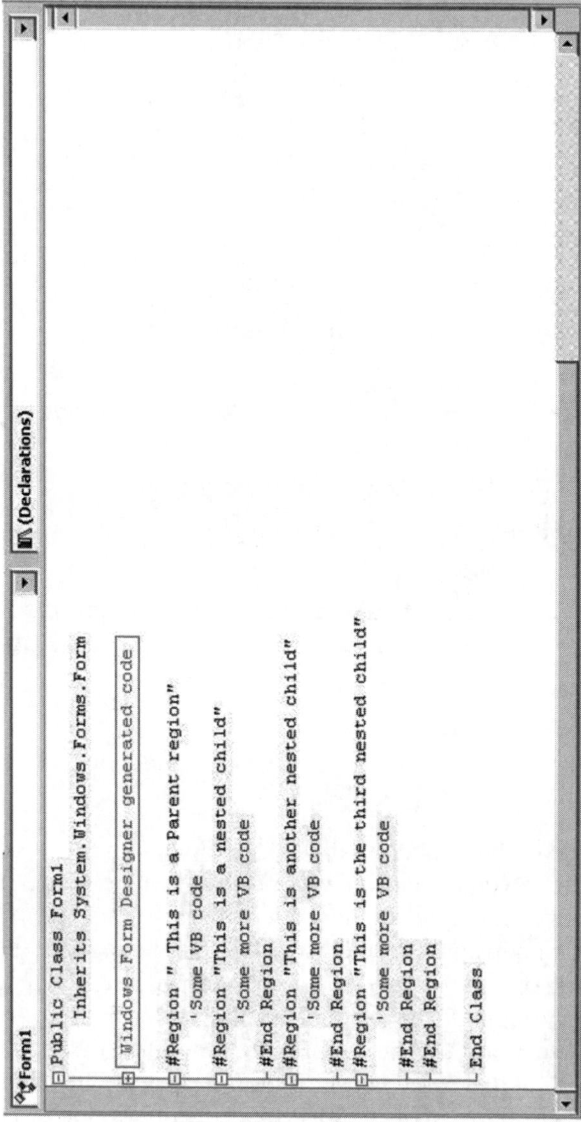


**Figure 3.5 A fully expanded nested region group.**

```
    End Function
    Public Function GetAge(ByVal txtAge As TextBox)
As Boolean
        On Error GoTo getAgeErrorHandler
        If txtAge.Text <> "" Then
            intAge = txtAge.Text
            getAge = True
        Else
            getAge = False
        End If
        Exit Function
getAgeErrorHandler:
        Debug.WriteLine(Err.Description)
    End Function
    Public Sub CalcAge(ByVal intAge As Integer, ByVal
retireAge As Integer)
        intAge = intAge + retireAge
        boolRespond = True
    End Sub
    Public Sub CalcAge(ByVal intAge As Integer, ByVal
votingAge As Integer, ByVal drivingAge As Integer)
        intAge = intAge + votingAge + drivingAge
        boolRespond = False
    End Sub
End Module
```

Now let us take this same module and block out the code using regions. There are several logical divisions that can be made using the `#Region` directive. Looking at the code we can place the functions, subroutines, and dimension statements into separate regions. Figure 3.6 illustrates the look of this module when the regions are collapsed.

Here we simply named the region after the code that appears within it. For the two functions that appear in the module, the name of the function was used as the name of the region it appears in. There is one region in Figure 3.6 that is named "Overloaded SubRoutines." Figure 3.7 shows this region expanded.

As we can see, the "Overloaded SubRoutines" region is a nested region that contains with it two other regions. These regions contain the two

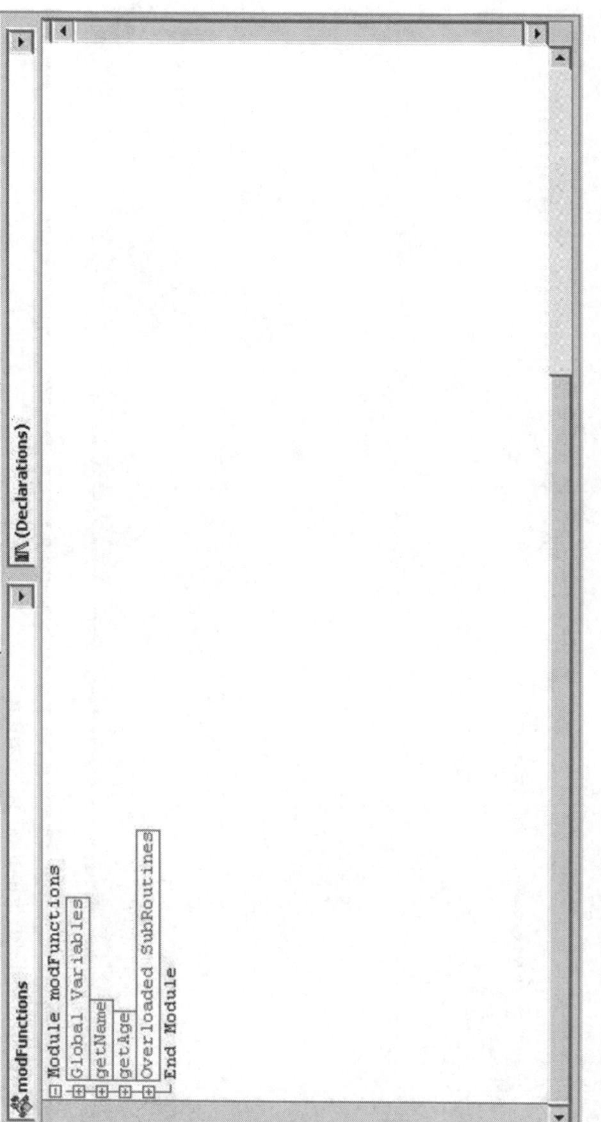


Figure 3.6 The VB.NET module using regions.

**Figure 3.7 The overloaded subroutines.**

overloaded subroutines from the original code. The full VB.NET code with all of the #Region directives intact should appear as follows.

**Listing 3.35: Two VB.NET Subroutines in Regions**

```
#Region "Global Variables"
     Public intAge As Integer
     Public stringName As String
     Public boolRespond As Boolean
#End Region
#Region "GetName"
     Public Function GetName(ByVal txtName As
TextBox) As Boolean
         On Error GoTo getnameerrorhandler
         If txtName.Text.ToString <> "" Then
             stringName = txtName.Text.ToString
             getName = True
         Else
             getName = False
         End If
         Exit Function
getnameerrorhandler:
         Debug.WriteLine(Err.Description)
     End Function
#End Region
#Region "GetAge"
     Public Function GetAge(ByVal txtAge As TextBox)
As Boolean
         On Error GoTo getAgeErrorHandler
         If txtAge.Text <> "" Then
             intAge = txtAge.Text
             getAge = True
         Else
             getAge = False
         End If
         Exit Function
```

```
getAgeErrorHandler:
        Debug.WriteLine(Err.Description)
    End Function
#End Region
#Region "Overloaded SubRoutines"
#Region "CalcAge2"
    Public Sub CalcAge(ByVal intAge As Integer, ByVal
retireAge As Integer)
        intAge = intAge + retireAge
        boolRespond = True
    End Sub
#End Region
#Region "CalcAge3"
    Public Sub CalcAge(ByVal intAge As Integer, ByVal
votingAge As Integer, ByVal drivingAge As Integer)
        intAge = intAge + votingAge + drivingAge
        boolRespond = False
    End Sub
#End Region
#End Region
```

You will find that as you use the `#Region` directive in your code, your code will be much easier to look through when it comes time to debug your code.

## Coding Standards

This section of the chapter examines coding standards. These standards govern how your code is written and ensure everything you write has a specific look and feel. A major benefit to using an adopted standard is that more programmers are likely to know it, and your code will be easier to work with when debugging. Think of a coding standard as a dialect of a language; although many people may speak the same language, they may speak it differently, adding to the amount of work and time needed to understand each other. Similarly, if everyone writes code to the same standard, other programmers will have an easier time looking at, editing, and debugging the code.

## *Older Standards*

Writing your code to a standard, like using regions, helps you when you need to quickly find problem points in your applications. When all of your code is written to a specific standard, governing how certain objects should look and be coded, it becomes much easier to recognize problem areas. For this reason, we will focus on coding standards in this section.

When Microsoft released its .NET programming platform, a lot more changed than just the languages we used to author our applications. A new way of thinking was required to use the platform to its fullest. One change that had to occur was in the standards we used to code by. That is, for a long time, programmers would follow certain standards, many of which were born in a time when code space was limited and a programmer really needed to keep an eye on how big a program was in terms of lines of code. Of course today space is not nearly the issue it was then. The coding standard that came of this era was known as Hungarian notation.

In Hungarian notation, variables were named according to the type of variable they were. Strings would be granted the prefix `str`; integers, `n`; and booleans, `b`. Therefore, if we have a program containing a string variable named `mystring`, the Hungarian notation name for the variable would be `strmystring`.

The following is a list of some Hungarian notation prefixes:

```
p   Pointer
str String
sz  Zero-terminated/null-terminated string
h   Handle
c   Character
by  Byte
n   Integer
f   Float
d   Double
b   Boolean
u   Unsigned...
w   Word or unsigned integer
l   Long
dw  Unsigned long integer
I   Interface
X   Nested class
```

```
x    Instantiation of a nested class
m_   Class member identifiers
g_   Global
v    Void
```

However, given that when we talk about these older programming standards the guiding force in their creation is space, `strmystring` would have been condensed further into `strmystr`. All methods, variables, functions, and most any other object would have been named similarly. A function called `GeneralPurposeFunctionForCounting-Chickens` would most likely have been written `GPFxnForCntngChckns` or `ChknCntFxn` to conserve space and make the code look tighter and neater — even at the expense of being a bit confusing.

Although we have now moved on in our programming technologies, and space is not nearly the issue it once was, many programmers still hold on to these old Hungarian notation standards. Even Microsoft, which once embraced Hungarian notation as its official standard, has moved forward, and away from the archaic coding practice.

The reason many programmers have moved away from Hungarian notation is that it really serves no purpose in today's programming environment. For one thing, space is no longer an issue, and within many languages there is no reason to identify the type of a variable within that variable's name. However, some features and standards created for older languages persist.

The standards that have been accepted by .NET programmers are very similar to those of other languages. By examining the .NET standards and some of those from other languages, we can find a common standard to be used across all languages and platforms.

## The New Standards

When examining the newer accepted standards in coding there are three terms we must be familiar with, and each describes a way of using upper- and lowercase letters when typing out your code. The terms *Pascal case*, *Camel case*, and *uppercase* are all derived from older programming standards and are all used today.

Pascal case is written so that the first letter of every word is capitalized, as in the following example:

```
MyNewClass
```

Camel case is similar to Pascal case; however, the first letter of the first word is lowercase. All remaining words are still capitalized.

```
myStringVariable
```

Finally, uppercase is as the term states, all letters in all words are capitalized:

```
jfdinclude.JFDLIBRARY
```

As we discuss different parts of code, we will also note if such items should be written in Pascal case, Camel case, or uppercase. Let us start with variable names.

There is no longer a need, as with Hungarian notation, to use any abbreviated type prefixes in the variable name. Now variable names should be as descriptive as possible and use Camel casing.

### Listing 3.36: VB.NET/VB6 Camel Casing

```
Dim queryStatement as String
Dim ageOfChildren as Integer
Dim executionFlag as Boolean
```

### Listing 3.37: C#/C++/Java Camel Casing

```
string firstLineOf Song;
int numberOfAliens;
```

Class, method, function, and subroutine names should always be written in Pascal casing. These items too should now be as descriptive as possible.

### Listing 3.38: VB.NET/VB6 Pascal Casing

```
Public Function MyAgeCalculator
End Function
Public Sub GetDatabaseSettings
End Sub
```

### Listing 3.39: C#/C++ Pascal Casing

```
public class LoadDataGrid
{
     void GetParameters()
{
}
}
```

**Listing 3.40: Java Pascal Casing**

```
public Class PostWebData
{
}
```

The last major item you should look at in terms of capitalization is a parameter. Parameters of methods and functions, being forms of variables, are also written in Camel casing.

When dealing with standards, capitalization is not the only important item to remember. There is also a way to visually form the code so that it becomes recognizable and is easy on the eyes. Code should be formed in a way that classes and other blocks follow a specific pattern of spacing and indentation. The first standard rule is to indent, using a tab space, all nested code. That is, your opening class, subroutine, or function should be aligned furthest to the left of your IDE. Any code that appears within this class, subroutine, or function should be indented one tab space.

In the event you are using a language that utilizes braces to mark the beginning and ending of classes and methods, these should be aligned under the class or method they belong to.

**Listing 3.41: VB.NET/VB6 Parameters**

```
Public Function AddSeveralIntegers(firstNumber as
Integer, secondNumber as Integer)
End Function.
```

**Listing 3.42: VB.NET/VB6 Alignment**

```
Public Function PostDataItems(itemOne as Integer)
     If itemOne > 5 Then
         Call PostLargeItem()
     End If
End Function
```

Compare the previous VB.NET code snippet with the following:

**Listing 3.43: C#/C++/Java Alignment**

```
public class PostData
{
     void PostLargeForm
     {
```

```
            for(x = 0; x < 10; x++)
            {
            }
        }
}
```

When you follow a standard in your code formation, the code is much easier to look at. The standardized code is admittedly easier to work with, and if you were looking for a potential bug, it would be much easier to find in such a block of code.

If you are using Microsoft's Visual Studio .NET (2002, 2003, or 2005) you will find that it does its best to standardize the spacing and indentation of your code for you. The IDE will automatically, depending on the language, close many code blocks for you, and properly indent them to nest correctly. The Visual Studio IDE will insert the `#End Region` directive on the next line after you type in the `#Region` directive. Little touches like this make keeping your code standardized even easier.

However, if you are using a simple C++ editor, or one of the many Java IDEs on the market, you may need to perform much of your own standardization. Keep this in mind as you work through these standards and put them into practice in your own code; the more thought and time you put into your code now, the easier any subsequent changes to that code will be.

## Functions, Subroutines, and Methods

In this section we will discuss the heart of most applications: the functions, subroutines, and methods that make those applications tick. There are some very specific steps you can follow to keep your code blocks as debugger-friendly as possible. Let us take a look at some of these steps. First, let us go over some simple rules for keeping your code clean and standardized.

> Being that we covered basic standardizing tips in the last section, all of the examples in the remainder of the book will show these standards, including comments.

### *Hardcoding Values*

In programming it is often the case where values are needed that the user should not be able to change, or otherwise has no knowledge of.

These values are often hard coded into application by the programmer. For example, an application that looks into a directory for a file to process may have that directory hard code because it never changes, as in the following code snippet:

**Listing 3.44: VB.NET Hard-Coded Directory Example**

```
Public Sub GetFileToProcess()
'**************************
'Subroutine gets processor file from director and
passes it to the parser
'    jfd
'    5/1/2005
'    v1.1
'**************************
Dim filePath as String
Dim fileName as String
filePath = "c:\processorfiles\"
fileName = Format(Now,"yymmdd") & ".prc"
'**************************
'Ensure file is not empty and pass on
If FileLen(filePath & fileName) > 0 Then
     FileParser(filePath & fileName)
End if
'**************************
End Sub
```

Notice, in this example, that we have hard coded the path to the file needed for processing. While you may think that the file location will never change, or you may not want the user to be able to change the path, your application has become very inflexible as a result. If the path to the file does change, without the user's knowledge, the program will no longer run correctly. This in itself can be considered a potential bug in the making.

Another problem that could arise from this situation is that if the program were to go through testing, the chances are very high that this path value would need to be changed to properly test the application. If so, the tester not only would need access to the code, but also would have to change the hard coded value, recompile, and remember to change the value back before the application went into production.

Therefore, we should try to keep all of our values flexible and not hard code any of them. There are several ways to do this. Within the .NET environment we can use a .config file. The .config file is an XML-based file that can be used to hold application settings.

### Listing 3.45: XML Configuration File

```
<?xml version="1.0" encoding="utf-8" ?>
<configuration>
<appSettings>
<add key="screenSize" value="large"/>
<add key="timeCode" value="EDT"/>
</appSettings>
</configuration>
```

To add an app.config file to your .NET project, press <Ctrl + Shift + A>. This will open the Add New Item dialog. Simply select the Application Configuration File and rename it if applicable. Visual Studio. NET will now add an XML file named App.config to your project. Double-click on the file to view its contents. The following is the contents of a typical App.config file upon creation:

### Listing 3.46: App.config File

```
<?xml version="1.0" encoding="utf-8" ?>
<configuration>
</configuration>
```

However, in its current state, the app.config file does you little good. You need to add the values that you want to retain to the XML file. Doing this requires a basic knowledge of XML and XML tags. Even if you are not proficient in XML, the process should be easy to follow.

Let us add a configuration setting for telling the applications which server to connect to. We will add a key named "productionServer" and give it a value of "MyServer." First, you must add the XML tag `<appSettings>`. Upon adding the opening tag, Visual Studio should automatically insert the closing tag. If Visual Studio does not add the closing tag, you will have to insert the `</appSettings>` tag manually.

### Listing 3.47: </appSetting> Placement

```
<?xml version="1.0" encoding="utf-8" ?>
<configuration>
```

```
<appSettings>
</appSettings>
</configuration>
```

Next we can add the key and value for our server name. The format is

```
<add key="<KEYNAME>" value="<VALUE>"/>
```

Let us call the key "productionServer" and the value will be "MyServer." Now to connect to the server, all we have to do is read this value into the program. If the server changes over the life of the application, no recompilation is needed; all you have to do is edit the app.config file and change the key value to the new server name.

**Listing 3.48: Server Parameter within App.config**

```
<?xml version="1.0" encoding="utf-8" ?>
<configuration>
<appSettings>
<add key="productionServer" value="MyServer"/>
</appSettings>
</configuration>
```

Now that the setting is created within the app.config file, we need to be able to read it out. This is a very easy process in .NET. The value is found in the method `System.Configuration.ConfigurationSettings.AppSettings`. The method can retrieve the values by string with the key name. The following code blocks retrieve the value for the key "productionServer" and assign it to a string variable:

**Listing 3.49: VB.NET Retrieve App.config settings**

```
Public Sub GetServerName()
     Dim serverName As String
serverName =
System.Configuration.ConfigurationSettings.AppSettings
("serverName")
End Sub
```

**Listing 3.50: C# Retrieve App.config Settings**

```
public GetServerName()
{
string serverName;
```

```
serverName =
System.Configuration.ConfigurationSettings.AppSettings
("serverName");
}
```

Another important thing to remember about your functions, methods, and subroutines is to try to limit what they do. Try not to create the Swiss Army Knife™ of code blocks. Keep your methods simple and divide larger code when possible. Most professionals suggest even keeping all functions, methods, and subroutines down to one main function. Doing so will help tremendously during debugging. If you can keep each block of code down to its primary functions, your code will be much easier to trace when it comes time to find the bugs.

Finally, if you are using a .NET language, you can use the `#if` and `#endif` directives to tell the processor to compile some blocks of code and not others. Using the `#if` directives, you can compile a setting for either the testing or production version of your code without having to change a lot of parameters. Although this method is not preferred over using the app.config file, it does pose a viable solution without having to use any external configuration setting.

The setting can be established as follows. Let us assume that our accounting application requires a specific username, password, and server name as a database connection string when used in production. The client is not intended to know these pieces of information, so they are hard coded into the application. However, when used in testing, the application should utilize a different username, password, and server name. The following example shows how that can be configured using the `#if...#endif` directives:

**Listing 3.51: VB.NET #if...#endif**

```
Public Const mode As String = "Test"
#If mode <> "Test" Then
     serverName = "TestServer"
     userName = "admin"
     passWord = "123ABC"
#Else
     serverName = "TestServer"
     userName = "guest"
     passWord = "guest"
#End If
```

Now if you need to recompile your application in a testing environment, you would simply change the constant mode to the string "Test," and this would compile with the program with the configuration settings for running in test mode. To compile the program with the settings needed to run in production mode, simply change the constant mode to anything other than "Test." This will force the compiler to use the production configuration.

The `#if...#endif` directive works by telling the compiler what code to compile and what code not to compile. Any code that is evaluated to be true by the `#if` statement is passed to the compiler; the remaining code is ignored.

There are many other uses for the `#if...#endif` directive, especially when it comes to debugging. However, we will be covering those in later chapters. Just keep in mind that this use for the directive exists and is completely acceptable.

## Reusable Code

In the final section of this chapter we will discuss the importance of reusable code. Reusable code is code that has been fully tested and debugged, performs a specific task, and can be easily ported from project to project. Reusable code is great when debugging because the chances are greater that the code has been fully debugged several times in the past, allowing you to focus your debugging efforts elsewhere.

Most programmers, even if it exists only in their head, have their own library of code that they refer to when needed. This code is built from experience and is often used over and over by the programmer in multiple applications. For example, one piece of reusable code that every programmer should have is an error logger.

An error logger is a function or class that simply creates a file or database entry containing the descriptions of any errors encountered by the application. The logger can then be called from anywhere in the application to record all errors. Because this is a function that all applications should possess, an error logger is a prime candidate for reusable code.

In making the error logger reusable, it is written and tested once. The code can then be cut and pasted, or included, in the current project. The following is an example of a simple error logging function:

**Listing 3.52: VB.NET/VB6 Error Logging Function**

```
Public Sub PostErrors(postMessage As String)
'****************************************
```

```
'5/1/2005
' jfd
'Function to display errors to screen
'****************************************
msgbox (postMessage)        'write error to screen
'****************************************
End Sub
```

**Listing 3.53: C#/C++ Error Logging Function**

```
private static void PostMessage(string postMessage)
{
    MessageBox.Show (postMessage, "Error",
MessageBoxButtons.OKCancel,
MessageBoxIcon.Asterisk);
}
```

To implement to logic, simply pass the error message to the method or subroutine, and it will be displayed in a message box. If you ever need to change your logic to then copy the error message to a database, you only need to change one method and the code will be updated. This is a perfect example of reusable code.

When writing your code, keep this concept in mind. You should try to write your code in such a way that as much of your application as possible can be reused in later applications, or can utilize previously written reusable code.

## Review Questions

1. Properly comment the follow VB.NET code:
   ```
   Public Sub HelloWorld(txtBox as TextBox)
   txtBox.Text = "Hello World!"
   End Sub
   ```
2. What is the purpose of introductory comments?
3. What is the name given to comments that run through your code blocks and explain lines of code as they are written?
4. Of the following languages, which two cannot use the `#Region` or `#region` directive: C#, VB.NET, C++, or Java?
5. What directive is used to close a C# `#region`?

6. What restriction is imposed on VB.NET users and `#Regions`?
7. What is the name of the original coding standard used by Microsoft?
8. Describe the three commonly used casing standards.
9. What is the name given to the .NET XML file used to hold application settings?
10. When debugging is concerned, what is the advantage to using reusable code?

## Looking Ahead

In Chapter 4 we will discuss the topic of error handling. Most programmers are not available 24 hours a day to watch over the clients using their software. For this reason, the application needs to be able to handle error in a graceful manner and then react appropriately to those errors. There are also times when the operating system's error capabilities are not as robust as you need, and you may have to develop your own error-tossing mechanism. Chapter 4 will cover all of these issues.

# Chapter 4

# Throwing Custom Exceptions

In the previous three chapters we discussed and examined some of the habits that you can change to make your code either more bug resistant or more debugger-friendly. However, these skills and techniques will probably not help you find the bug in the first place. One of the keys in debugging is, as elementary as it sounds, finding the bugs. That is, we must realize that a bug exists before we can attempt to extract it from the code. Some bugs can be blatant, in that they will seize processing, freeze the operating system, or even crash the computer. Other bugs can by subtle and simply throw up a cryptic error code, many of which are overlooked if they do not appear to affect operation.

This chapter will walk you through the different techniques and concepts for handling error messages thrown by external systems, throwing your own errors, and allowing your applications to react appropriately. This means that we will look into trapping and handling errors that an operating system is throwing in reaction to your application. We will also examine what it takes to throw your own errors, alerting the user that something may be wrong within the application. Most importantly, we will look at allowing your application to react in the proper manner when an error is encountered.

There is a subtle difference in the terms *error handling* and *error trapping*. The difference comes in the inference of the terms. Error handling pays no mind to the root or meaning of an error at all. In error handling, an application is concerned only with the fact that an error has occurred and it must now react in a prescribed manner. Error trapping, on the other hand, although it may be implemented through error handling, is concerned only with the error itself. Error trapping allows the user, programmer, or support person the ability to look at what the exact error was and what may have caused it.

## Unstructured Error Handling

Error handling, like commenting, is often overlooked by programmers as one of those things that are just too time-consuming to take part in. Many programmers think that writing error logic is too distracting, and they also think that if an application tests properly, there should be no reason to handle errors. This can be flawed logic.

Even in the most basic of applications it can be nearly impossible to predict if or when an error could occur. Once the application is written and compiled, you no longer have any control over the workings of that application. That is, once the program is in the hands of the user, anything can happen. To compound problems, you have little to no control over the user's environment. The user may have a corrupted system to begin with, he or she may be running software that you are unaware of, or he or she may even attempt to use your application in ways you did not anticipate.

Being aware that an error has occurred is one thing; however, there is another piece of the puzzle to consider. Simply knowing that an error has been encountered will do you little good if your code does not react accordingly.

The appropriate reaction of your code to any error, anticipated or not, is key in your application's survival of a bug. In the case of shrink-wrapped or commercially available software, the way an application responds when it encounters an error could (literally) make or break the product. What would you rather see — an application that froze and then crashed your system when it encountered an error, or an application that simply notified you an error was encountered and allowed you to continue? Chances are you have come across both scenarios at least once, and chances are the more graceful handling of the problem left a better impression on you.

In this section we will discuss the different techniques that can be employed in error handling. These techniques, when integrated into your applications, should allow your program to gracefully handle most errors and problems that it encounters. The first error-handling technique we will look at is `On...Error` as used by VB.NET and VB6. In the next section we will explore the `try...catch` and `try...catch...finally` statements used by C#, VB.NET, and Java.

Users of both Visual Basic 6 and Visual Basic .NET can utilize a very powerful tool when handling errors. This tool is the statement

```
On Error { GoTo [ line | 0 | -1 ] | Resume Next }
```

The `On Error` statement is considered to be an example of unstructured error handling. Unstructured error handling is that which can accept and react to a wide variety of errors, as opposed to structured error handling, which is tailored to a specific error type. Being unstructured, the `On Error` statement can help your application handle the widest variety of errors.

The `On Error` statement is used to direct the execution of your application to or through certain areas of your code when an error is encountered. By placing the `On Error` opening statement at the beginning of a block of code, you can then control what your application will do if an error is triggered by that block of code. This means that an `On Error` statement will only work for the block of code it appears in. You will need to put an `On Error` statement in every block of code you need error handling in.

To use the `On Error` statement you need to first provide the parameters needed to direct the action of your code. The least invasive iteration of the `On Error` statement is to couple it with the `Resume Next` parameter:

```
On Error Resume Next
```

Let us look at the following block of VB.NET code. This code utilizes the `On Error` statement with `Resume Next`.

#### Listing 4.1: Using the `On Error` Statement

```
Public Function GetTenth(ByVal txtNumber As TextBox)
As Integer
'**********************************************
'Function to get 1/10 of given number
'jfd
'5/1/2005
```

```
'*********************************************
    Dim oneTenthOfNumber As Integer
'*********************************************
    On Error Resume Next    'Error Handler
    If txtNumber.Text.ToString <> "" Then
       oneTenthOfNumber = txtNumber.Text.ToString/10
       GetTenth = oneTenthOfNumber
    Else
       GetTenth = 0
    End If
End Function
```

This function is being called from a form containing one text box and one button. The following is the code behind this form:

```
Private Sub Button1_Click(ByVal sender As
System.Object, _
 ByVal e As System.EventArgs) Handles
GetTenthBtn.Click
    MsgBox(GetTenth(GetTenthTxt))
End Sub
```

Now we have a function that takes a text box and extracts from that a value. The value is then divided by 10 to compute 1/10th of that value. The 10th is then returned to the form where it is displayed in a message box.

> Looking at the function as it is, you may notice some obvious flaws with its code. This is being done purposely so we can test some error logic.

You should attempt running this small example, or try following along with the code. Place the number 10 in the text box and click on the button `GetTenth`. You should see the following message box. Figure 4.1 illustrates the returned message box.

The return is `1`, which is what would be expected given the input of `10`. The text box containing the value `10` is passed to the function `GetTenth`. The function extracts the value through the `txtNumber.Text.ToString` property. The extracted value, in this case `10`, is then divided by `10` and returned to the form. You will notice that in the case

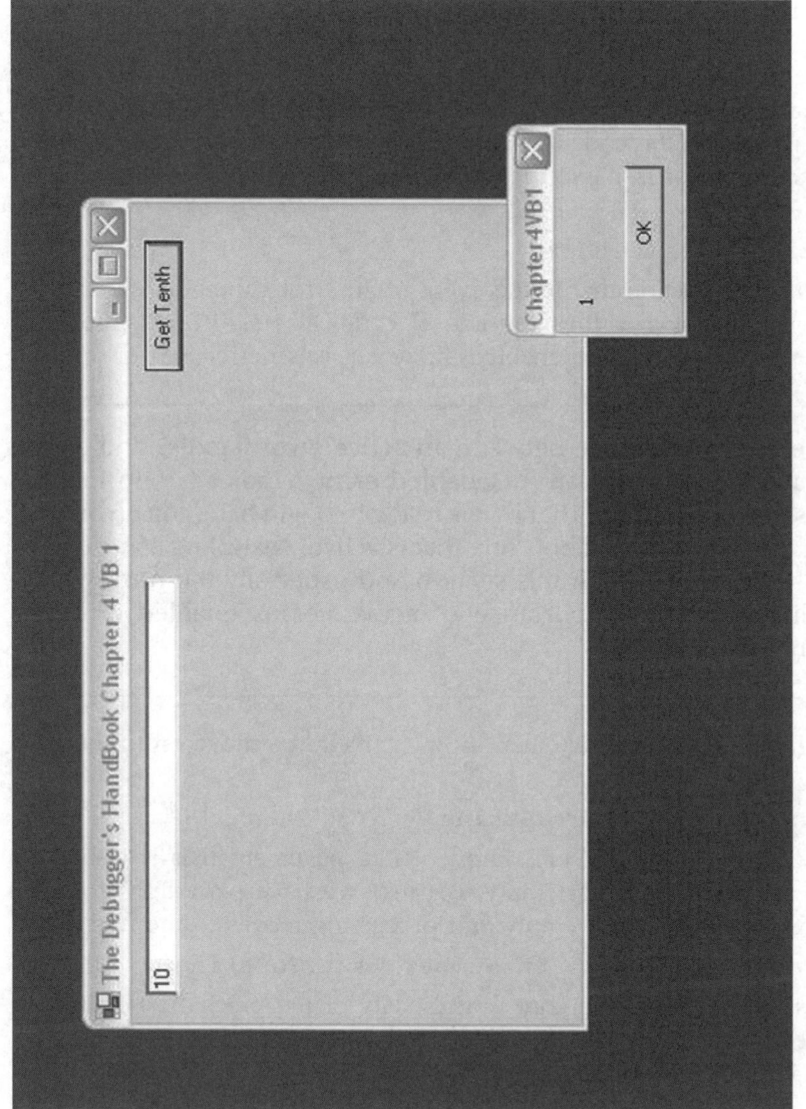


**Figure 4.1 The return of `GetTenth` with 10.**

of the text box being blank, the `If...Then...End IF` statement will return the default value of `0`.

Because we have determined that the function works properly given the correct parameters, let us see what happens if we put an `H` in the text box rather than a number. Logic would tell you that the function would fail because H cannot be divided by 10. However, if you run the sample program, you will see that the result is not what would be expected. Figure 4.2 illustrates the message box that is returned.

Here we can see that the function returned 0 rather than an error. We can step through the code to discover why. When the `GetTenth` button is clicked, control is passed to the `GetTenth` function. The following line executes:

```
On Error Resume Next
```

This tells the function that in the event of an error condition, `On Error`, continue processing at the next line of code, `Resume Next`. The error handler is now said to be enabled; however, it is not active.

> There is a difference between an active error handler and an enabled error handler. An enabled error handler is one that has been turned on. That is, it is ready to begin handling errors. An active error handler is one that is actively handling an error. As we move through this section and especially the next, we will discuss the importance of active versus enabled error handlers.

With the `On Error` statement now enabled, we move on to the next line of code:

```
If txtNumber.Text.ToString <> "" Then
```

Here we have a simple `If...Then...Else` statement that is testing to ensure the text box is not empty. Because we have placed an `H` in this text box, it is clearly not empty and processing moves to the next line:

```
oneTenthOfNumber = txtNumber.Text.ToString / 10
```

On this line we have the core functionality of the block. The H is now extracted from the text box and divided by 10. This line generates an `InvalidCastException` error. The description of the error is

```
Cast from string "H" to type 'Double' is not valid.
```

The full exception is listed below for you to examine. Regardless of what the exception is, the error handler now takes over.

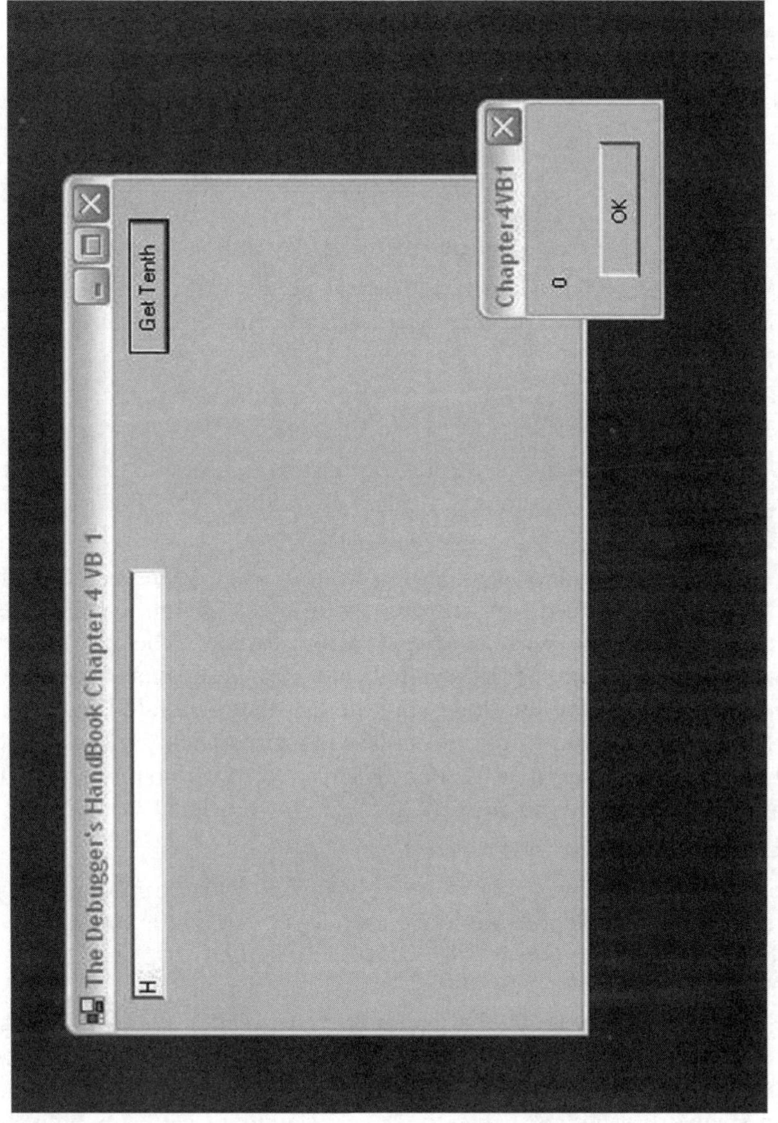


**Figure 4.2 The result of H/10.**

**Listing 4.2: Exception Output**

```
System.InvalidCastException: Cast from string "H" to
type 'Double' is not valid. --->
System.FormatException: Input string was not in a
correct format.
 at Microsoft.VisualBasic.CompilerServices.
DoubleType.Parse(String Value, NumberFormatInfo
NumberFormat)
 at Microsoft.VisualBasic.CompilerServices.
DoubleType.FromString(String Value, NumberFormatInfo
NumberFormat)
 --- End of inner exception stack trace ---
 at Microsoft.VisualBasic.CompilerServices.
DoubleType.FromString(String Value, NumberFormatInfo
NumberFormat)
 at Microsoft.VisualBasic.CompilerServices.
DoubleType.FromString(String Value)
 at Chapter4VB1.NumericAndErrorFxns.GetTenth(TextBox
txtNumber) in C:\Documents and Settings\My Documents\
Chapter4\Chapter4VB1\NumericAndErrorFxns.vb:line 13
```

The On Error statement now moves from enabled to active. The On Error statement, having been activated with an exception, looks at its parameters to determine what course of action to take. The parameters we have supplied, Resume Next, tells the On Error statement to continue processing at the line following the line that generated the error. After returning processing to the line following that which generated the error, the On Error statement is then deactivated, but remains enabled. The application continues to process at the following line:

```
GetTenth = oneTenthOfNumber
```

Given that nothing was stored in oneTenthOfNumber because of the error, and that the default value for an integer variable is 0, the value 0 is passed back to the form. The value of 0 is then displayed in the message box.

One key thing to note in this example is that after the On Error statement passes control back to the Next line, it is deactivated but not disabled. This is important because of how On Error and the runtime environment work together. Each On Error statement can only actively handle one error at a time. If the application were to encounter a second exception while the On Error statement was active, processing would not be able to utilize that On Error.

In this situation, the processing would then move back to the calling function, that is, the function that called the block of code with the active `On Error` statement. It would then attempt to activate the `On Error` statement of that block of code. If no `On Error` statement exists, the application will crash. However, if there is an `On Error` statement that is enabled, but not active, the processor will use it to process the current error. In the event that this `On Error` statement is also active, the processor will continue moving from calling function to calling function until it either finds an inactive `On Error` statement or reaches the highest-level calling function.

In the simple example used above, we told `On Error` to, in the case of an exception being thrown, resume processing at the next line. However, this may not always be possible. In many functions or subroutines, the processing of the next line may depend fully on the results provided by the line previous to it. That is, using `Resume Next` may leave you no better off than crashing from an error. In these situations we may want to use the `GoTo` parameter of `On Error`.

`GoTo` allows you to specify a section of code to process in the event of an error. The section of code that the `On Error` statement passes to can do anything from alternative processing to gracefully exiting the error-generating code block. The usage of the `On Error` statement with `GoTo` is as follows:

```
On Error Goto [line | 0 | -1]
```

> Do not use the 0 or –1 parameters for right now; we will discuss those later in this section.
>
> The line parameter is the section of code you want processing to move to in the event of an error. To use the line parameter, we must designate a line in our function as the one that we want `On Error` to move to. To do this, we name the line with a plain English name followed by the : character.
>
> `MoveToThisLineOnError:`

Let us look at our `GetTenth` function and define a line for `On Error` to move to. Use the version of `GetTenth` provided on the CD to try this at home. Start by erasing the line `On Error Resume Next`, as seen in the following code block. Then add a line for the `On Error` statement to move to.

### Listing 4.3: Using `On Error GoTo`

```
Public Function GetTenth(ByVal txtNumber As TextBox)
As Integer
```

```
'*******************************************
'Function to get 1/10 of given number
'jfd
'5/1/2005
'*******************************************
    Dim oneTenthOfNumber As Integer
'*******************************************
    If txtNumber.Text.ToString <> "" Then
       oneTenthOfNumber = txtNumber.Text.ToString/10
       GetTenth = oneTenthOfNumber
    Else
       GetTenth = 0
    End If
GetTenthErrorHandler:
End Function
```

Here we simply identified the line of code we want processing to move to and flowed it with the : character. Following the logical flow of the application, if an error is encountered in the `GetTenth` function, processing will move to the line `GetTenthErrorHandler:`, which will simply exit to the calling function. To enable the `On Error` statement, begin to type `On Error Goto`. At this point you should see `GetTenthErrorHandler:` as a `GoTo` option. Figure 4.3 illustrates the `GoTo` options menu.

Select `GetTenthErrorHandler:` from this menu and your code will be ready. The finished code will appear as follows:

**Listing 4.4: Complete GoTo Statement**

```
Public Function GetTenth(ByVal txtNumber As TextBox)
As Integer
'*******************************************
'Function to get 1/10 of given number
'jfd
'5/1/2005
'*******************************************
    Dim oneTenthOfNumber As Integer
'*******************************************
    On Error Goto GetTenthErrorHandler
    If txtNumber.Text.ToString <> "" Then
```

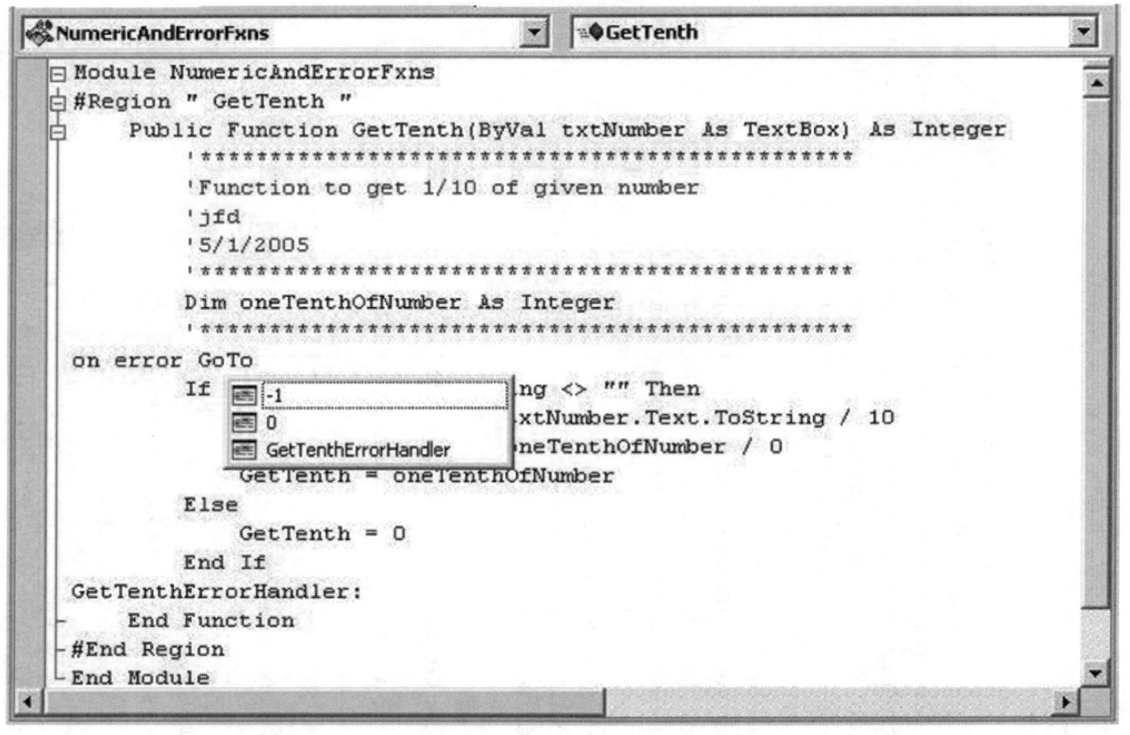
NumericAndErrorFxns
GetTenth
Module NumericAndErrorFxns
#Region " GetTenth "
Public Function GetTenth(ByVal txtNumber As TextBox) As Integer
'*************************************************
'Function to get 1/10 of given number
'jfd
'5/1/2005
'*************************************************
Dim oneTenthOfNumber As Integer
'*************************************************
on error GoTo
If
ng <> "" Then
xtNumber.Text.ToString / 10
neTenthOfNumber / 0
GetTenth = oneTenthOfNumber
Else
GetTenth = 0
End If
GetTenthErrorHandler:
End Function
#End Region
End Module
-1
0
GetTenthErrorHandler

Figure 4.3 The GoTo options menu.

```
        oneTenthOfNumber = txtNumber.Text.ToString/10
        GetTenth = oneTenthOfNumber
    Else
        GetTenth = 0
    End If
GetTenthErrorHandler:
End Function
```

If you run this new version of our sample program, you will see that given the input H, a 0 still appears in the message box. This is because after the `On Error` statement is activated, processing moves to the `GetTenthErrorHandler` line. The only piece of code following this line is `End Function`. From here, the code passes back to the form where `MsgBox(GetTenth(GetTenthTxt))` is finished. Because nothing was assigned to `GetTenth` as an integer value, the default 0 is still applied to the message box.

What if you wanted the message box to display a different number if an error was reached? One of the most useful features of `On Error` is that, after `GoTo` executes, you can have it execute any code you want. You can insert code after the `GetTenthErrorHandler` line assigning a different value to `GetTenth` in the event of an error. For example, in the following version of the `GetTenth` function we will have the code `GetTenth` set to 1234.

### Listing 4.5: Displaying a Message Box on `Error`

```
Public Function GetTenth(ByVal txtNumber As TextBox)
As Integer
'**********************************************
'Function to get 1/10 of given number
'jfd
'5/1/2005
'**********************************************
    Dim oneTenthOfNumber As Integer
'**********************************************
    On Error Goto GetTenthErrorHandler
    If txtNumber.Text.ToString <> "" Then
        oneTenthOfNumber = txtNumber.Text.ToString/10
        GetTenth = oneTenthOfNumber
    Else
```

```
        GetTenth = 0
    End If
GetTenthErrorHandler:
    GetTenth = 1234
End Function
```

When this code executes, you should be able to pass H to the `GetTenth` and it will return 1234. Try this on your own, replacing H with a few different values. What do you find?

> Even if you cannot compile this code to work along with the example, follow the code with your eyes and see if you can pick up on a bug.

The current iteration of the `GetTenth` function actually contains a bug, a bug caused by our error-handling logic. If you were able to execute this code and tested it with a few different values, you should have noticed that every value now returns 1234. This is because even if `On Error` is never activated, the processor still runs the code that appears after the `GetTenthErrorHandler` line. Just because you want this line to run when there is an error does not mean the opposite condition will be met.

To prevent this line from executing when `On Error` is not active, we need to insert an `Exit Function` before the `GetTenthErrorHandler` line.

**Listing 4.6: Exiting a Nonactive Error Statement**

```
Public Function GetTenth(ByVal txtNumber As TextBox)
As Integer
'*********************************************
'Function to get 1/10 of given number
'jfd
'5/1/2005
'*********************************************
    Dim oneTenthOfNumber As Integer
'*********************************************
    On Error Goto GetTenthErrorHandler
    If txtNumber.Text.ToString <> "" Then
        oneTenthOfNumber = txtNumber.Text.ToString/10
        GetTenth = oneTenthOfNumber
```

```
    Else
        GetTenth = 0
    End If
    Exit Function
GetTenthErrorHandler:
    GetTenth = 1234
End Function
```

The `Exit Function` command tells the processor to, under normal conditions, exit the function and return to the calling function at this point, ignoring the `GetTenth = 1234` line. However, in the event an error is encountered before the `Exit Function`, processing will move to the `GetTenthErrorHandler` line and `GetTenth = 1234` will be executed.

Running the application with this line in place will generate a more acceptable outcome. Correct values will be divided by 10 (even if the modulus is not taken into account), and if an error is encountered, the application returns 1234. However, 1234 really does not tell us that much about what happened. To return more information about what happened in the application during an error condition, we need to change some code.

Rather than set `GetTenth` to 1234, we can force the application to display details about what happened to the user. To do this, we can use one of three pieces of information, all of which are parts of the Err object. We can use `Err.Description`, `Err.GetException`, or `typename(Err.GetDescription)`. All of these will return different but useful pieces of information.

`Err.Description` will return a plain English description of the error:

```
Cast from string "H" to type 'Double' is not valid.
```

`Err.GetException`, on the other hand, returns the full error:

### Listing 4.7: Err.GetException Full Output

```
System.InvalidCastException: Cast from string "H" to
type 'Double' is not valid. --->
System.FormatException: Input string was not in a
correct format.
    at Microsoft.VisualBasic.CompilerServices.
DoubleType.Parse(String Value, NumberFormatInfo
NumberFormat)
    at Microsoft.VisualBasic.CompilerServices.
DoubleType.FromString(String Value, NumberFormatInfo
NumberFormat)
```

```
    --- End of inner exception stack trace ---
    at Microsoft.VisualBasic.CompilerServices.
DoubleType.FromString(String Value, NumberFormatInfo
NumberFormat)
    at Microsoft.VisualBasic.CompilerServices.
DoubleType.FromString(String Value)
    at Chapter4VB1.NumericAndErrorFxns.GetTenth
(TextBox txtNumber) in C:\Documents and Settings\My
Documents\Chapter4\Chapter4VB1\NumericAndErrorFxns.
vb:line 13
Finally, typename(Err.GetException) will return the
type of exception that was thrown in string format.
InvalidCastException
```

When making a decision about which of these to use, consider following these guidelines. If the error is being displayed to users, you should keep the message as simple as possible and use `Err.Description`. If, however, you are saving these errors to a technical log, then you would want as much information as possible. That could mean saving even all three pieces of data concatenated.

Let us edit our `GetTenth` function to pop a message box with the `Err.Description` in it rather than the code 1234. To do this cleanly, we should also change `GetTenth` from an integer-returning function to a string-returning function.

### Listing 4.8: Outputing the `Err.Description`

```
Public Function GetTenth(ByVal txtNumber As TextBox)
As String
'*********************************************
'Function to get 1/10 of given number
'jfd
'5/1/2005
'*********************************************
    Dim oneTenthOfNumber As Integer
'*********************************************
    On Error Goto GetTenthErrorHandler
    If txtNumber.Text.ToString <> "" Then
       oneTenthOfNumber = txtNumber.Text.ToString/10
       GetTenth = oneTenthOfNumber
```

```
    Else
       GetTenth = 0
    End If
    Exit Function
GetTenthErrorHandler:
    GetTenth = Err.Description
End Function
```

If you run this new version of the GetTenth application, attempting to pass the function, an H should now yield an error message. This message is illustrated in Figure 4.4.

Displaying the error, even in plain English, is one way of alerting the user that a potential bug has been encountered. However, the majority of software users would admittedly not know what to do at this point. The error provided may not mean anything to them, or they may just not realize what channels should be followed to correct the situation. For this reason, it may be more productive and helpful to create an error logger.

An error logger will retain critical information about exceptions thrown by the system. Information about these errors can be placed into a database or other file system to be used by debuggers and testers in evaluating the application. Let us examine how to use an error logger in conjunction with the On Error statement.

First, a decision has to be made about what, if anything, to display to the user at the time an error is encountered. To get the most out of our example, let us decide to display a generic message stating "An error has been encountered" to the user. The remaining critical data will be passed through the logger. Make the following changes to the GetTenth function:

**Listing 4.9: Notifying the User on Error**

```
Public Function GetTenth(ByVal txtNumber As TextBox)
As String
    '*********************************************
    'Function to get 1/10 of given number
    'jfd
    '5/1/2005
    '*********************************************
    Dim oneTenthOfNumber As Integer
    '*********************************************
    On Error Goto GetTenthErrorHandler
```

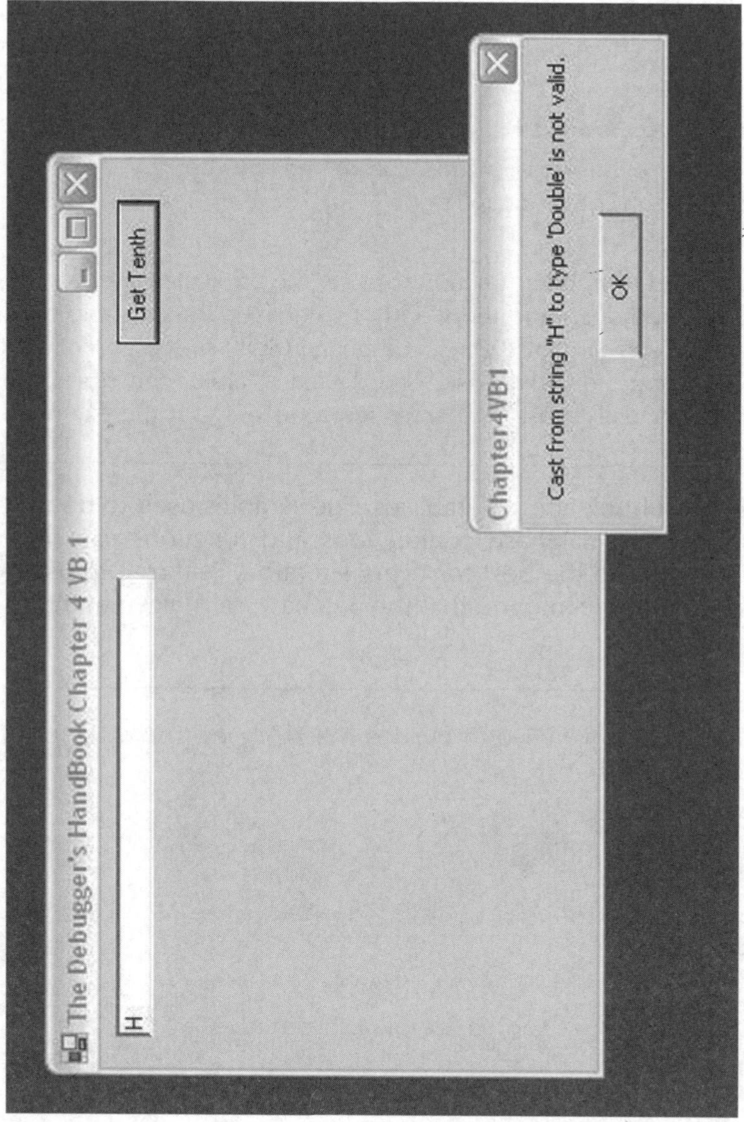


**Figure 4.4 Displaying the error message to the user.**

```
    If txtNumber.Text.ToString <> "" Then
       oneTenthOfNumber = txtNumber.Text.ToString/10
       GetTenth = oneTenthOfNumber
    Else
       GetTenth = 0
    End If
Exit Function
GetTenthErrorHandler:
 GetTenth = "An error has been encountered. Please
contact technical support"
End Function
```

Now we need to build a function to write the error messages to a log. Without diving too deep into the world of databases, the example on the CD uses a Microsoft Structure Query Language (SQL) stored procedure to write the error data to a database. The database, table, and stored procedure do not actually exist, and are referred to only for the example.

> This is not a book about databases. The samples used to demonstrate where database connections and functions can be used may not be the best for every situation. Feel free to use the code, keeping in mind that the database calls may need to be tweaked.

The first function we need to build is called logger. The code for this function is as follows:

**Listing 4.10: Logger**

```
Public Function Logger(ByVal message As String) As
Boolean
    '*********************************
    'function to log errors to database
    'jfd
    '5/1/2005
    '*********************************
    Dim conn As SqlClient.SqlConnection = New
SqlClient.SqlConnection()
```

```
    Dim command As SqlClient.SqlCommand = New
SqlClient.SqlCommand()
    '********************************

    If IsConnectable(conn) = True Then 'if connection
is made continue
        command.Connection = conn
        command.CommandText = "LoggerSP"
        command.Parameters.Clear()
        command.Parameters.Add("message", message)
        command.ExecuteNonQuery()
        command.Dispose()
    End If
End Function
```

Simply, this function accepts a string message as a parameter and then passes that string to a stored procedure named `LoggerSP`. We can assume that `LoggerSP` places the string in a database. However, looking at the `If...Then` statement, you can see a call to `IsConnectable`. This is another function that ensures the connection object is currently attached to a database.

Going back to the last chapter's discussion about functions, subroutines, and methods, each of these objects should perform only one function. Therefore, we will break out the code establishing the database connections into a second stand-alone function.

## Listing 4.11: Function with More Than One Purpose

```
Public Function IsConnectable(ByVal conn As
SqlClient.SqlConnection) As Boolean
    '***************************************
    'function to check for database connection
    'jfd
    '5/1/2005
    '***************************************
    IsConnectable = False
    conn.Close()          'close the current
connection
    conn.ConnectionString = _
System.Configuration.ConfigurationSettings.AppSettin
gs("connectionString")
```

```
    conn.Open()              'open new connection
    IsConnectable = True
End Function
```

Notice that the IsConnectable function gets its connection string from the app.config file. This makes changing setting both before and after the compile very easy. The app.config was set up as follows:

### Listing 4.12: New App.config Setting

```
<?xml version="1.0" encoding="utf-8" ?>
<configuration>
    <appSettings>
        <add key = "connectionString" value =
"USR=Guest,PWD=GuestPass,Server=MyServer"/>
    </appSettings>
</configuration>
```

With these two functions in place, all you have to do is pass the Err.Description, and any other information, to the Logger function from your On Error statements.

### Listing 4.13: Passing Control from On Error to Logger

```
Public Function GetTenth(ByVal txtNumber As TextBox)
As String
    '*******************************************
    'Function to get 1/10 of given number
    'jfd
    '5/1/2005
    '*******************************************
    Dim oneTenthOfNumber As Integer
    '*******************************************
    On Error GoTo GetTenthErrorHandler
    If txtNumber.Text.ToString <> "" Then
        oneTenthOfNumber = txtNumber.Text.ToString/10
        GetTenth = oneTenthOfNumber
    Else
        GetTenth = 0
```

```
    End If
    Exit Function
    '*********************************************
GetTenthErrorHandler:
    '*********************************************
    'write error to error log
    GetTenth = "An error has been encountered. Please
contact technical support"
    Logger(Err.Description)
    '*********************************************
End Function
```

Before we can end our discussion of `On Error` and unstructured error handling, there are two more parameters that we should examine. `On Error Goto` can also except a 0 or –1 as a parameter.

Keep in mind that each `On Error` statement can only handle one exception at a time; if the current `On Error` statement is active and another exception is encountered, the application will crash. `On Error Goto -1` can be used to clear the current error condition from the current `On Error` statement, whereas `On Error Goto 0` is used to disable the current `On Error` statement altogether.

> The current `On Error` statement will be both cleared and disabled when the block of code it appears in is exited. This is essentially the same as using `On Error Goto 0` and `On Error Goto -1`.

`On Error` is an unstructured error handler, meaning that it reacts to a broad range of exceptions as opposed to a specific exception. However, this does not mean that you cannot use `On Error` to react in different ways depending on the exception encountered. Once `On Error` has been activated, you can test for certain exception criteria and tailor your application's response accordingly.

For example, let us say that when the user passes a letter to `GetTenth` we want to have `GetTenth` ask the user to use a numeric value, but all other error conditions should be logged. We can test the `Err` object to see if it is of the type `InvalidCastException`. Then we can have `GetTenth` issue the new statement; otherwise, it will pass the error to the logger.

**Listing 4.14: Testing for `InvalidCastException`**

```
Public Function GetTenth(ByVal txtNumber As TextBox)
As String
    '********************************************
    'Function to get 1/10 of given number
    'jfd
    '5/1/2005
    '********************************************
    Dim oneTenthOfNumber As Integer
    '********************************************
    On Error GoTo GetTenthErrorHandler
    If txtNumber.Text.ToString <> "" Then
       oneTenthOfNumber = txtNumber.Text.ToString/10
       GetTenth = oneTenthOfNumber
    Else
       GetTenth = 0
    End If
    Exit Function
    '********************************************
GetTenthErrorHandler:
    '********************************************
    'test if error is a cast exception
    If typename(Err.GetException()) =
"InvalidCastException" Then
       Msgbox "Please use a numeric value"
    Else   'write error to error log
    GetTenth = "An error has been encountered. Please
contact technical support"
    Logger(Err.Description)
    End If
    '********************************************
```

> There are other methods for ensuring the user puts a numeric value in a text box. However, because it is an easy error for a user to make, it is a good example to demonstrate the `On Error` statement's capabilities.

The GetTenth function now utilizes the typename() function to get the type of exception being handled by On Error:

```
typename(Err.GetException())
```

This VB function, when passed a valid, active Err object, will return the type of exception being handled in string form. We then test the type name, and if it is an InvalidCastException, we issue the new message to the user. The following is a list of the different exception types that you can test for:

## Listing 4.15: Microsoft Exceptions

```
AmbiguousMatchException
AppDomainUnloadedException
ArgumentException
ArithmeticException
ArrayTypeMismatchException
BadImageFormatException
CannotUnloadAppDomainException
CodeDomSerializerException
ConfigurationException
ContextMarshalException
CryptographicException
DataException
DBConcurrencyException
ExecutionEngineException
ExternalException
FormatException
IndexOutOfRangeException
InstallException
InternalBufferOverflowException
InvalidCastException
InvalidComObjectException
InvalidOleVariantTypeException
InvalidOperationException
InvalidPrinterException
InvalidProgramException
IOException
```

```
LicenseException
ManagementException
MarshalDirectiveException
MemberAccessException
MissingManifestResourceException
MulticastNotSupportedException
NotImplementedException
NotSupportedException
NullReferenceException
OdbcException
OracleException
OutOfMemoryException
PolicyException
RankException
ReflectionTypeLoadException
RegistrationException
RemotingException
SafeArrayRankMismatchException
SafeArrayTypeMismatchException
SecurityException
SerializationException
ServerException
ServicedComponentException
SoapException
SqlCeException
SqlException
SqlTypeException
StackOverflowException
SynchronizationLockException
ThreadAbortException
ThreadInterruptedException
ThreadStateException
TimeoutException
TypeInitializationException
TypeLoadException
TypeUnloadedException
```

```
UnauthorizedAccessException
VerificationException
WarningException
XmlException
XmlSchemaException
XmlSyntaxException
XPathException
XsltException
```

Now that we have discussed and examined unstructured error handling, we can move on to structured error handling. The next section of this chapter will introduce you to the `Try...Catch` and `Try...Catch...Finally` statements.

## Structured Error Handling

In the last section we discussed unstructured error handling in VB using the `On Error` statement. Although unstructured error handling is a good option for catching a broad range of exceptions, there is another tool available to users of VB.NET, C#, C++, and Java.

The `Try...Catch` and `Try...Catch...Finally` statements can be used within VB.NET, C#, and Java.

The `Try...Catch` statement is an example of structured error handling. This means that `Try...Catch` is used to test for, trap, and react to specific exception types. Where in the last section we used `On Error` to trap any exception thrown to it, `Try...Catch` will only react to a specific exception type. The exception type to be trapped is specified at design time and cannot be changed.

`Try...Catch` is a very powerful tool in fighting bugs and detecting errors. However, the statement works differently in VB.NET than it does in C# and Java. Let us first explore how `Try...Catch` is used in VB.NET, and then we will examine its uses in the other languages.

Going back to the example we were using in the last section, let us apply the use of `Try...Catch` to the `GetTenth` function. In VB.NET the structure of `Try...Catch` is as follows:

**Listing 4.16: Try/Catch Block**

```
Try
    <Block of Code to execute>
Catch <exception> as Exception
```

```
    <Block of Code to execute on error>
End Try
```

The GetTenth function appears as follows using Try...Catch:

### Listing 4.17: GetTenth Using Try/Catch

```
Public Function GetTenth(ByVal txtNumber As TextBox)
As String
    '*********************************************
    'Function to get 1/10 of given number
    'jfd
    '5/1/2005
    '*********************************************
    Dim oneTenthOfNumber As Integer
    '*********************************************
    Try
        If txtNumber.Text.ToString <> "" Then
            oneTenthOfNumber = txtNumber.Text.ToString/
10
            GetTenth = oneTenthOfNumber
        Else
            GetTenth = 0
        End If
    Catch getTenthException as exception
 GetTenth = "An error has been encountered. Please
contact technical support"
            Logger(getTenthException)
    End Try
 End Function
```

Notice that the If...Then statement has been placed in the Try block of the Try...Catch statement. This represents the code that VB.NET will try to execute. In the event that an exception is thrown during the execution of the If...Then statement, the application will catch the exception and handle it with the code that appears in the Catch block. The current iteration of the GetTenth function operates exactly as the version that is utilized On Error.

There are two optional parameters that can be used with `Try...Catch`; these are `Finally` and `When`.

The `When` option is used to tell the `Catch` block only to execute if a certain criterion evaluates as true. This lets you conditionally use the `Catch` portion of the `Try...Catch` statement. In the following example we will tell the `Catch` block to execute on an error only if the text box being evaluated is not a numeric value.

**Listing 4.18: Catching a Nonnumeric Value**

```
Public Function GetTenth(ByVal txtNumber As TextBox)
As String
    '*******************************************
    'Function to get 1/10 of given number
    'jfd
    '5/1/2005
    '*******************************************
    Dim oneTenthOfNumber As Integer
    '*******************************************
    Try
       If txtNumber.Text.ToString <> "" Then
          oneTenthOfNumber = txtNumber.Text.ToString/
10
          GetTenth = oneTenthOfNumber
       Else
          GetTenth = 0
       End If
    Catch getTenthException as exception When
IsNumeric(txtNumber.Text) = False
 GetTenth = "An error has been encountered. Please
contact technical support"
          Logger(getTenthException)
    End Try
 End Function
```

In our testing of the `GetTenth` function we found that an error was thrown if the user placed an alpha character in the form's text box. Now we have told our `Try...Catch` statement that it only needs to evaluate the exception if the contents of the text box are indeed alpha.

The `Finally` block in the `Try...Catch` statement contains code that will execute after the `Try` block is evaluated. If an exception is thrown in the `Try` block, the `Finally` block will be executed after the `Catch` block.

Let us add a `Finally` block to our `GetTenth` function that clears the text box.

#### Listing 4.19: Using `Finally`

```
Public Function GetTenth(ByVal txtNumber As TextBox)
As String
    '*********************************************
    'Function to get 1/10 of given number
    'jfd
    '5/1/2005
    '*********************************************
    Dim oneTenthOfNumber As Integer
    '*********************************************
    Try
        If txtNumber.Text.ToString <> "" Then
            oneTenthOfNumber = txtNumber.Text.ToString
/ 10
            GetTenth = oneTenthOfNumber
        Else
            GetTenth = 0
        End If
    Catch getTenthException as exception When
IsNumeric(txtNumber.Text) = False
    GetTenth = "An error has been encountered. Please
contact technical support"
            Logger(getTenthException)
        Finally
    txtNumber.Clear
        End Try
    End Function
```

The `Try...Catch` statement works slightly differently on C# and Java. The C# structure for running `Try...Catch` is as follows:

### Listing 4.20: C#/Java Try/Catch

```
try
{
    <Block of Code to execute>
}
catch ( <ExceptionType> | <e>)
{
    <Block of Code to execute on error>
}
```

The following is our `GetTenth` VB function rewritten in C# and using the `Try...Catch` statement. `GetTenth` has been rewritten slightly to throw on a specific exception. This is to make the two examples operate a similarly as possible.

### Listing 4.21: C# `GetTenth`

```
private int GetTenth(TextBox txtNumber)
    {
        try
        {
            if (txtNumber.Text.ToString() != "")
            {
                return (Convert.ToInt16( txtNumber.Text)/
10);
            }
        }
        catch (FormatException e)
        {
MessageBox.Show (e.ToString(),"Error" , _
MessageBoxButtons.OKCancel,
MessageBoxIcon.Asterisk);
            return 0;
        }
        return 0;
    }
```

Notice the slight change in syntax between the VB.NET and C# iterations of the statement. Where VB.NET allowed for a general exception declaration to catch any errors in the `Try` block, the C# version forces the programmer to specify the exception being trapped.

> Refer to the list of exception types in the last section.

The syntax of the `Try...Catch` statement in Java is the same as that of C#. You must declare the type of exception you are trying to catch. The following is a partial list of the exceptions that can be trapped in Java:

**Listing 4.22: Java Exceptions**

```
AclNotFoundException
ActivationException
AlreadyBoundException
ApplicationException
AWTException
BackingStoreException
BadLocationException
CertificateException
ClassNotFoundException
CloneNotSupportedException
DataFormatException
DestroyFailedException
ExpandVetoException
FontFormatException
GeneralSecurityException
GSSException
IllegalAccessException
InstantiationException
InterruptedException
IntrospectionException
InvalidMidiDataException
InvalidPreferencesFormatException
InvocationTargetException
IOException
```

```
LastOwnerException
LineUnavailableException
MidiUnavailableException
MimeTypeParseException
NamingException
NoninvertibleTransformException
NoSuchFieldException
NoSuchMethodException
NotBoundException
NotOwnerException
ParseException
ParserConfigurationException
PrinterException
PrintException
PrivilegedActionException
PropertyVetoException
RefreshFailedException
RemarshalException
RuntimeException
SAXException
ServerNotActiveException
SQLException
TooManyListenersException
TransformerException
UnsupportedAudioFileException
UnsupportedCallbackException
UnsupportedFlavorException
UnsupportedLookAndFeelException
URISyntaxException
UserException
XAException
```

These exceptions are those thrown from `java.lang`.

## Throwing Custom Errors

One of the most powerful and flexible aspects of error handling is the ability to define and throw your own errors. Throwing your own custom errors allows you to be as specific, or as vague, as you want to be when explaining the reason behind and possible resolutions to any problems the application may encounter. There are two ways to throw custom exceptions. The first is to override an existing exception and throw the overridden version, while the second is to create your own exception and throw it when necessary. Let us first look at the process for overriding and throwing an existing exception.

The `Throw` function is used to send an exception to the error handler. This is true whether the exception is an existing one or one that is custom defined by the programmer. The key in throwing an existing exception yourself is that you can control the message and the information passed to the user. The following code snippets in C# and VB.NET show a fictitious `Try...Catch` statement that throws an `OutOfMemoryException()`:

**Listing 4.23: VB.NET Catching `OutOfMemoryException`**

```
Try
    'perform a large amount of work
Catch e As OutOfMemoryException
    Throw New OutOfMemoryException ("Please check
your equation parameters and try the calculation
again.")
End Try
```

**Listing 4.24: C# Catching `OutOfMemoryException`**

```
try
    {
//perform a large amount of work
    }
catch (OutOfMemoryException e)
    {
    throw new OutOfMemoryException ("Please check
your equation parameters and try the calculation
again.");
```

```
    return 0;
    }
```

Now, when the exception is thrown, the user will be presented with the additional information that you added to the existing exception message. However, there are times when an existing error does not work for your situation. Let us look at the procedure for creating a custom exception.

All exceptions are inherited from the `System.Exception` class. Therefore, to create your own exception class, all you need to do is create a class that inherits `System.Exception`. The class can perform cleanup functions, gather and log information, or simply display information. Take a look at the following two custom exceptions, one in VB.NET and the other in C++:

**Listing 4.25: VB.NET Forming Custom Exception**

```
Public Class myCustomException
    Inherits System.Exception
    Public Sub New(ByVal message As String)
        MyBase.New(message)
    End Sub 'New
End Class
```

**Listing 4.26: C# Forming Custom Exception**

```
public class myCustomException:System.Exception
{
        public void myCustomException (string Message)
        {
        }
}
```

The procedure for throwing the custom exceptions is the same for throwing an overridden one. You simply call the `Throw` function from the code to send your exception to the error handler. Custom exceptions give you a great deal of flexibility when it comes to alerting your users about bugs and other anomalies in the application.

## Review Questions

1. What are the two numeric (optional) parameters for the `On Error Goto` statement?
2. Modify the following error logger we created to log to a file if no database is available.

```
Public Function Logger(ByVal message As String)
As Boolean
   '*********************************
   'function to log errors to database
   'jfd
   '5/1/2005
   '*********************************
   Dim conn As SqlClient.SqlConnection = New
SqlClient.SqlConnection()
   Dim command As SqlClient.SqlCommand = New
SqlClient.SqlCommand()
   '*********************************
   If IsConnectable(conn) = True Then 'if
connection is made continue
        command.Connection = conn
        command.CommandText = "LoggerSP"
        command.Parameters.Clear()
        command.Parameters.Add("message", message)
        command.ExecuteNonQuery()
        command.Dispose()
   End If
End Function
```

3. Describe the difference between an active and an enabled error handler.
4. What languages can use the `Try...Catch` statement for error handling?
5. Describe the difference between structured and unstructured error handling.
6. What will happen if your application throws an exception and your current error handler is already active?
7. In a `Try...Catch` statement, what parameter needs to be specified in the `Catch` block?

8. What form of the `On Error` statement is used to deactivate the current error handler?
9. When using the `Try...Catch` block, at what point is the `Finally` block executed?
10. What is the `When` parameter of the `Try...Catch` block used for?

## Looking Ahead

So far in *The Debugger's Handbook* we have examined and discussed tips and techniques for performing two different functions. We have looked at ways of writing your code to either make potential bugs easier to find or help prevent bugs in the first place. Now that we have made our applications as debugger-friendly as possible, it is time to discuss the topics that will help you debug these applications. Chapter 5 will walk you through the process of using the programming IDE to look for bugs in applications as you are coding.

# Chapter 5

# Design Time Debugging

The first experience most programmers have with debugging comes at design time, the point before application code is compiled. Most popular programming IDEs have some debugging tools built in for use during the design and coding of an application. These tools help you to look for and remove bugs before your application is compiled.

> Though not as easy, there are different tools for finding bugs in applications during runtime, after they have been compiled. Many of these tools are third-party tools, and one should do the appropriate research before deciding on a runtime debugger. We will not be discussing such tools in this book, as our main focus will be on design time debugging.

Some of the tools we will be discussing, such as breakpoints and watches, can help a programmer step through his or her code methodically and pinpoint areas where there may be problems. These tools help you zero in on potential bugs and offer ways to test different scenarios in an effort to determine where problems exist. In this chapter we will examine these tips and sharpen our debugging skills.

In the last few chapters we have covered all of the topics related to organizing your thoughts before you write code. This includes all things related to the bug-free planning of a project and the physical act of writing the code itself. The debugging techniques and skills we have covered thus far, for the most part, have been more antibug in nature. That is, what we have discussed has not been geared toward removing a specific existing bug or bug condition. Rather, the skills acquired to date have been for avoiding general bugs throughout your writing. You should now, with a fair degree of confidence, be able to write some code while confidently avoiding bugs.

Now that you have been introduced to some of the skills that will help you avoid bugs, you need the skills necessary to find the bugs that may have slipped into your code anyway. Because, no matter how aware we are or how diligently we work, it is very difficult to get everything correct the first try. Even for the most seasoned programmer, bugs will find a way of working into our code.

Therefore, to think that you will never have another bug in your code again is a bit premature. No matter how hard we try, or how long we have been programming, bugs really are inevitable. Whether they are major or minor in nature, a bug will be in your code somewhere, at some time. This chapter will focus on finding and removing the bugs that do exist. More importantly, we will focus on removing such bugs before our application is compiled.

## Benefits of Removing Bugs at Design Time

There are clear benefits to removing bugs before an application is compiled. The first benefit to removing bugs at design time is the fact that the processes, code, and over-target goals are still fresh in your, the programmer's, mind. Waiting until days, or even weeks, into the testing process, well after an application has been compiled, can mean that you or any other programmers involved have lost your train of thought in relation to the block of code in question.

Programming is a skill that requires a fair amount of foresight and thought. It is not uncommon to hear programmers being referred to as "in the zone" while coding. This often refers to the fact that programmers must know where they intend to end up at the time they start to code. That is, for most programmers, the complete picture of what the code should do is usually in their head at all times. This thought or reference point, concerning why a specific block of code was programmed in a specific way, may be lost if problems are not tested and dealt with at design time.

Although it may not seem like a major issue at first, being in the right frame of thought is one of the most important things to a programmer. Programming, much like writing a book, is done over time, and although you may know where a block of code is going, if you do not keep track of your thoughts, you may lose them. Because of the amount of concentration required, a programmer will be best served by performing extensive debugging prior to an application being compiled.

However, the most compelling reason for performing design time debugging is to ensure that all future code written for that application is not written over untested, bad code, possibly worsening the process of debugging and making it harder to locate and remove bugs. The longer you go before identifying and removing a bug, the more of a chance there is for basing more code on that bug.

By being constantly aware of your code, and running it often in debug mode during the design process, the easier your job will be the farther into the application you get. The more often you run your code in the design time debugger, the better your chances will be in finding a problem with a specific part of code before you have a chance to base any other blocks of code on that bug.

The process of design time debugging will begin with interpreting build errors. We will discuss how to interpret build errors and research the problems behind them. After we look into build errors, we will examine different IDE-level tools for removing the bugs that caused the error. Breakpoints, code stepping, book marks, and other tools will help you find, remove, and replace bad code.

When most people think about the compiler and build errors, they immediately think of the runtime environment. Although it is true that the compiler marks the major difference between the design and runtime environments, it is not used only in runtime situations. All code, whether in design or run environments, must be compiled before it can be run, even if it is just being run in the debugger. Therefore, we still pass the code through the compiler before we can run the code in debug mode.

In the following examples, and those throughout the remainder of this chapter, we will be using Microsoft's Visual Studio .NET. The major version we will be using is the more common Visual Studio 2003, and the new Visual Studio 2005. However, where we approach a topic where there are major differences in the way the two versions operate, we will offer examples and instructions from both.

There are two major versions of Microsoft's Visual Studio .Net currently in use and covered in this book. The more common and more widely used of the two is Microsoft's Visual Studio 2003. This version has been around longer and is used by more programmers. However, the newer Microsoft's Visual Studio 2005 (deep into the beta process at the time of this book's production) offers some changes that should make it widely accepted.

One difference between VS 2003 and VS 2005 that affects this chapter in particular, and has turned out to be a very popular change with VB.NET users, is the debug time code editing of VS 2005. If you are familiar with VB6, you no doubt have used this feature. That is, when a VB6 application is run in debug mode, you can pause the execution of that application and edit the code directly in the debugger. This feature was removed in VS 2003, much to the dismay of many programmers. However, this feature has been restored in VS 2005, which will be covered more in the next chapter.

## Debugging in Visual Studio 2003

Being that the major IDE we will be using for this chapter is Microsoft's Visual Studio 2003, with Microsoft's Visual Studio 2005 covered later in this chapter; let us examine the IDE's main graphical user interface (GUI). Figure 5.1 illustrates the Visual Studio 2003 IDE.

Figure 5.1, although it may not be immediately obvious, contains most of the information we will be covering is that chapter. We will examine, among other aspects of the IDE, most of the debug windows, as that is where the bulk of the debugging tools reside. These windows include the following:

- Breakpoints/tracepoints
- Watch
- Immediate window
- Modules

As a contrast, look at this screen shot from Visual Studio 2005. Although the over functions are still in place, you will notice some subtle differences. In fact, Visual Studio 2005 has more of the look and feel of Visual Studio 6 than that of Visual Studio 2003. Figure 5.2 illustrates the Visual Studio 2005 interface.

Some differences to note include that the compiler mode options, available in Visual Studio 2003, are now gone from the menu bar in 2005. Also, one of the tools we will be examining in 2003, watches, is no longer available in 2005. However, all the functionality available in watches is still present in the IDE; it has just been incorporated into other areas of the IDE.

To start off the chapter, let us now examine the first indication many programmers will have that there is a problem with their code — build errors.

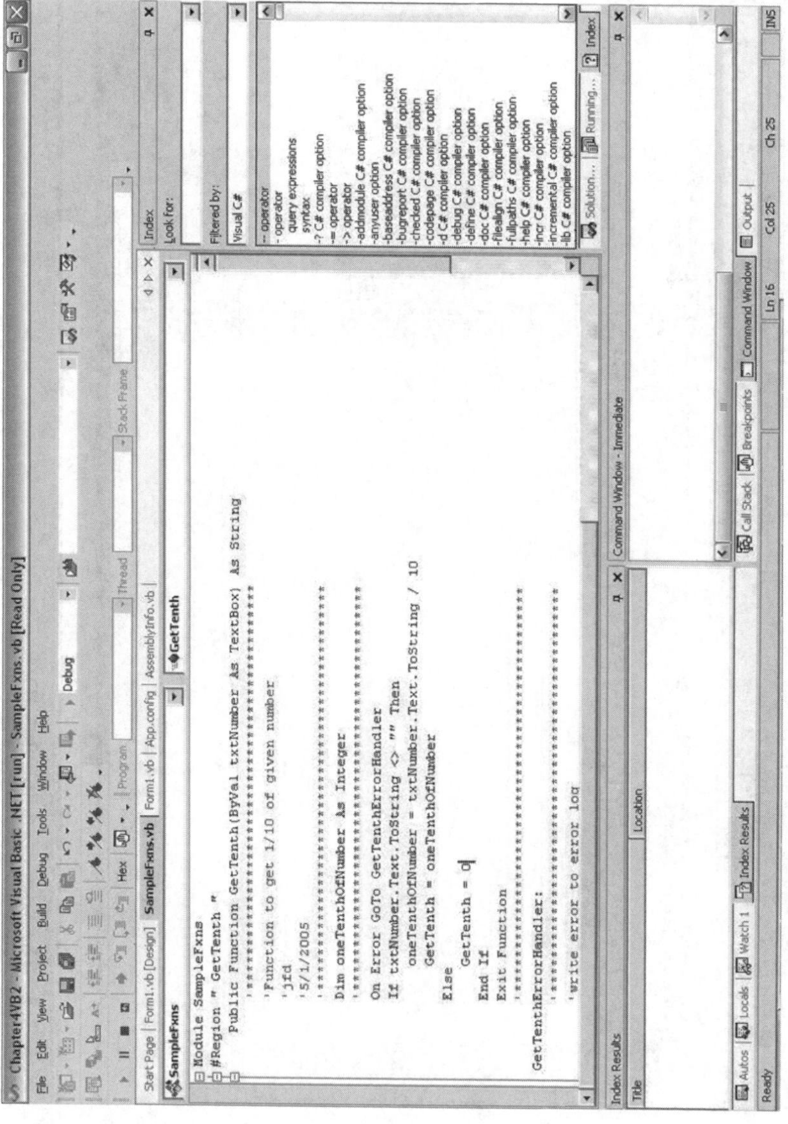


**Figure 5.1 The Visual Studio 2003 IDE.**

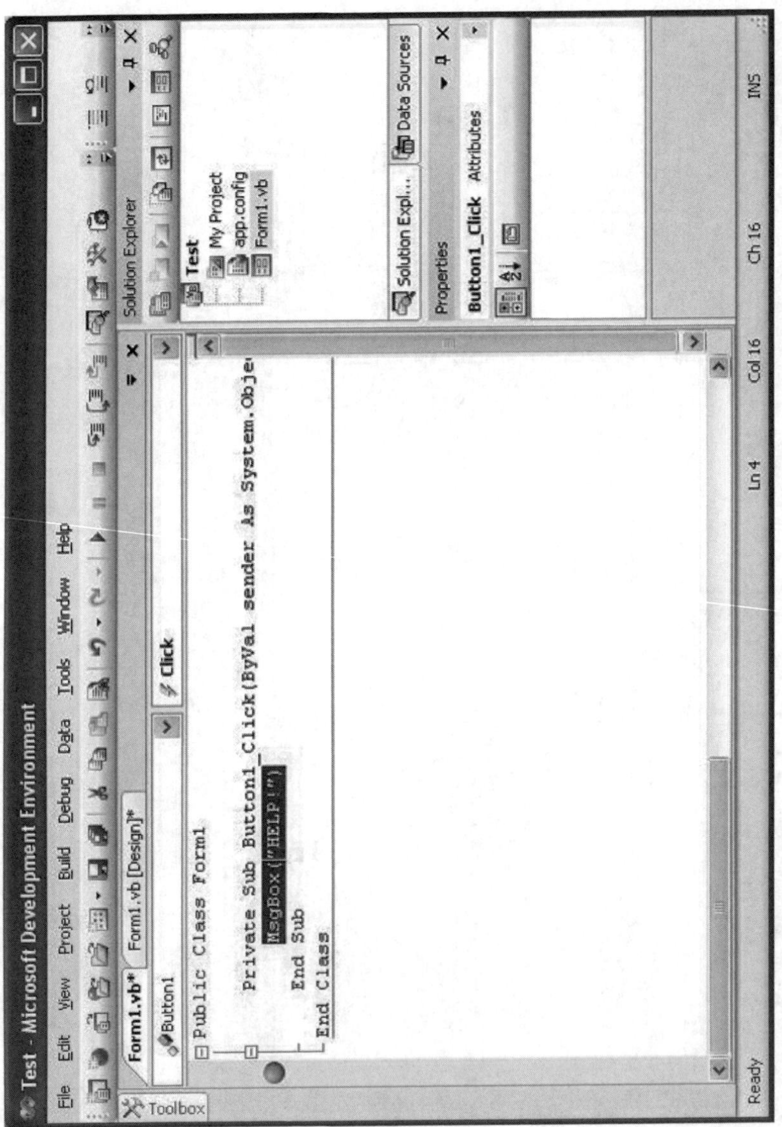


Figure 5.2 The Visual Studio 2005 IDE.

## *Build Errors*

By their design, most compilers will throw an error when they attempt to compile bad code, or attempt to compile code that contains a bug. For this reason, the compiler is your first line of defense in the bug battle.

It is important to note that whether you are running your application in debug mode or compiling it to run stand-alone, the code is still passed through the compiler. Therefore, every time you run your code it is being processed by the compiler; thus, the compile has a chance to throw errors when something goes wrong.

> Depending on the IDE, your compiler errors and build errors may be presented in a slightly different way than described here. However, many of the concepts will still hold true.

The compiler, on its most basic level, takes the code that you have written and translates it into a form that your processor can read and understand. Therefore, if there is even the slightest problem in your code, the compiler will not be able to correctly interpret the code, and the compile will fail. This is a way of protecting the underlying system from potentially harmful code.

In the event that your code does fail at the compile level, the compiler will return a fairly detailed description of the error and possibly a location within the code as to where the offending operation is. To demonstrate this, we need to use a piece of code that contains an error. To keep everything relevant, we will use a modified version of the `GetTenth` function that we used as an example in the last chapter.

#### Listing 5.1: `GetTenth` with Error

```
Public Function GetTenth(ByVal txtNumber As TextBox)
As String
    '*******************************************
    'Function to get 1/10 of given number
    'jfd
    '5/1/2005
    '*******************************************
    Dim oneTenthOfNumber As Char 'this line now
contains an error
    '*******************************************
```

```
    On Error GoTo GetTenthErrorHandler
    If txtNumber.Text.ToString <> "" Then
       oneTenthOfNumber = txtNumber.Text.ToString/10
       GetTenth = oneTenthOfNumber
    Else
       GetTenth = 0
    End If
    Exit Function
    '********************************************
GetTenthErrorHandler:
    '********************************************
    'write error to error log
    GetTenth = "An error has been encountered. Please
contact technical support"
    Logger(Err.Description)
    '********************************************
 End Function
```

To force the compiler into throwing a build error, we have changed the following dimensioning statement:

```
Dim oneTenthOfNumber As Integer
```

The new dimensioning statement has `oneTenthOfNumber` being declared as a `Char`, or character data type, rather than an integer. Because we attempt to pass this character variable an integer value, compiling this function will force an error. Figure 5.3 illustrates the error message displayed by the compiler when we attempt to build this function.

Now we can clearly see that the compiler has generated an error. The error reads as

```
Value of type 'Double' cannot be converted to 'Char'.
```

This tells us that the compile encountered a value of one type being passed to a value of another type, and the two types are not compatible. Because the compiler also gives us the line number where the error occurs, we can now search through the code for the offending line and fix it. However, what if we are dealing with a few hundred lines of code? Some programs, even from the best of us, can produce tens of build errors from the compiler. You need to have a specific process in place to fix these bugs. Let us discuss a process for using the build errors to methodically work through our code and fix it.

This error message on its own, although it explains the root cause of the problem, really does not tell us where or why — that is, where the

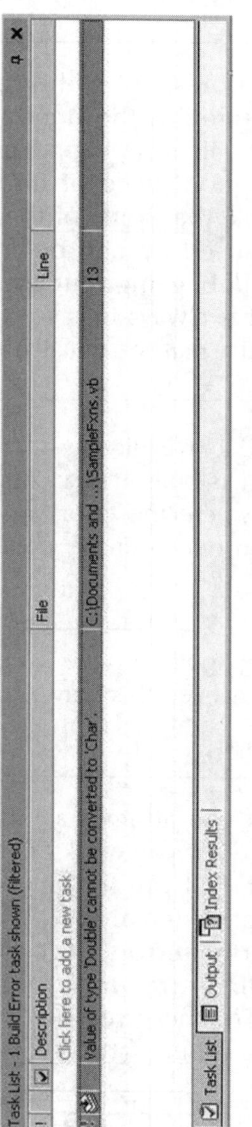


**Figure 5.3 A "Build" error message.**

problematic line of code is and why it is a problem. The one clue we have is in the column-marked line. This column tells us that the error occurred when compiling line 13 of our program. Although for this particular example it would be quite easy to locate line 13; if you have to find line 496 in a 617-line module, it might take a little longer.

> The compiler will always present build errors in the order in which they are encountered in the program. Therefore, the first errors encountered will always appear toward the top of the task list. This is a good piece of information to know because it is very possible that some of the later errors in the list could have been caused by one or more of the earlier errors. Therefore, when debugging your applications based on compiler build errors, it is always best to start at the top and work down. This will ensure that you get all of the errors in order.

There is an easier way to move directly to the problematic line of code. The Visual Studio IDE has built in a way that allows you to move directly to the line of code where the error was generated by double-clicking on the build error. In our example, double-clicking on the line that reads

```
Value of type 'Double' cannot be converted to 'Char'.
```

will take you directly to the point in the code where the compiler encountered the problem. However, this may not correspond directly to the line you need to fix.

> It is recommended that you attempt a rebuild of your code after every bug or build error you work on. The reason for this is twofold. First, the bug that you fix may have been the root of most or all of the errors listed after it. Therefore, fixing that error may clear up all further errors. Second, just the opposite may occur. Fixing the first error may cause different errors further down the line. For these reasons, it is always recommended that you issue a rebuild after every bug fix.

Now that we have identified the first build error, and in this case the only build error, let us see what happens when you double-click on the build error message in the task list. Figure 5.4 shows the results of double-clicking on our sample build error.

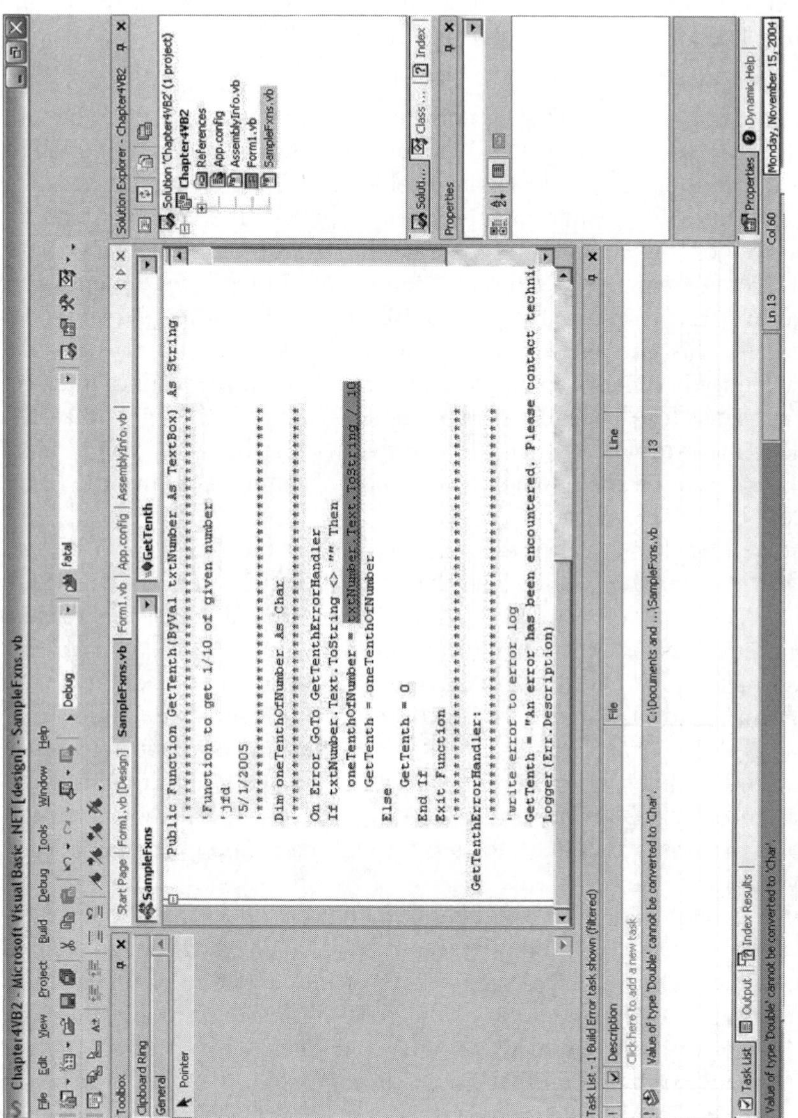


**Figure 5.4 The problematic line of code.**

In this example, the compile ran into a problem on line 13. We may need to do some debugging detective work, however, because line 13 features the following highlighted code:

```
txtNumber.Text.ToString / 10
```

This compiler seems to be mistaken, because we already know that the offending line of code is the one that reads

```
Dim oneTenthOfNumber As Char
```

It is in situations such as this that having the code and the programmer's intent fresh in your head during debugging helps. The compile is actually correct in pointing to line 13 as the problematic line. This is because the function of line 13 puts into use the incorrectly declared variable. Line 11, the line we actually changed to generate the error, by itself does not have any problems in it. It is, after all, completely correct to dimension a variable as `Char` for use by your application. Therefore, the compiler cannot mark this line as an error. The problem is what you do with that variable after you dimension it. The one thing the compiler cannot interpret is intent. Therefore, because the compiler cannot determine that the variable is incorrect rather than the line that uses it, the error will actually occur later on in the code, when the application attempts to use the `Char` variable.

In following through the code, and looking at the build error, we can see that the compiler is telling us that it cannot convert a double value to a char. The double is created by the division operator. For this reason, the compiler sees the mathematic operation as the root of the problem.

It is in situations like this that having well-commented code comes in handy. For example, had this function been longer, we could have dimensioned the Char variable at the top of the function, but not used it until a hundred lines, or more, into the function. We would then have to track the root of the problem using the comments, and if they were not available, we would be forced to step through each line programmatically until we noticed the error.

The compiler cannot be counted on to find all of the bugs in an application. In fact, the compiler really will not find all bugs with a program; it will locate and define syntax errors, and find potential bugs that affect the internal operation of the code during execution. These are errors in the way a program was written, literally. Keep in mind that for a bug to manifest, the code that generates it has to work; therefore, most of your bug code will generally be good code as far as the compiler is concerned. The bugs of an application are generally found after the program is compiled.

After you have removed all of the build errors from your code and are able to fully compile, it is time to do some serious debugging. With the IDE mode set to debug mode, the compiler is now ready to help you find any bugs that have slipped through.

## Debug Mode

The compiler can only be relied on to find the most glaring and basic of code problems. However, to find actual bugs, you need to use and test your code in a mode that allows you to locate and identify potential issues. This mode is known as debug mode.

Stepping through code is the best way to test and debug your applications. To use the IDE in debug mode, ensure that it has been set correctly. In Visual Studio 2003, the solution configuration mode can be set to either Release or Debug; we want it set to Debug. Figure 5.5 shows where this configuration setting is made.

However, if you are using Visual Studio 2005, the process is slightly different, and more like that of Visual Studio 6. Figure 5.6 illustrates the menu bar of Visual Studio 2005. Notice that the Release/Debug option is no longer available.

In Visual Studio 2005, like Visual Studio 6, the mode is set to debug by default. Therefore, to start debugging your application, all you have to do is click on the green "play" arrow.

In debug mode, you can step through the execution of your code one line at a time. This allows you to execute small pieces of code and identify potential bugs. The advantage to this is that you can control the execution of specific lines of code to see why certain blocks may or may not be executing correctly. Tools such as breakpoints, watches, and the immediate window let you view what is happening in the application as it is being executed.

Let us take our project from the last chapter and use it to work out a scenario. Before we use the project, we need to make a quick edit to the code. Because we do not want to be hunting down more than one error in the example, we are going to clean one section of the code. In the `GetTenth` function, we need to comment out the line in the error handler that calls the logger. We already know that the error logger does not work, and at this point, it would only get in the way of the example. The modified `GetTenth` function is as follows:

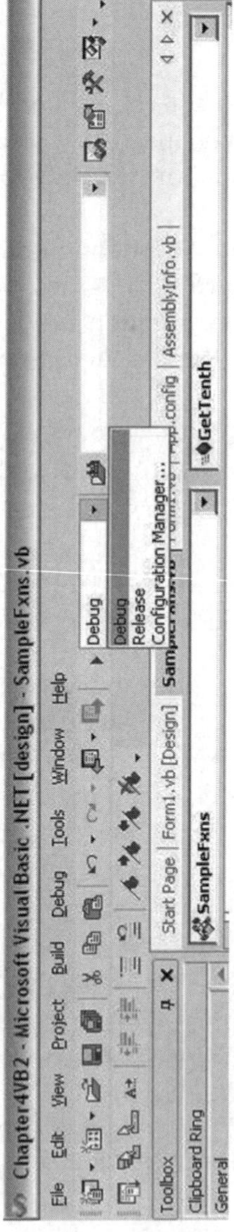


Figure 5.5 Setting the IDE for debug mode.

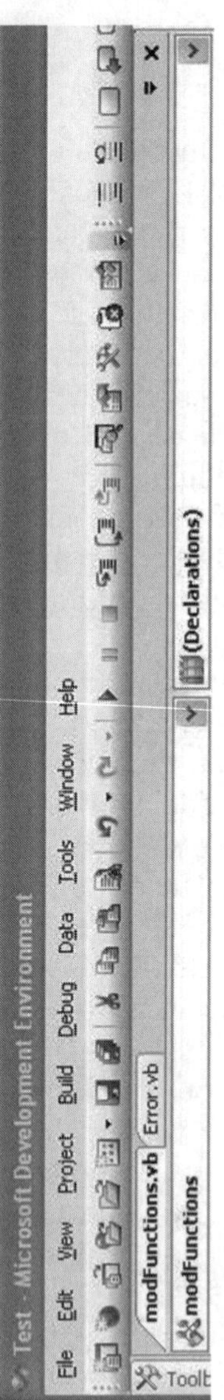


Figure 5.6 Visual Studio 2005 menu bar.

**Listing 5.2: Modified `GetTenth()`**

```
Public Function GetTenth(ByVal txtNumber As TextBox)
As String
    '*******************************************
    'Function to get 1/10 of given number
    'jfd
    '5/1/2005
    '*******************************************
    Dim oneTenthOfNumber As Integer
    '*******************************************
    On Error GoTo GetTenthErrorHandler
    If txtNumber.Text.ToString <> "" Then
       oneTenthOfNumber = txtNumber.Text.ToString/10
       GetTenth = oneTenthOfNumber
    Else
       GetTenth = 0
    End If
    Exit Function
    '*******************************************
GetTenthErrorHandler:
    '*******************************************
    'write error to error log
    GetTenth = "An error has been encountered. Please
contact technical support"
    'Logger(Err.Description) !comment out this line
    '*******************************************
 End Function
```

For the purposes of this example, let us say a user has notified you that while using the application he or she received the following error:

```
An error has been encountered. Please contact
technical support.
```

Our job is to now find out what is causing this bug and correct it.

With the bolded line commented out, we should be able to compile and debug the application. With the solution configuration set to Debug, hit F5 and the application will be run in the debug mode. While running the application in debug mode, open the code view of Form1.vb. Now we will set a breakpoint at the first line of execution in the program.

To insert the breakpoint, highlight the line that reads

```
MsgBox(GetTenth(GetTenthTxt))
```

Once this line is highlighted, right-click over it and select Insert Breakpoint from the menu. Another way to insert a breakpoint is to single-click in the shaded region to the left of the code window, as illustrated in Figure 5.7.

When a breakpoint is properly inserted, it will highlight the code in red and add a red circle to the left side of the code window.

With the breakpoint set, bring up the application window and click on the button `GetTenth`. When you do, focus should then shift to the breakpoint. The IDE is now paused and is waiting for you to decide how to execute the code. The breakpoint should appear yellow, meaning it is active.

The following chapter will refer to two ways of navigating through your code: stepping through your code and running through your code. When using breakpoints, there are two different keystrokes for performing these functions. To step, or walk, through your code, press F11. This allows you to execute one line at a time, regardless of the location of any breakpoints. To run through your code, use F5. F5 will continue to execute lines of code until it reaches a breakpoint or the end of the code.

Try hitting the F5 key to run through the code. The application should continue executing as normal. Clicking on the `GetTenth` button again will bring you back to the breakpoint. Now try stepping through the code. Pressing F11 will send you to the first line of the `GetTenth` function. Experiment by navigating around the code. This will get you familiar with using breakpoints. However, now that we can use the breakpoint to pause the execution of the code, we need a way to extrapolate some useful data from the application. The next section of this chapter will show you how to extract information from the application in conjunction with using the breakpoints.

## Visual Basic Debug Mode Editing

If you are familiar with Visual Basic, and Visual Studio 6, then you may be aware of a helpful tool known as debug mode editing. This feature allowed Visual Basic 6 users to edit and make changes to their code while it was being executed in debug mode. Unfortunately, this feature had

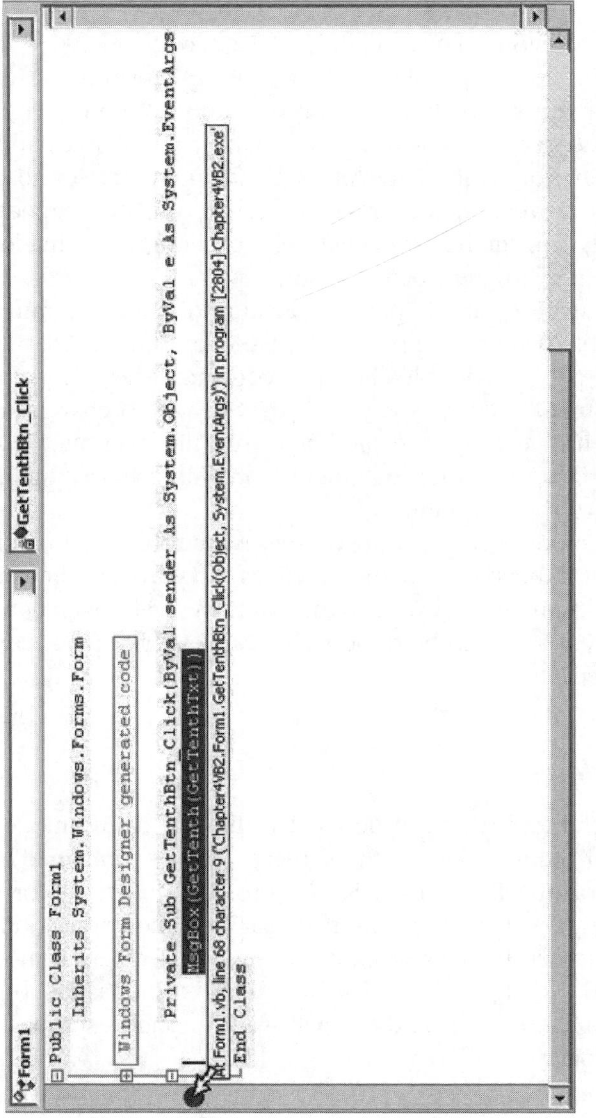


Figure 5.7 Inserting a breakpoint.

been removed in subsequent versions of Visual Studio .NET. That is, until Visual Studio 2005.

With the release of Visual Studio 2005, Visual Basic users again have the ability to pause the execution of their code and make changes to it in debug mode. This allows for a faster debug cycle, and the ability to quickly try different code scenarios.

In previous versions of Visual Studio .NET (2002 and 2003) you would have to locate a line of problematic code using a breakpoint (or similar tool), and then you would have to stop execution of your program. After the program had been halted, you could make your changes and start the debug mode environment again. Although this may not sound like a big deal, it can be a very tedious process to stop, make changes to, and restart very large programs, especially if the change you made requires some setup in the program before testing.

To use this feature, simply pause execution of your program in debug mode (preferably with a breakpoint, discussed later in this chapter). When execution has paused, double-click the code to insert your cursor and make your changes. The only caveat is that if you do change something constant that has already executed and remained in memory, like a function name or a dimension statement, you will have to stop and restart the execution of the program.

The debug mode editor is a great timesaving tool in VB6 and VB.NET 2005. However, to keep our editing practices standard, and because Visual Studio 2003 is more widely used right now, we will cover debug mode editing the way it needs to be done in VS 2003, by stopping, editing, and restarting projects.

## Debug Windows

There are several tools that can be used within the debug mode environment of Visual Studio 2003. Each of these tools is contained within its own window on the IDE. Visual Studio provides functions for manually executing lines of code that are not necessarily in the application, looking into variables to see their values, and seeing what external modules are being accessed, among others. The following sections will outline the uses of each of these tools, and we will walk through each of them with our sample project.

## Breakpoints

Because we have already set up breakpoints, this will be a good place to start. However, there is more functionality that we can put behind the

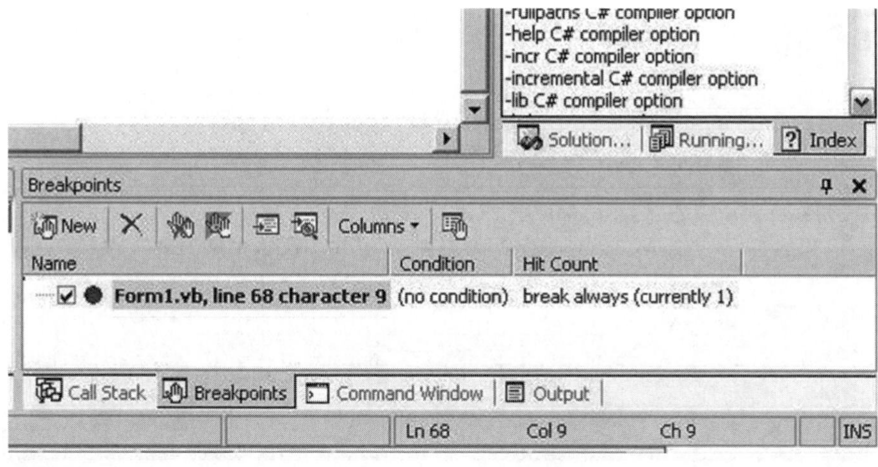


**Figure 5.8 Figure the breakpoint window.**

breakpoints. We can specify when the break should fire and use it to give us information about the line of code it has stopped on.

The first step is to set the breakpoint window. The breakpoint window is located in the lower-right-hand section of the IDE, as illustrated in Figure 5.8. By default, this window may not be displayed or set to view a different pane. Simply click on the Breakpoint tab to show the correct pane.

This window will display all of the breakpoints you have added throughout your code. From here you can adjust any of the properties of those breakpoints. The most useful properties of breakpoints are Condition and Hit Count. These two properties are extremely useful when evaluating large blocks of code. They control how and when a breakpoint gets activated.

The Condition parameter allows you to set a Boolean condition and attach the condition to the activation of a breakpoint. The breakpoint will not activate unless this condition evaluates as true. For example, if we only wanted the breakpoint to pause the program when we put an H in the text box, we could use the following expression as a condition:

```
getTenthTxt.text.tostring ="H"
```

When this expression evaluates as true (we put an H in the text box), the breakpoint will activate and pause the code. Otherwise, the code will continue to execute, ignoring the breakpoint.

To specify a condition on a breakpoint, right-click the breakpoint and select Breakpoint Properties. This will open the breakpoint properties

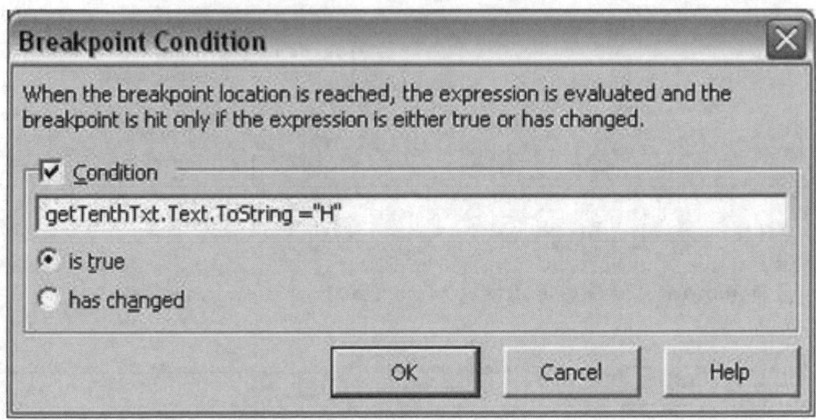


**Figure 5.9 The breakpoint condition dialog.**

dialog. Click on the Condition button to enter a condition. Figure 5.9 illustrates the Breakpoint Condition dialog box.

The Hit Count parameter allows you to specify a finite number of passes you want the code to make before activating the breakpoint. This is very useful when you have a breakpoint on a `For...Loop` or `Do...While` statement. For example, assume you are debugging a program that reads through a flat file. The code that reads in each line of the file is nested in a `Do...While` statement. You have noticed that the program encounters problems after it reads 237 lines. You could step through your program 237 times using the F11 key, or you could use the Hit Count parameter of the breakpoint to specify that you do not want the breakpoint to activate until it has been passed 237 times. The Hit Count dialog is accessed from the same properties dialog box as the Condition dialog. Figure 5.10 shows the Hit Count dialog.

## Watch

A watch is an expression that can be identified in the debugger by the programmer. The debugger will then publish the value of the expression set in the watch. A watch can contain a variable, object, or expression. When the program executes to a point where the object in the watch is encountered, the watch will be updated to show all of the pertinent information about that object. For example, if we wanted to see how the value of `GetTenthTxt` changed during testing, we could set up a watch containing `GetTenthText`.

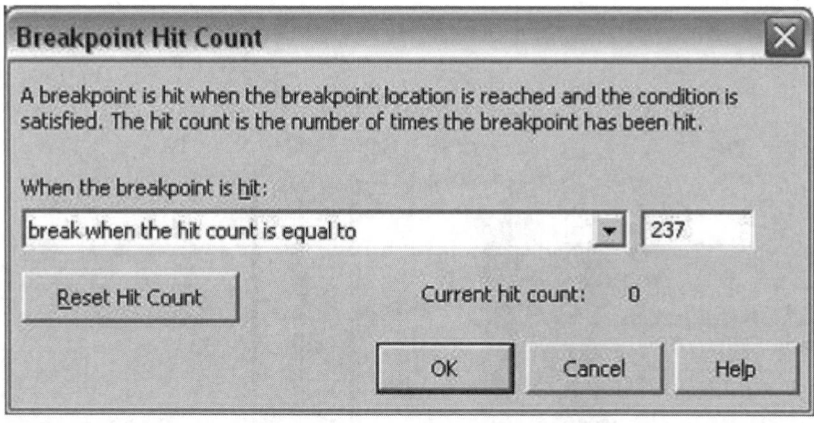


**Figure 5.10 The hit count dialog.**

To set up a watch, run your application in debug mode and break it. While the application is paused, click on the Watch1 tab located on the lower-left-hand side of the debug window. The watch pane is illustrated in Figure 5.11.

If the Watch1 pane is not visible, it can be accessed through the menu by going to

```
Debug>Windows>Watch.
```

Click into the watch pane to add a new watch. In our example we will be adding `GetTenthTxt`. Figure 5.12 shows a watch on `GetTenth-Txt`.

Examining Figure 5.12, we can see that almost every property of the text box `GetTenthTxt` is accessible from the watch. You can see exactly how the object is configured and what the text property is.

> If you are using Visual Studio 2005, you may have trouble locating the watches. This is because as a stand-alone item, watches have been removed from Visual Studio. However, most of the functionality that watches provided has been rolled into Breakpoints. Therefore, the ability to set conditions and hit counts is now inherent to breakpoints, and watches has been dropped from the IDE.

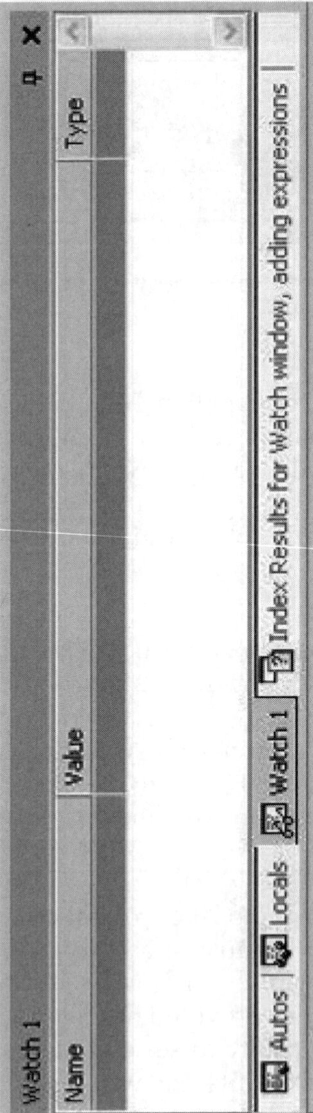


**Figure 5.11** The watch pane.

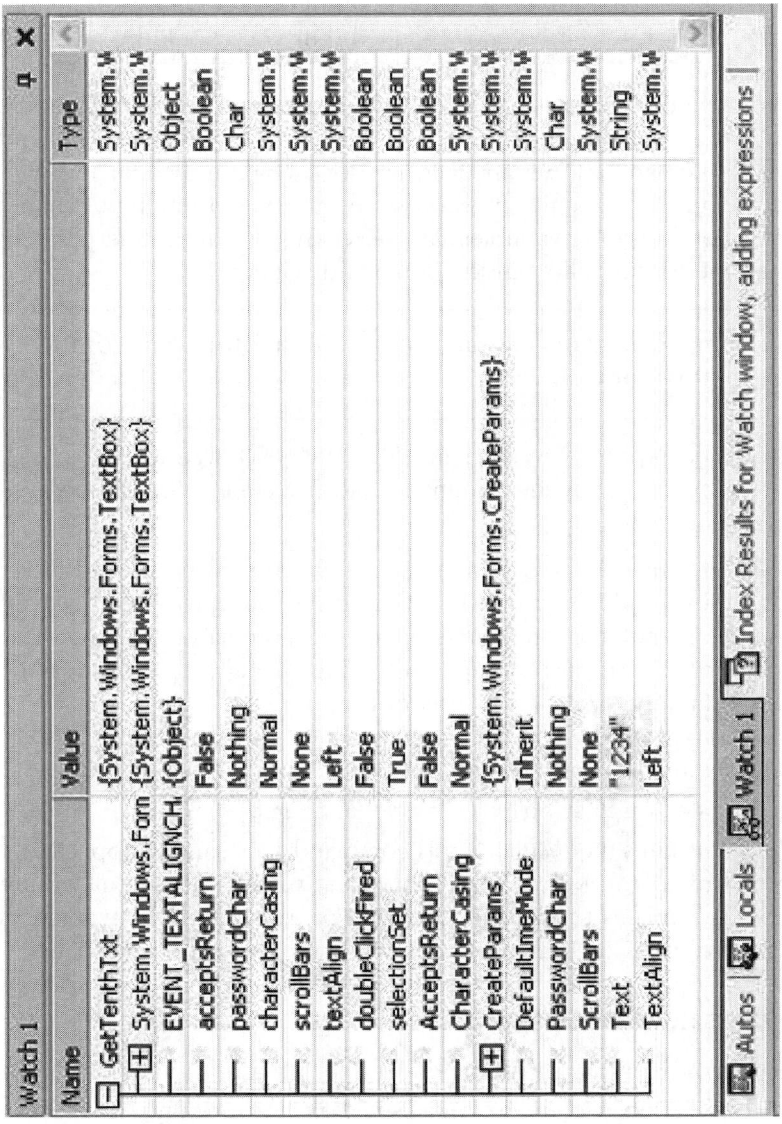

Watch 1

| Name | Value | Type |
|---|---|---|
| GetTenthTxt | {System.Windows.Forms.TextBox} | System.W |
| System.Windows.Forn | {System.Windows.Forms.TextBox} | System.W |
| EVENT_TEXTALIGNCH | {Object} | Object |
| acceptsReturn | False | Boolean |
| passwordChar | Nothing | Char |
| characterCasing | Normal | System.W |
| scrollBars | None | System.W |
| textAlign | Left | System.W |
| doubleClickFired | False | Boolean |
| selectionSet | True | Boolean |
| AcceptsReturn | False | Boolean |
| CharacterCasing | Normal | System.W |
| CreateParams | {System.Windows.Forms.CreateParams} | System.W |
| DefaultImeMode | Inherit | System.W |
| PasswordChar | Nothing | Char |
| ScrollBars | None | System.W |
| Text | "1234" | String |
| TextAlign | Left | System.W |

Autos | Locals | Watch 1 | Index Results for Watch window, adding expressions

**Figure 5.12** The `GetTenthTxt` watch.

## *Command Window/Immediate Window*

In another change, much like that of the debug mode editing capabilities of Visual Basic, Microsoft attempts to keep programmers on their toes by renaming the console window (which was called the immediate window in Visual Studio 6) back to the immediate window. The general functionality of the windows itself has not changed, but you should be aware of the new name.

The command window is one of the most commonly used and versatile tools in the debugger. In previous versions of Visual Studio, the command window was known as the immediate window. Using the command window, the debugger can enter in expressions or call up different runtime properties. For example, variables can be changed, parameters entered, and dumps performed all from the command window.

> The command window can be accessed as another pane of the breakpoint window.

While at a breakpoint, we can change the value of `GetTenthTxt.Text` to 17 by typing the following command into the command window:

```
GetTenthText.Text = 17
```

This same format of `<expression> = <value>` can be used to set most properties in your application during the debug process. However, setting values is not the only function of the command window. The command window can also accept use of the debug set of commands, the most commonly used of which is `debug.write`.

To print into the command window the value of `GetTenthTxt.Text`, the debug command could be used as follows:

```
debug.write GetTenthTxt.Text.ToString
```

Figure 5.13 illustrates the results of this command on a sample application.

`Debug.write` can be used to display any value of the result of any expression as it relates to your application. For example, if we wanted to find out how the `If...Then` statement from our application evaluated:

### Listing 5.3: `If...Then` Statement

```
If txtNumber.Text.ToString <> "" Then
 oneTenthOfNumber = txtNumber.Text.ToString/10
 GetTenth = oneTenthOfNumber
Else
 GetTenth = 0
End If
```

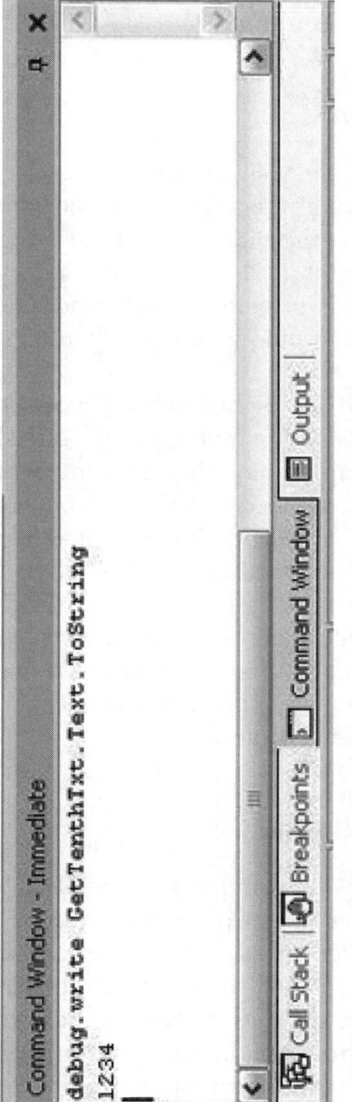


**Figure 5.13 The debug.write command.**

we can use the command window to tell us if the `If...Then` statement evaluated as true or false by issuing the following command in the command window:

```
debug.write txtNumber.Text.ToString <> ""
```

The command window will display either true or false, depending on how the application has been evaluated.

## Modules

The final debugger tool we will discuss in this chapter is the module window. The module window is used to display the external files that are being accessed by your application, and the order in which they are accessed. This is important in helping you track problems in larger applications, or interactions in other libraries and .dlls.

To display the module window, select it from the Debug>Windows> Module Window menu.

In Figure 5.14 we can see eight modules accessed by the Chapter 4 VB application. This information, although not directly important to the execution of our sample application, becomes much more useful in larger applications, where the one piece you are debugging may rely on 30 other custom .dlls to run correctly. Using the module window, you can see what .dlls have been accessed and what symbols were loaded during the execution.

If you need to edit a file used by the application being debugged, you can continue your debugging session without having to restart. Simply right-click on the module that you edited and select Reload Symbols. This will reload the newly changed module.

## Compiler-Generated Errors

Now that you are ready to compile your application for the runtime environment, you can start to keep an eye on the compiler errors. The good thing about compiler errors during a release compile is that they can not only indicate a potential bug in your application, but also alert you to problems in the compile itself. That is, the compiler will throw an error if there is an incorrect option provided, memory problem, or any other bug that may keep the application from executing in a release environment. What follows is a list of some common compiler errors and some solutions.

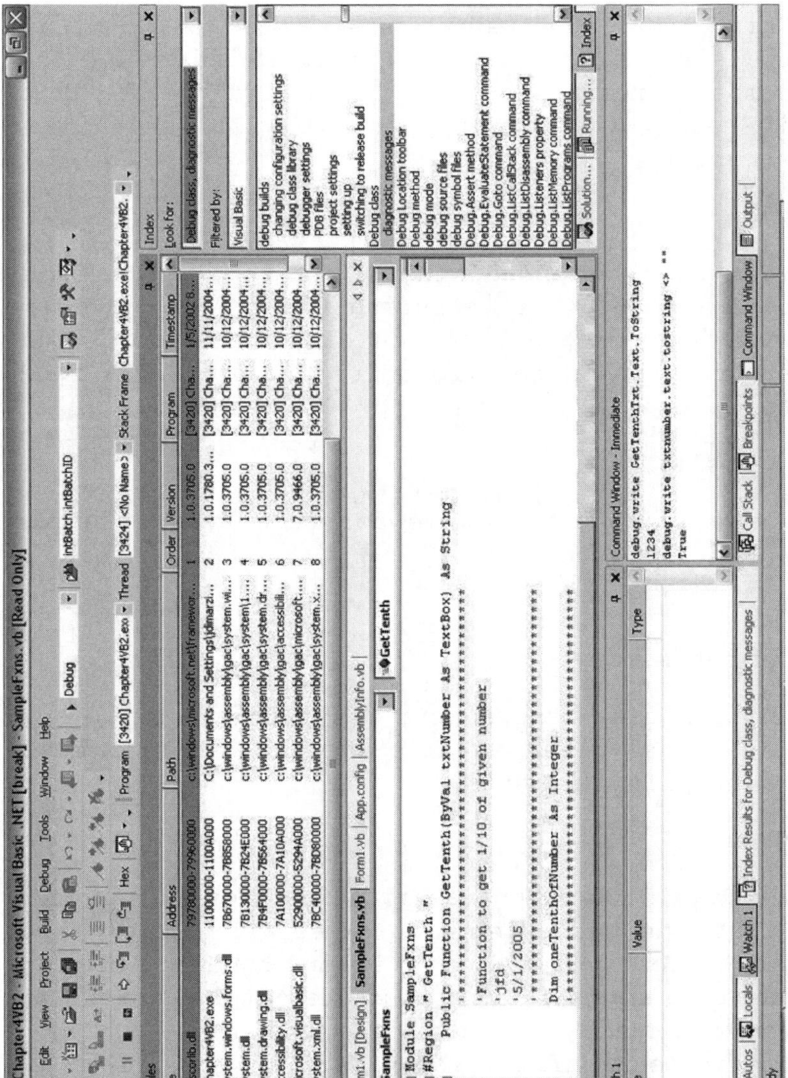

Figure 5.14 The module window.

**Listing 5.4: Common Compiler Errors and Solutions**

```
Error

    Internal compiler error

    This error, as frustrating as it may be, is more
    or less the catchall of compiler errors. If the
    compiler reaches a point in the translation that
    it really cannot get past, it will issue this
    error.

Solution

    Your best bet in fixing it is to step through
    each line of code, ensuring there is no problem
    with your program. If you can verify that your
    program should compile correctly, you will need
    to look into reinstalling Visual Studio.

Code sample

    There is no code sample for this type of error.


Error

    Out of memory

    In this case, there were insufficient resources
    for the compiler to allocate the memory needed
    to compile the code.

Solution

    There are two potential solutions for this issue.
    First, you can attempt to close all windows that
    you currently have open. Closing unneeded windows
    may free up some memory for the compiler. Second,
    you can attempt to increase the size of your
    machine's pagefile. The pagefile can be used by
    the compiler for larger operations; therefore,
    increasing its size will help it run.

Code sample

    There is no code sample for this type of error.
```

Error

Metadata file '<dll_name.dll>' could not be found

This error, as the name implies, occurs when you attempt to use resources in your application that are derived from an external .dll file, but that .dll file cannot be located by the compiler.

Solution

The best solutions for this error are check that the .dll file is correctly added as a reference to the project, and to ensure that the .dll file name is spelled correctly.

Code sample

There is no code sample for this type of error.

Error

A user-defined namespace is conflicting with an imported type name.

Being fairly descriptive, this error is generated when a namespace you are trying to import into an application has the same name as a defined type within the application.

Solution

Change or rename the namespace you created.

Code sample

```
// This code causes the error.
//***************************
namespace System.Int32
{
//remaining code
}
//***************************
// corrected code
//***************************
```

```
Namespace MyNewNamespace
{
//remaining code
}
//***************************
```

Error

Required file '<file>' could not be found

While on the surface a file is a file, this error is not necessarily referring to a file used by your application. This could be a file used by the compiler, or Visual Studio.

Solution

Unfortunately, the best solution in this case is to ensure Visual Studio is installed correctly.

Code sample

There is no code sample for this type of error.

Error

Could not write to output file '<file>' – '<reason>'

If you get this error, a file used by your application cannot be accessed. For example, you may not have file- or directory-level permissions to access the file, or it could be in read-only mode.

Solution

Ensure that all required permissions for the file are in place, and attempt to open the file manually. This will let you know if there are read issues with the file. Keep in mind, the file itself may even be corrupted; therefore, attempting to open it manually will give you a better idea of what the problem is.

Code sample

There is no code sample for this type of error.

Error

Operator '<operator>' cannot be applied to operands of type '<type>' and '<type>'

An example of this kind of error would be:

Operator '*' cannot be applied to operands of type 'Char' and 'Int'

Solution

The solution for this kind of error would be to change the type of the operands involved in the operation.

Code sample

```
'This code produces the error
'***************************
Public Sub operandTest()
Dim operand1 as Char
Dim operand2 as Integer
    product1 = operand1 * operand2
End Sub
'*****************************
'this code is corrected
'*****************************
Public Sub operandTest()
Dim operand1 as Integer
Dim operand2 as Integer
    product1 = operand1 * operand2
End Sub
```

Error

A binary operator is operating on data types for which it was not designed.

One common place this error occurs is when you attempt to pass multiple parameters to an attribute that is only designed to accept one.

Solution

Select only one of the parameters to be passed.

Code sample

```
// this code produces the error
//*************************************
public class MyClass
{
 [System.Diagnostics.ConditionalAttribute("DEBUG" ||
"TRACE")]
}...
//*************************************
//this code corrects the error
//*************************************
public class MyClass
{
 [System.Diagnostics.ConditionalAttribute("DEBUG")]
<or>
 [System.Diagnostics.ConditionalAttribute("TRACE")]
}...
//*************************************
```

Error

Division by constant zero

A division by zero error occurs when you attempt to divide any integer by zero (0).

Solution

The solution for this error is to edit your formula.

Code sample

There is no code sample for this error.

Error

Operator '<operator>' cannot be applied to operand of type '<type>'

This error occurs when you attempt to use an operator on a variable of a type that does not take an operator.

Solution

The solution for this error is to remove the operator or check your variable type.

Code sample

```
//***************************
// the code produces the error
//***************************
{
   public class helloWorld
   {
      public static void Main()
      {
         string helloMessage = "Hello World";
         helloMessage = -helloMessage;
      }
   }
}
//****************************
// the code fixes the error
//****************************
{
   public class helloWorld
   {
      public static void Main()
```

```
        {
           string helloMessage = "Hello World";
           //helloMessage = -helloMessage; //this line
could be removed
        }
    }
}
//*****************************
```

Error

Cannot implicitly convert type '<type>' to '<type>'

When this error is generated, it is an indication that you are trying to assign a value to a variable that is defined as a type that does not correspond to the value you are assigning to it.

Solution

The solution for this error is to either cast your value to equal the variable you are placing it in, or redefine the variable to match the value.

Code sample

```
//***************************
// the code produces the error
//***************************
{
    public class intAssign
    {
       public static void Main()
       {
          int int1;
          long long1;
          int1 = 45;
long = int1;
       }
```

```
    }
}
//****************************
// the code fixes the error
//****************************
{
    public class helloWorld
    {
       public static void Main()
       {
//****************************
//solution 1
//****************************
          int int1;
          int long1;
          long1 = 256;
int1 = long1;
//****************************
//solution 2
//****************************
          int int1;
          long long1;
          long1 = 256;
int1 = (int) long1;
       }
    }
}
//*****************************
```

```
Error

   Cannot access a nonstatic member of outer type
   'type1' via nested type 'type2'

Solution

   The solution for this error is to edit your
   formula.
```

```
Code sample

    There is no code sample for this error.
```

This short list of common compiler errors should help you in many situations. If you are having trouble with an error that you do not see listed here, check the reference guides in the back of the book. These reference guides contain a much more comprehensive list of exceptions, both design and runtime.

The next chapter covers the newer features of Visual Studio .NET 2005. Microsoft has taken some time to add in new features, many of which are geared specifically for debugging. Some of these features are brand new, and others are either enhanced or were previously removed and returned.

## Review Questions

1. What is the function of the compiler?
2. What happens when you double-click on a compiler error?
3. In Visual Studio, what are the two solution configuration modes?
4. What keystroke is used to step through your code in debug mode?
5. Name three of the debug windows.
6. What parameter is used to keep a breakpoint from activating until a given expression evaluates as true?
7. What debug command is used to display the contents of an object in the command window?
8. What can a watch be applied to?
9. What was the command window called in previous versions of Visual Studio?
10. When using the module windows, how can you reload a module?

## Looking Ahead

Now that we have been fully introduced to the arsenal of tools available in the debugger we can use them to debug a full program. Chapter 6 is going to take a full program and run it through the Visual Studio debugger. Using breakpoints, watches, and the immediate window, we will debug this program to find three pre-compiled bugs.

# Chapter 6

# Debugging and Visual Studio 2005

## Debugging with the New Features in Visual Studio 2005

Although we touched upon this earlier, there were some key changes made to Visual Studio .NET 2005. These changes can affect the way in which you debug your applications within the IDE. Although we will not cover every change that Microsoft made to the product, for the fact that many may not have anything to do with your debugging, we will cover the major changes that directly impact debugging procedures.

These changes include:

- Tracepoints
- Design time debugging
- Debug mode code editing
- Edit Tracking
- Snippet Manager
- Just My Code™ debugging
- Breakpoint filters for processors
- Exception Assistant
- Unused Variable Notification

Let us examine all of these features, and you can use each in debugging your code.

## Tracepoints

One of the newer features of Microsoft's Visual Studio .NET is called tracepoints. If you have used Visual Studio .NET 2005, you may have noticed that a very useful item is conspicuously missing. Earlier in this book we examined how to work with watches in Visual Studio .NET 2003. Watches as an individual item no longer exists in Visual Studio .NET 2005. However, the functionality that watches provided has been distributed across other components of the interface.

The functionality that watches once provided has been used to enhance the functionality already provided by breakpoints. However, not all of the functions of watches fit well within the scope of what a breakpoint was — hence the two items being separated in the first place. Therefore, a new tool was developed with some of its own functionality. This new tool is known as a tracepoint. As you use them you will find tracepoints to be extremely useful in your everyday debugging. Let us examine what tracepoints can be used for, and then we will take a look at an example of tracepoints in action.

Tracepoints offer debuggers the opportunity to assign a tag to a breakpoint-style line in a block of code. This tag, or tracer, is then evaluated during specific debugging situations; the consequence of such is a customizable set of events. In other words, you can use a tracepoint for instructing the compiler to supply particular information about the highlighted code, under distinct conditions.

To insert a tracepoint in your code, right-click over the line you want to add the tracepoint to. Click on <Breakpoint>, then <Insert Tracepoint>, as seen in Figure 6.1.

> To make things easier for yourself, you just have to think of tracepoints as being breakpoints. The marker used in the margin, a red circle, is the same for tracepoints and breakpoints. Also, the window used to configure your tracepoint is called the "When Breakpoint Is Hit" window, thus begging the question: Why have two separate entities when they are completely interchangeable? Unfortunately, we really do not have a good answer for this, and being that this book was written using an advanced copy of Visual Studio .NET 2005, the names may change when Microsoft releases the final compile of Visual Studio .NET.

Selecting the Insert Tracepoint option will force the When Breakpoint Is Hit window to be displayed. This window will be displayed with all

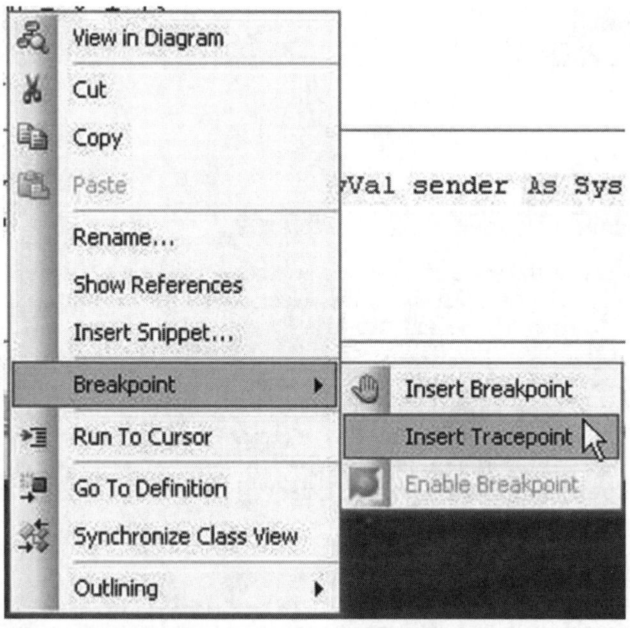


**Figure 6.1 Insert tracepoint menu.**

of the standard options selected. Figure 6.2 illustrates what the When Breakpoint Is Hit window looks like with the standard options selected.

The When Breakpoint Is Hit window allows you to specify one of two actions for your tracepoint. The first function you can assign to your tracepoint allows it to print a custom message to the immediate window. This can be a very powerful tool in debugging your code, and it is very close to the functionality provided by watches, yet much more powerful. Where watches would only show you static information about the object being watched, tracepoints can be customized to display many different things.

Tracepoints have eight predefined pieces of information, represented by keywords, which can be displayed about the environment in which a tracepoint runs. These keywords and their associated information are listed as follows:

## Listing 6.1: Tracepoint Keywords

```
$ADDRESS – Current instruction being processed
$CALLER – Name of the function that called the block
of code containing the tracepoint
```

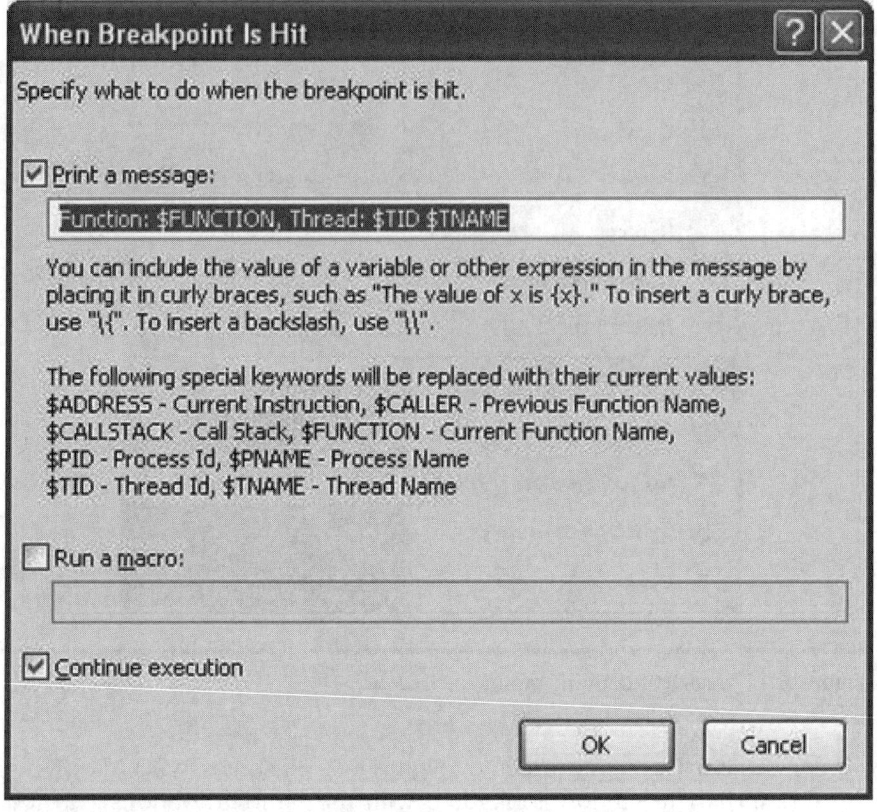


**Figure 6.2 The When Breakpoint Is Hit window.**

`$CALLSTACK – Current call stack`

`$FUNCTION – Name of the function containing the block of code being traced`

`$PID – Current process ID`

`$PNAME – Current process name`

`$TID – Current thread ID`

`$TNAME – Current thread name`

The default instruction for a tracepoint when it is created is

```
Function: $FUNCTION, Thread: $TID $TNAME
```

If you do not edit this line, when the tracepoint is activated, it will print into the immediate window the name of the function containing the tracepoint, the thread ID, and the thread name (if applicable). The following VB subroutine is named ComplicatedMath. This function was used in our tracepoint examples.

**Listing 6.2: VB.NET Code `ComplicatedMath()` Subroutine**

```
Public Sub ComplicatedMath()
'***************************
'Meaningless sample math function
'***************************
    Dim x As Integer
    Dim y As Integer
    For x = 1 to 100
       y = x + 12
       y = y * 2
       y = y + 7
       y = y / 2
    Next
'***************************
End Sub
```

If you have inserted this function into your own Visual Basic .NET project, insert a tracepoint at the line that reads `For x = 1 to 100`. Accepting the standard options for the "Print a Message" option, let us debug the function and see what happens. Figure 6.3 illustrates the results of the tracepoint being fired.

> Pay close attention to the checkbox that appears at the bottom of the When Breakpoint Is Hit window. The checkbox is labeled "Continue Execution." When most people think of breakpoints or tracepoints, the assumption is that the debugging will pause when a point is hit. That is not necessarily the case anymore. The Continue Execution checkbox is selected by default, meaning that when the tracepoint is encountered, the configured message will print into the immediate window, but the debugger will not pause at the line containing the tracepoint. Therefore, if you do want the debugger to halt execution, you must be sure to uncheck the Continue Execution checkbox.

As you can see from Figure 6.3, the tracepoint provided the following line to the immediate window:

```
Function: Test.Form1.ComplicatedMath(), Thread: 0x550
<No Name>
```

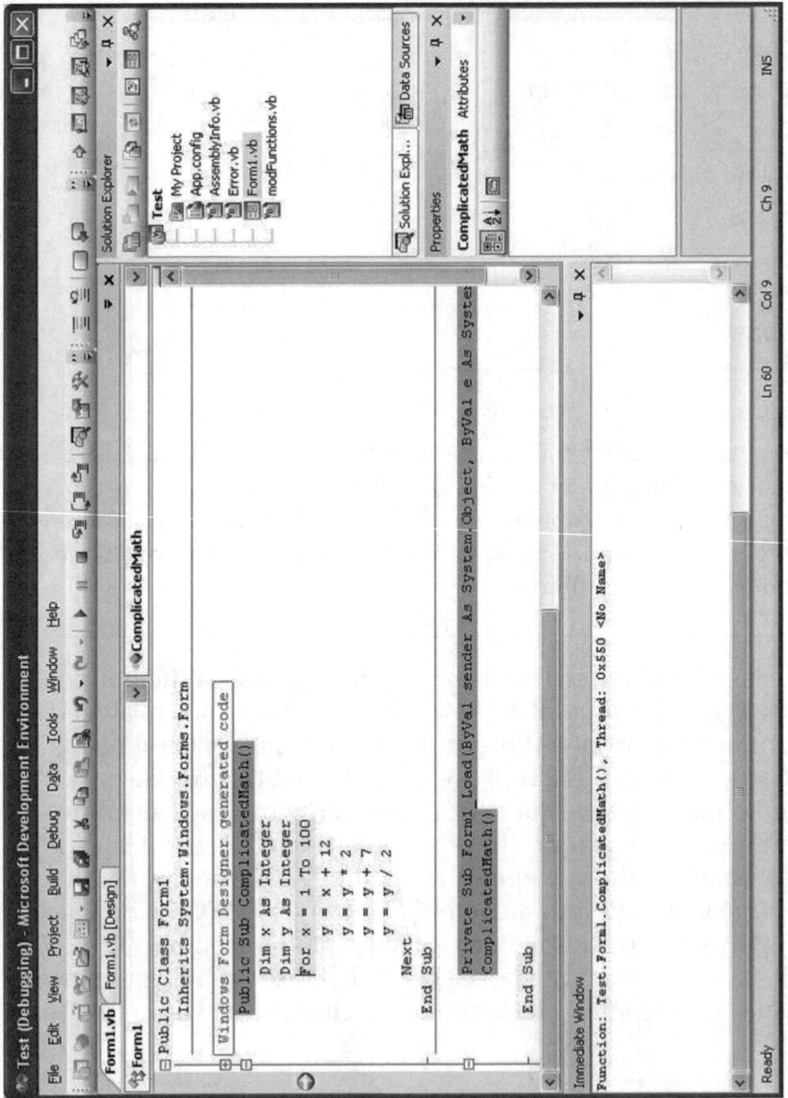


**Figure 6.3 The results of a standard tracepoint.**

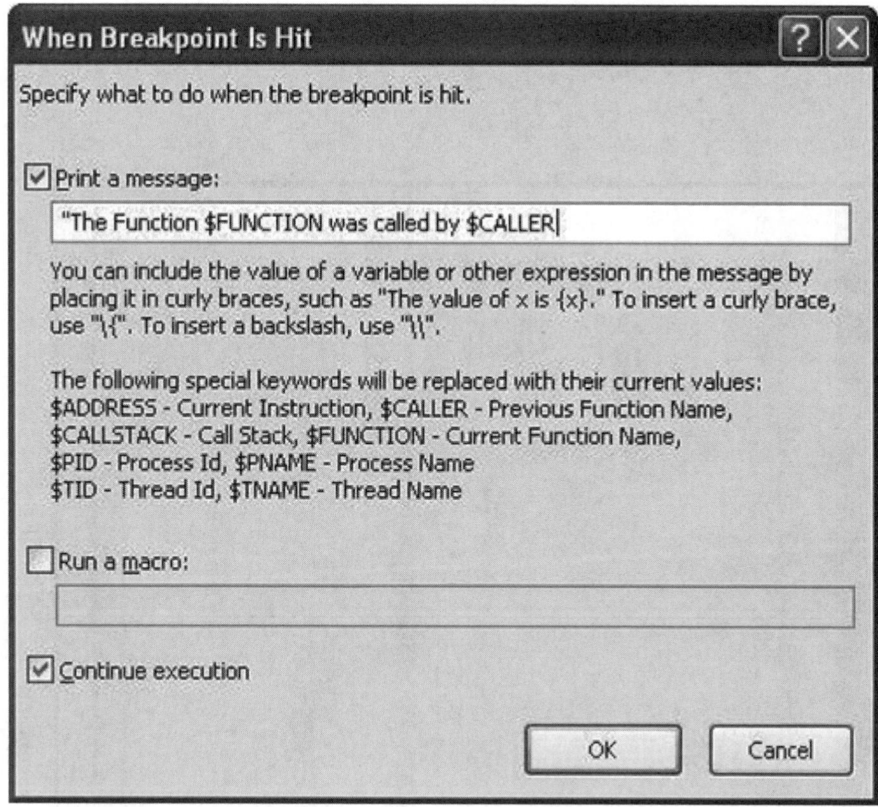


**Figure 6.4 The When Breakpoint Is Hit window with custom text.**

As mentioned earlier, the display message can be customized to display many different pieces of information. In fact, the way the message is presented can be customized as well. Text can be added to the message to give it specific meaning. This can be useful if you are using multiple tracepoints and they are all set to continue execution. Adding custom text will allow you to identify the output of each tracepoint. Figure 6.4 illustrates how text can be used in concert with the tracepoint keywords to create more meaningful output.

Figure 6.4 shows that we have created a custom message for the tracepoint to display when it is fired. In this example we want the tracepoint to display "The Function Test.Form1.ComplicateMath() was called by Test.Form1.Form_Load." To do this, we simply type in the added text around the keywords in the message box. The text we added to achieve this result was "The Function $FUNCTION was called by $CALLER." Figure 6.5 shows the output of this message.

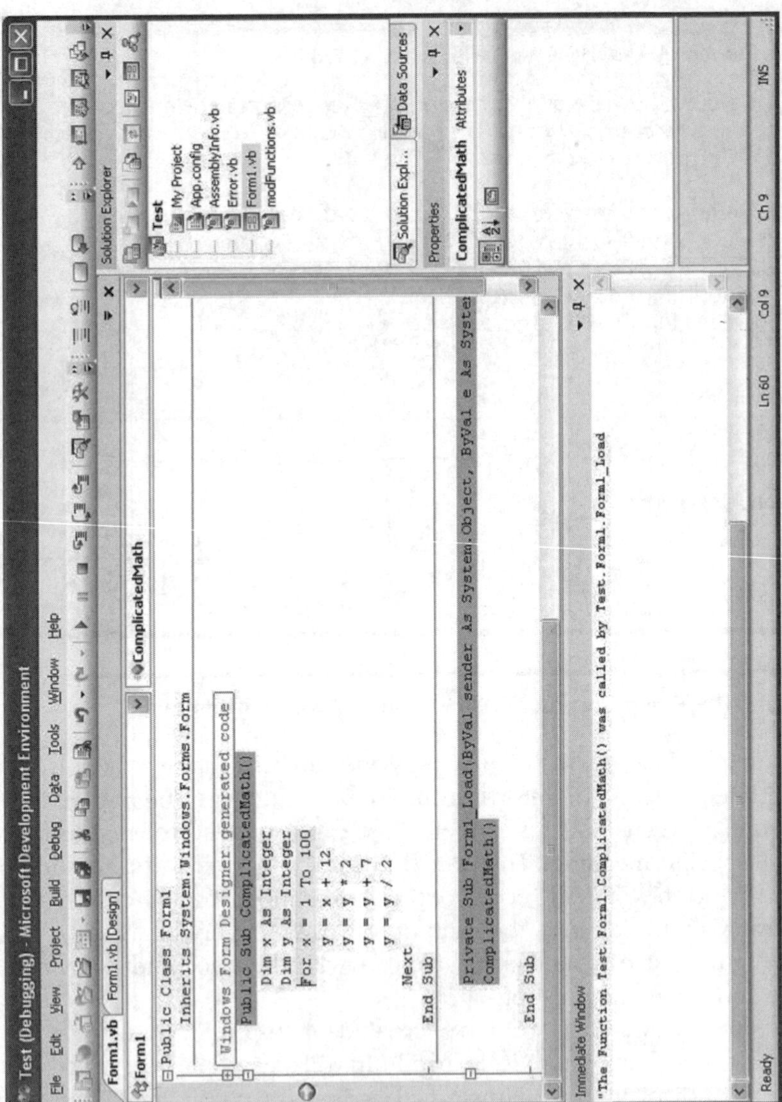


Figure 6.5 The results of the customized tracepoint.

If we were to use all of the keywords available to us, the tracepoint would print out the following when it was executed:

### Listing 6.3: Output from All Tracepoint Keywords

```
Address: Test.Form1.ComplicatedMath() + 0x00000007
Caller: Test.Form1.Form1_Load
CallStack: Test.Form1.ComplicatedMath
    Test.Form1.Form1_Load
    System.Windows.Forms.Form.OnLoad
    System.Windows.Forms.Form.OnCreateControl
    System.Windows.Forms.Control.CreateControl
    System.Windows.Forms.Control.CreateControl
    System.Windows.Forms.Control.WmShowWindow
    System.Windows.Forms.Control.WndProc
    System.Windows.Forms.ScrollableControl.WndProc
    System.Windows.Forms.ContainerControl.WndProc
    System.Windows.Forms.Form.WmShowWindow
    System.Windows.Forms.Form.WndProc
    System.Windows.Forms.Control.ControlNativeWindow.
OnMessage
    System.Windows.Forms.Control.ControlNativeWindow.
WndProc
    System.Windows.Forms.NativeWindow.
DebuggableCallback
    [Native to Managed Transition]
    [Managed to Native Transition]
    System.Windows.Forms.Control.SetVisibleCore
    System.Windows.Forms.Form.SetVisibleCore
    System.Windows.Forms.Control.Visible.set
    System.Windows.Forms.Application.ThreadContext.
RunMessageLoopInner
    System.Windows.Forms.Application.ThreadContext.
RunMessageLoop
    System.Windows.Forms.Application.Run
    Test.Form1.Main
    [Managed to Native Transition]
```

```
    System.AppDomain.ExecuteAssembly
    VSHostUtil.HostProc.RunUsersAssembly
    System.Threading._Thread.ThreadStart_Context
    System.Threading.ExecutionContext.Run
    System.Threading._Thread.ThreadStart
PID: 0x7D0
PNAME: .NET
```

> Keep in mind that not all computers will execute identically, and information such as ProcessID and ThreadID will differ from computer to computer.

Although this information can be very useful, sometimes you may need to know what is going on inside of a variable to debug a situation. Tracepoints can also be used to display information from within variables directly to the immediate window. That is, in the same way watches could be used to monitor what information was in a variable at difference stages of the application's execution, a tracepoint can be used to display the contents of block variables.

To have a tracepoint print out the value of a variable, simply enclose that variable's name in braces within the message string. For example, take a look at the following VB.NET code:

**Listing 6.4: VB.NET Tracepoint Variable Print**

```
Public Function VariableExample()
'*******************************
'Sample function that doesn't really do much
'jfd
'5/05/2005
'*******************************
Dim Counter as Integer
Dim Marker as Integer
Dim Result as Integer
Dim x as Integer
Counter = 100
X = 0
```

```
Marker = 100
Result = 0
For x = 1 to Counter
'this will generate a divide by zero error
    Result = 100 / Marker
    Marker = Marker - 20
Next
'********************************
End Function
```

The preceding code, if run, will eventually generate a divide-by-zero error. Although it may be evident why just by looking at the code, if you did not know when or why the error was generated, you could use a tracepoint to print out the values of the variables involved. Let us insert this line in our tracepoint message:

```
Marker: {Marker} X: {x}
```

The result of this message would be as follows:

**Listing 6.5: Tracepoint Output of x**

```
Marker: 100 X: 1
Marker: 80 X: 2
Marker: 60 X: 3
Marker: 40 X: 4
Marker: 20 X: 5
Marker: 0 X: 6
```

Experiment with tracepoints and use them to gather information about your applications. Tracepoints truly provide a great tool in Visual Studio .NET 2005 for assisting debugger in tough situations. In the next section, we will look at another new tool in Visual Studio .NET 2005, design time debugging.

## Design Time Debugging

Design time debugging is one of the more powerful and timesaving features added to Visual Studio .NET 2005. This is a new feature that was unavailable in previous versions of Visual Studio .NET. However, you will find it very valuable in your debugging efforts.

The concept of design time debugging takes advantage of one existing tool in the Visual Studio .NET arsenal that has been modified, and although the modification made may seem insignificant on the surface, it makes a big difference in the way you will debug applications. The tool is the immediate window, and the added functionality is offline access.

First let us take a look at the immediate window as it stands in Visual Studio .NET 2002–2003. We have covered some aspects of the immediate window or command window in this chapter already, and if you are even slightly familiar with programming in the Visual Studio .NET environment, you most likely consider the immediate window to be one of the most valuable tools in your Visual Studio toolbox.

In the earlier versions of Visual Studio .NET, the immediate window was renamed the command window — immediate. However, even with the new name, much of the functionality remained intact. Both the command window and the older immediate window were used during the debug mode execution to display information and run commands against the executing application.

In Visual Studio .NET 2005, the command window has been separated from the immediate window once again. Now there are two entities within Visual Studio .NET: the command window and the immediate window. Figure 6.6 illustrates the immediate window in Visual Studio .NET 2005.

Although the placement of the immediate window in Figure 6.6 may look familiar to users of older versions of Visual Studio, Microsoft has made one major change to welcome back its keystone tool. The newest incarnation of the immediate window, unlike its predecessors, can be used offline. This means that much of the functionality present in the immediate window is available to you without having to put the IDE into debug mode. How can having the use of something as seemingly simplistic as the immediate window change the way you debug your application? That question is best answered by looking at the current procedure, in a nutshell.

One change to note that is present in the new and improved immediate window of Visual Studio 2005 is that it can execute functions without the program being run. That is, if you are working on a function, without executing the entire program in debug mode, you can call up the immediate window and execute the specific function in the window.

The immediate window will then pass just that function, and its related lines of code, to the compiler, compile it in memory, and execute the function, returning the results back to the immediate window. Although this function does have its limitations, it can prove to be exceedingly valuable for programmers who are trying to debug one part of a larger application.

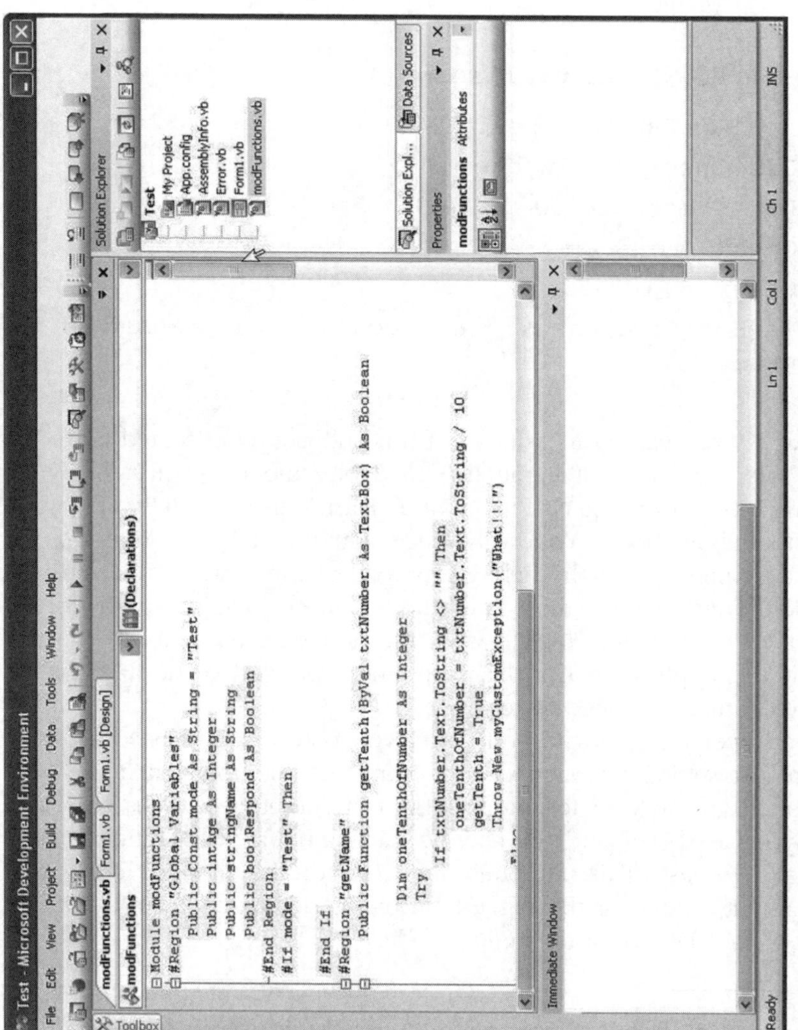


**Figure 6.6** The Visual Studio .NET 2005 immediate window.

In a standard debugging situation, you would have your code written in the IDE Text Editor. However, not much can be told about the debugging status of the application at this point. The application is only a collection of words in a text editor. Now it is time to run your application in debug mode to start the debugging process. Let us look at the following code sample; it will be the basis of this example.

**Listing 6.6: VB.NET `InitializeApp()`**

```
Public Sub InitializeApp()
    Dim Check As Integer
    Dim CheckDate As Date
    CheckDate = Now
    Check = 10045
    MsgBox("The check " & Check & " was cashed on "
& CheckDate)
End Sub
```

Now, if you wanted to find out if this subroutine executed correctly, you would need to switch the IDE to debug mode — most likely by selecting Debug from the tool menu, then Start. This process would switch you into debug mode. You will notice that the IDE can take a good amount of time to start the debugger, as all of the written code must be compiled. Therefore, the more code there is in the Text Editor, the longer it will take to start up. Finally, when the debugger has started, you run through the application from start-up until you get to the area of the application that you need to test.

When everything is said and done, you could have wasted valuable time in just setting up your test environment. Multiply that across the number of days in your testing cycle and the number of times you need to run your debugger, and you may be wasting hours just getting to places you need to test. This, although the core of the modern debugging environment, is one of the biggest problems debuggers face: the inefficiency of the IDE when debugging code.

> If you think about it from a strictly machine point of view, the inefficiency makes sense. The IDE must create a separate environment space for the code to run in, it must compile the code, and it must run the code in a way that allows the programmer to view and work with internal processes. Basically, the IDE wants to do what the operating system (OS) is not used to doing.

As programmers, we no longer need to endure the long load times or the agony of getting our application to a particular point five windows into the application, just to test one function. In fact, the latest enhancement offered by Microsoft — the functionality of the immediate window — is not available to programmers without having to enter debug mode.

Let us say that you wanted to check the functionality of the subroutine `InitiateApp()` from the previous code listing. In previous versions of Visual Studio, if you wanted to perform this procedure, you would need to go into debug mode and run through the application until you got to the place in the code where `InitiateApp()` is called. However, with the new offline immediate window you can simply call up the immediate window and execute that subroutine.

When you execute a function in the offline immediate window, the IDE will quickly compile only the code needed to run the subroutine or function and display any results. For example, to test `InitiateApp()` we would click on Debug>Windows>Immediate. With the immediate window displayed, simply type `InitiateApp`. At this point, the IDE quickly compiles `InitiateApp()` and runs it in memory.

If you were to attempt to run a function in this manner in a previous version of Visual Studio .NET, you would receive the following error:

```
The expression cannot be evaluated while in design
mode.
```

However, we notice that Visual Studio .NET 2005 handles the process quite well.

Using the code sample `InitiateApp()`, the immediate window will simply stop processing when the subroutine has completed. This is because the subroutine offers no output or result. To make things a bit more interesting, let us take a look at a function that has some output.

### Listing 6.7: VB.NET `Caps()` Function

```
Public Function Caps(ByVal word As String) As String
    If IsNumeric(word) = False Then
       Caps = UCase(word)
    Else
       MsgBox("No numbers please")
    End If
End Function
```

Although it is very simplistic, and mocks the functionality of the `UCase()` function in VB, the sample function `Caps()` will be used to demonstrate how the offline immediate window can be used to display function results. As you can tell from the code, this small function will take in any string and output it in all uppercase letters. To now run this function in the immediate window, type the following line:

```
Debug.Print(Caps("test"))
```

This command in the immediate window will compile just the `Caps()` function, send it the parameter test, and print the results back to the immediate window — all without the use of tracepoints, breakpoints, or the debug mode. Figure 6.7 illustrates the resulting output.

As you can see in Figure 6.7, the result of running the function in the immediate window is TEST printed to the window. However, looking at the code you can see that it has been written to throw a message box if the value of the parameter word is a number. Therefore, let us try running this again with the value 123 passed to `Caps()`. Because we are not expecting any output from the function itself in this case, we do not need to use the `Debug.Print` argument. Now try running the following in the immediate window:

```
Caps(123)
```

The immediate window, using the same process as before, now compiles and runs `Caps()` with the parameter 123. Rather than showing any output, a message box is generated. Figure 6.8 illustrates the message box that was displayed as a result of running the function command `Caps(123)`.

Examining Figure 6.8, you can see that the immediate window was able to run the function `Caps()` and consequently produce the correct message box. This example shows the power of the offline immediate window. As you progress through a debugging session, you will find that the new functionality of the immediate window is one of the greatest tools at your disposal. You can now, on demand, execute and test functions without having to worry about whether the remaining code in the application will compile correctly. This allows you to focus completely on each section of your project.

However, the fact that you can subjectively choose what to test, leaving other unfinished behind, is also the one aspect of the offline immediate window that you need to be careful of. This attitude of not finishing pieces of code because you do not have to can lead to unrealized code and bugs. So although you may now have a very powerful tool, be careful that other aspects of your applications do not suffer as a result of its use.

In the next section we will look at a feature that is new in Visual Studio .NET 2005; however, it may be very familiar to some VB programmers.

## Debug Mode Code Editing

This feature of Visual Studio 2005 will come as a welcome addition to many Visual Basic programmers. Before Visual Studio .NET — in fact,

**Figure 6.7 The result of running the `Caps()` function in the immediate window.**

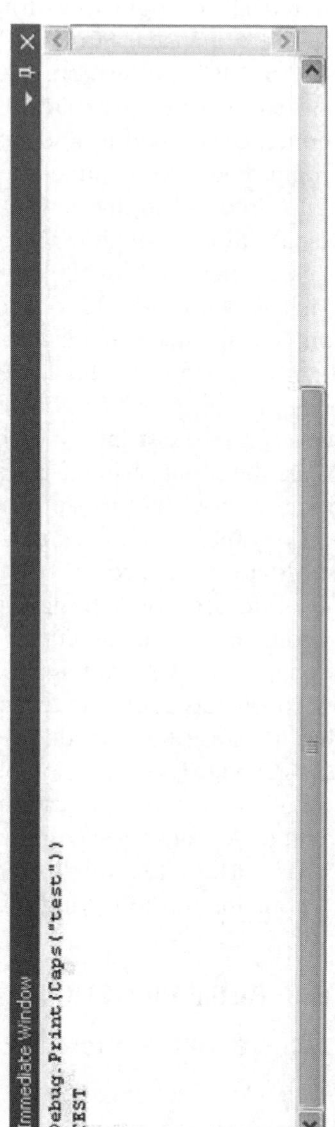


**Figure 6.8 The `Caps()` message box.**

before the .NET framework — Visual Studio 6 was the biggest programming platform. Some may argue that for those companies who have yet to adopt the .NET platform, Visual Studio 6 is still the preferred programming environment. For Visual Basic programmers, Visual Studio 6 especially offered all the right tools to get the job done.

If you were a Visual Studio 6/Visual Basic user who jumped on the Visual Studio .NET bandwagon, you were probably caught off guard early on. Visual Studio .NET was lacking a tool that Visual Basic 6 users had grown quite accustomed to and may have taken for granted. Most Visual Basic programmers were quite surprised the first time they threw Visual Studio .NET into debug mode and tried editing their code.

In Visual Studio 6, within Visual Basic, a programmer had the ability to edit his or her code while in the process of executing it in debug mode. That is, with the IDE in debug mode, a programmer could pause execution (usually with a breakpoint) and then edit certain parts of the code. After the code was edited, the execution could be resumed from that point. This process proved to be very valuable to Visual Basic debuggers.

However, as we got into Visual Studio .NET, one discovery would be made clear: the ability to edit code while in debug mode was removed. A programmer now had to stop the debugger, switch back to the editor, edit the code, and switch back to the debugger to make and test changes. This proved to be a process that was very inefficient and took some getting used to for Visual Basic 6 programmers.

Microsoft, proving its ability to keep us on our feet, has changed the way we use Visual Basic yet again. With the release of Visual Studio .NET 2005, Microsoft has returned to where it began and given programmers the ability to pause the execution of an application in debug mode, and then edit the code. The execution of the application can then be continued. Figure 6.9 illustrates an application in debug mode being edited.

Take a look back at Figure 6.5. Figure 6.5 shows the subroutine `ComplicatedMath()`. In this figure, the subroutine `ComplicatedMath()` contains the following block:

**Listing 6.8: Partial VB.NET Code Block**

```
Partial VB.NET code block
For x = 1 to 100
    y = x + 12
    y = y * 2
    y = y + 7
    y = y / 2
Next
```

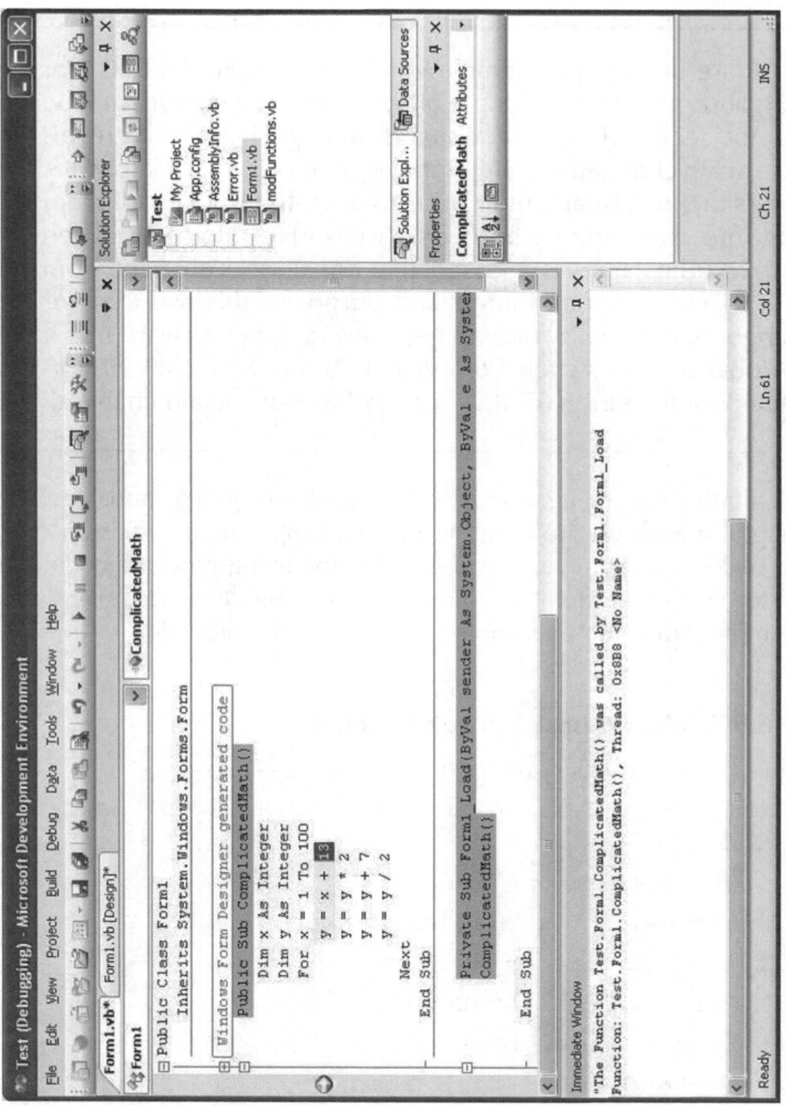


**Figure 6.9 Debug mode editing.**

We ran this code in Visual Studio .NET 2005 and set a breakpoint to pause execution at the line `y = x + 12`. Figure 5.23 picks up at this point, and as you can see, we were able to change the 12 to a 13 without exiting the debug mode. After the change was made, we simply continued execution by pressing <F5> or <F8> or selecting Debug>Start.

> If you are used to programming in Visual Studio .NET 2002 or 2003, and notice something a bit off in the last statement, you are not seeing things. In Visual Studio .NET 2005, Microsoft once again changed the Step Into key from <F11> back to <F8>. In versions of Visual Studio prior to .NET, the hot key for stepping into code line by line was always <F8>. However, when Visual Studio .NET was released, that hot key was changed from <F8> to <F11>. For all intents and purposes, this was a minor change that was fairly easy to get used to. Just be aware that if you now plan to switch from Visual Studio .NET 2002–2003 to Visual Studio .NET 2005, this hot key has once again changed.

Little things, like being able to edit code from debug mode, can be very helpful when you are trying to make settings changes or tweaks to lines of code. For example, if you had the following block of code and wanted to change the number you are using as the `TimerMarker`, you could simply pause the execution and change the value:

### Listing 6.9: VB.NET `Timer1_Tick` Function

```
    Private Sub Timer1_Tick(ByVal sender As
System.Object, ByVal e As System.EventArgs) Handles
Timer1.Tick
        CurrentTime = Time
    TimerMarker = (Val(TimerMarker) - 1)
    If TimerMarker <= 0 Then
        DirA = File1.ListCount
        DirB = File2.ListCount
            If DirA <> DirB Then
            DirSource = Dir(DirSource + "\")
            For t = 1 To DirA
                SourceA = SourceB
                DestinationA = DestinationB
```

```
            FileCopy (SourceA + "\" + DirSource),
(DestinationA + "\" + DirSource)
            Listbox1.Items.Add (CurrentTime + "
Files were successfully copied from " + SourceA + "
to " + DestinationA)
            File1.Refresh
            File2.Refresh
            DirSource = Dir
         Next t
         TimerMarker = 10
      Else
         Listbox1.Items.Add (CurrentTime + " No Files
were added to " + SourceA)
         Listbox1.Items.Add (CurrentTime + " No Files
copied")
         File1.Refresh
         File2.Refresh
         TimerMarker = 10
      End If
   End IF
End Sub
```

Please note that there are variable definitions not included in the previous code block. Let us assume that the preceding code block was part of your overall application. Its purpose is to copy files from one location to another at a set interval. However, in running the application, it has been seen that there is another application accessing some of the files when this function wants to copy them, meaning that some files do not get copied. You have been asked to adjust the value of `TimerMarker` to coincide with when the files are not being accessed; however, you do not have any other details about what the interval should be.

The best way to approach this situation would be to run the application in debug mode and set a breakpoint at the beginning of the subroutine. Then, utilizing the debug mode editing feature, you can pause the execution of the application and adjust the value of `TimerMarker` until you find the correct setting. In this situation, the debug mode editing feature of Visual Studio 2005 is a great asset because it allows you to make otherwise quick and small changes without having to reestablish the entire debugging environment for each one.

One major change has been made to distinguish the Visual Studio .NET iteration of the debug mode editor from that of earlier version of

Visual Studio. That is, along with being resurrected from the depths of the "removed features" bin, the debug mode editor is also an enhanced feature. Although the original tool stands on its own as a valuable part of the Visual Studio .NET 2005 IDE, the added feature makes the debug mode editor even more valuable.

In Visual Studio .NET 2005, you can not only edit your code while in debug mode, but also rearrange objects on your forms. In previous versions of Visual Studio, before .NET was released, the design view of an application was not available to you while your application was in debug mode. Therefore, if you needed to make a change to the interface design of your application, you had to exit debug mode and return to design mode. Your changes could then be made and you could restart debug mode to test them. Figure 6.10 illustrates the error message earlier versions of Visual Studio produce if you attempt to move an object in debug mode.

With the latest change to the debug mode edition, all of the Form Design tabs are available to you in debug mode. Therefore, you can move and resize objects when your application is paused in debug mode. Figure 6.11 shows an application paused in debug mode, while Figure 6.12 shows an object being moved. These figures represent the newest feature of the Visual Studio .NET debug mode editor.

As you can see, Visual Studio .NET 2005 allows the programming the ability to move and interact with the design aspects of the application while in debug mode. This power does have its limitations though. The debug mode editor has its overall limitations, and not just those related to moving objects during debug.

Much like in Visual Studio 6, there are things that are just not possible to do in the Visual Studio 2005 debug mode editor. After we discuss these items, it will become clearer why the editor has such limitations. Being

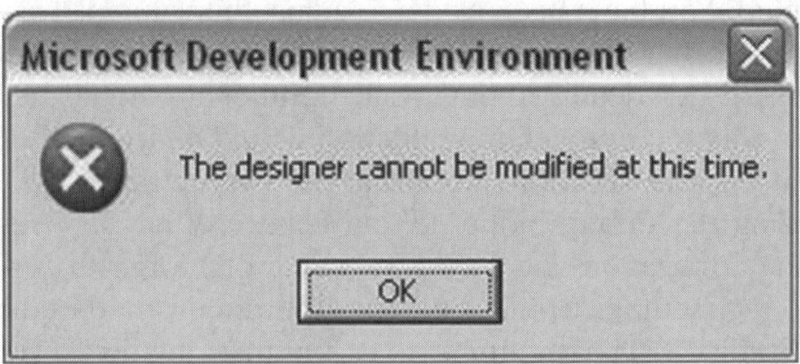


**Figure 6.10 Error received when object move attempted.**

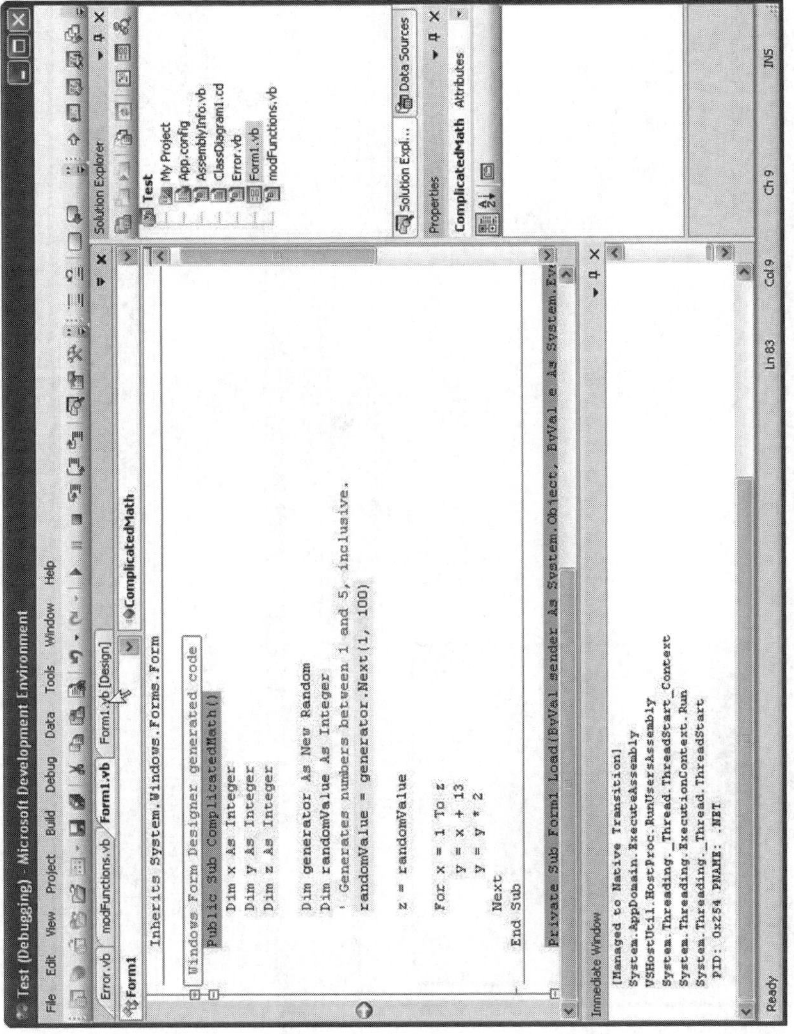


**Figure 6.11** An application paused during debug mode.

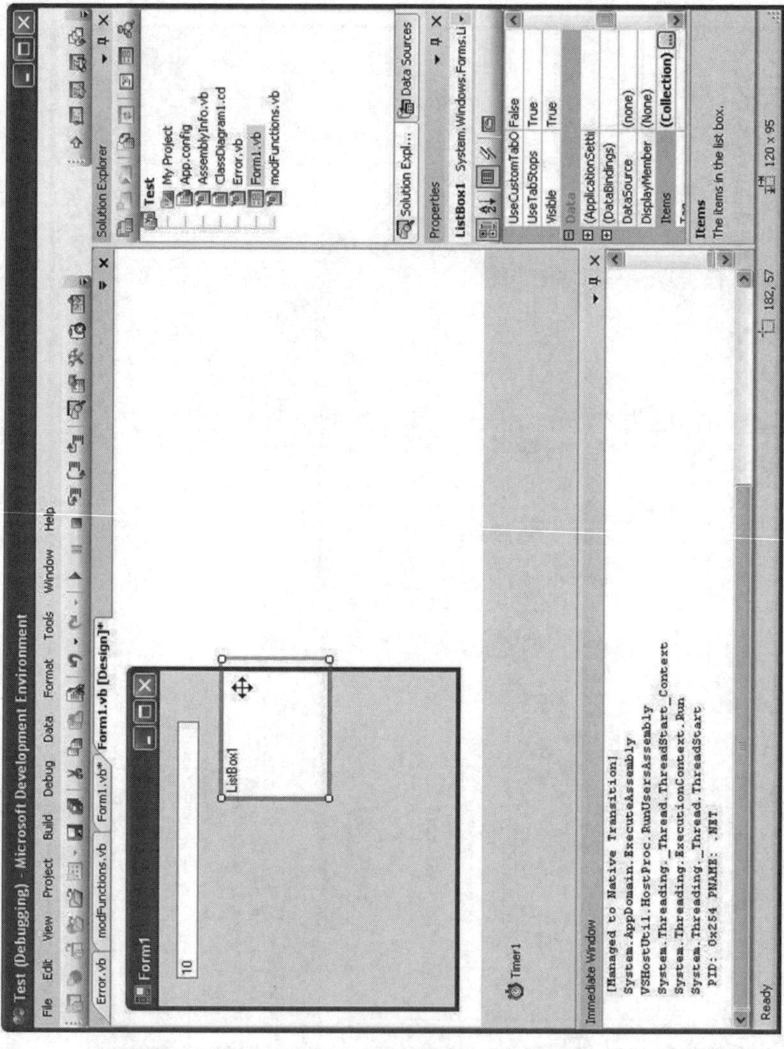


**Figure 6.12 Moving an object while in debug mode.**

that we are on the subject of moving objects with the debug mode editor, let us discuss the limitations there first.

> The following limitations were observed using an advanced copy of Visual Studio .NET 2005. This situation described may change when the final product is released. Because this particular feature is not present in any other version of Visual Studio .NET, there is really nothing to compare it to.

In the current build of Visual Studio .NET 2005, when you move an object while in debug mode, you must recreate the form that the object is on to see the results. If your application only consists of one form, this could mean stopping and restarting debug mode to have your changes take effect. However, if your application has multiple forms and the form you modified is not the main form of the Form_Load, you can simply destroy and recreate the form to see the changes.

> If you are not familiar with the terms or the process, you must destroy and create the form to get the changes to show up. Hiding and showing the form will not let you see the changes. The difference here is that hiding and showing the form does not reload it. When a form is hidden, it is not destroyed; all of the information about that form is retained in memory, including the location of the objects on the form. Think of hiding more as just making the form invisible.

The other limitation of using the debug mode editor is that it really cannot be used on everything. That is, there are some things that you still are not allowed to edit using the debug mode editor. If you used the old debug mode editor from Visual Studio 6, you may already be aware of what you can or cannot edit while in debug mode. However, if you are not familiar with it, it is worth knowing.

The general guideline is that if the object, value, or item that you are attempting to modify is loaded in the compiler as a setting of the application, it cannot be changed without exiting from debug mode. In other words, things such as dimension statements, declarations, function and subroutine parameters, and redirects cannot be changed using the debug mode editor of Visual Studio 2005.

Therefore, if you wanted to edit

```
Dim TimerMarker as Integer
```

to be

```
Dim TimerMarkerTest as Integer
```

or

```
Dim TimerMarkerTest as Byte
```

you would need to stop the debugger and exit debug mode. After exiting debug mode, you can make the changes and restart the debugger. Restarting the debugger will reload those items that you edited.

In the next section we will discuss another new feature in Visual Studio .NET 2005. This feature, while new to Visual Studio .NET, was taken from another Microsoft product that you should be very familiar with.

## *Edit Tracking*

Arguably one of the most popular Microsoft products is its Microsoft Office suite of tools. Within Office, Microsoft Word is most likely the application most people are familiar with. Whether you have a technical background or not, chances are you have used Microsoft Word at some point in your personal or professional life. From school papers to employee handbooks to reports, most electronic word processing is done using Word. Even this book was written using Microsoft Word.

If you have used Word extensively, you may be familiar with its edit tracking capabilities. Used extensively in the production of many multi-contributor documents, including this one, edit tracking is a tool within Word that allows document owners to track who made specific changes within a document. For example, we can create a document with hundreds of pages in it, like the one used to produce this book. That document then needs to be sent to an editor. The editor will make syntax and voice changes, correct spelling, and add his or her own personal thoughts. That editor may then send the document to a second editor to correct some technical data within the document, who may then forward the document to a layout person. With all of these changes going on, it may be hard to figure out who made what changes, where, and what the original intent of the author was. Therefore, Word allows you to track these changes by the person who made them and not lose track of the original thoughts.

Using the Track Changes option in Word, you can see who made what changes in your document, when they made the change, and what the original statement was before the change. Figure 6.13 illustrates the use of Track Changes in Word.

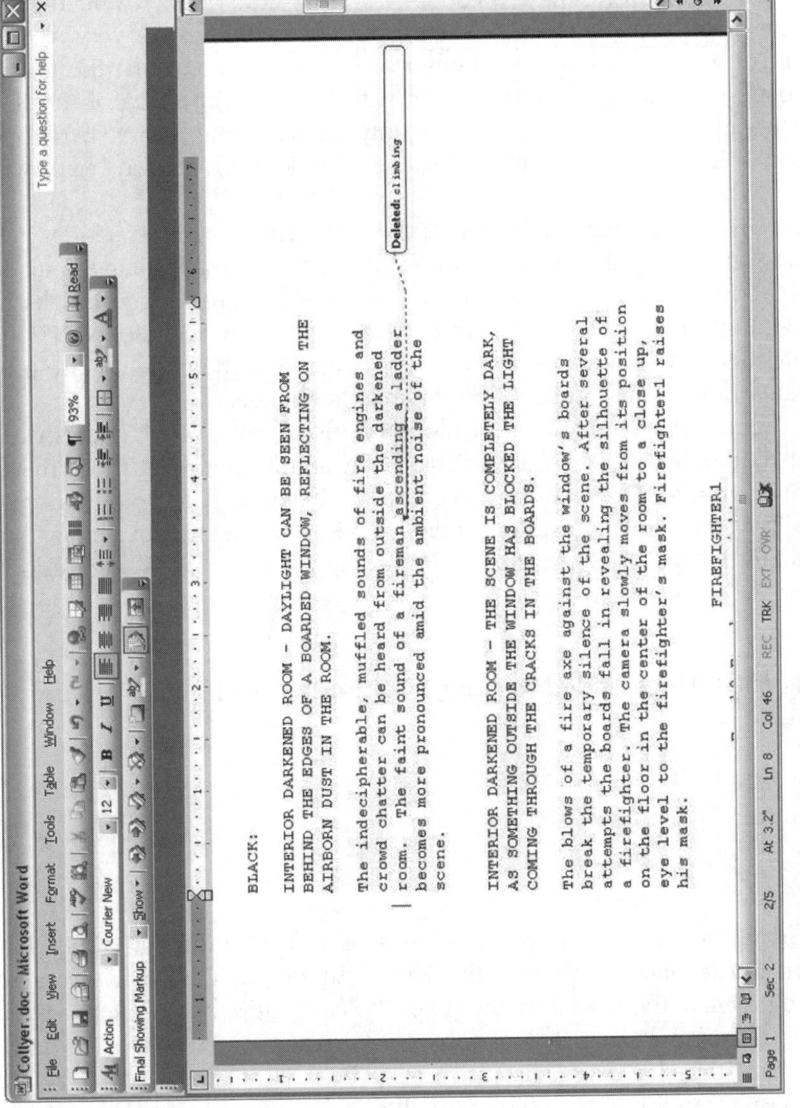


Figure 6.13 A change made using Track Changes.

In Figure 6.13, you can see that we have a document created in Word. This document has Track Changes enabled. A second author, other than the document creator, has made a change to the document. Microsoft Word clearly shows that the word `climbed` was changed to `ascended` in the document.

On the most basic level, the IDE of Visual Studio .NET, and that of most programming platforms, is just a modified text edited, very similar to Word. It is not until after you enter and edit your code that the text is passed on to the compiler. Therefore, with the main interface of the IDE being no more than a text editor, it only makes sense that at least one of Microsoft Word's text-editing features would find its way to Visual Studio .NET 2005.

Another new feature of Visual Studio .NET 2005 is Edit Tracking. Edit Tracking gives you the opportunity to, as in Word, track changes made to your code. This can be helpful if you work on fairly large blocks of code and often move around from code to code. Visual Studio .NET 2005 will highlight when and where a change is made to the code. Figure 6.14 illustrates how Visual Studio .NET highlights changes.

In Figure 6.14 you can see a block of Visual Basic .NET code in the Visual Studio .NET 2005 editor. The code in this figure is the familiar `ComplicatedMath()` subroutine that we have used for other discussions. However, in this example Edit Tracking has been activated within Visual Studio .NET 2005. In this example the following lines were added to `ComplicatedMath()`:

**Listing 6.10: Lines Added to `ComplicatedMath()`**

```
...
Dim Changes As Boolean
Changes = False
...
Changes = True
```

Looking at Figure 6.14, you can see that Visual Studio .NET 2005 has marked the location of those edits. Visual Studio .NET 2005 has created shaded boxes in the left-hand margin of the code, adjacent to the modified blocks of program data. Because this image has been replicated in black and white, the shade area is just a gray box. However, when you are using Visual Studio .NET 2005, you will see that when a change is made, the markers that appear in the left-hand margin are actually yellow. If you were to now save the application, the edit markers would appear as

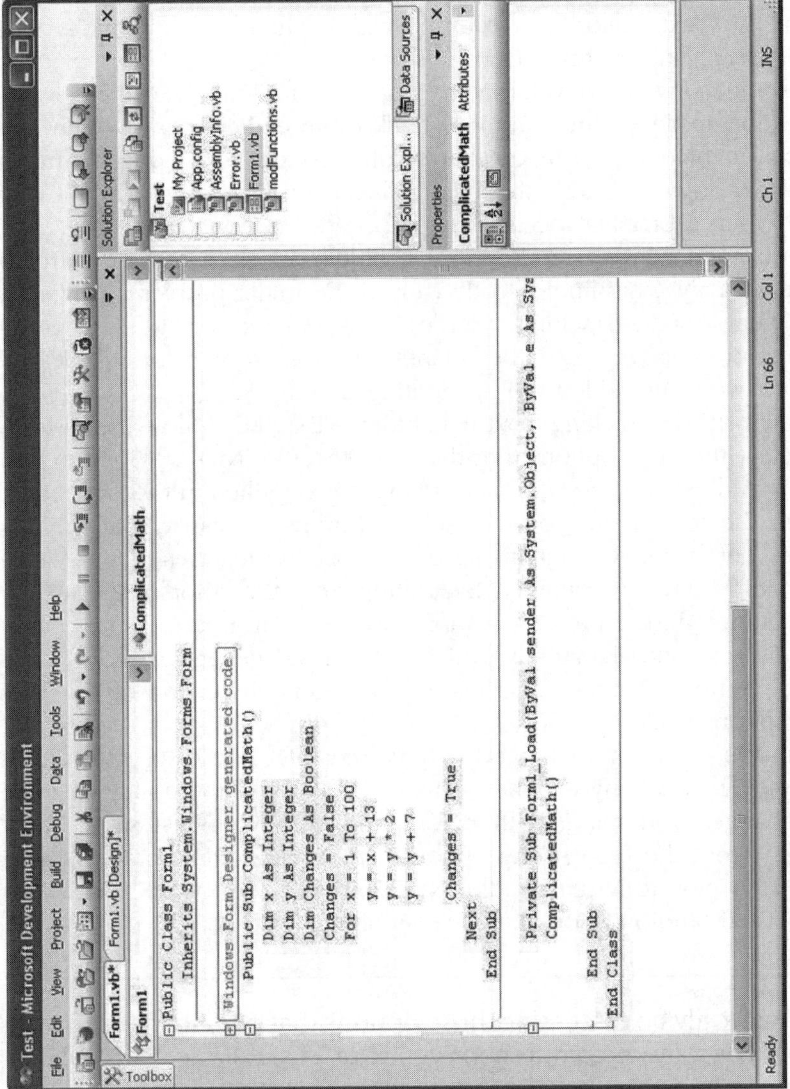


**Figure 6.14 A tracked change in Visual Studio .NET 2005.**

green rather than yellow to indicate that the change was made before your last save.

This allows you as the programmer to keep a sense of control over who has made what changes to your code by simply highlighting those changes and making them easier to recognize. Now, by looking at your code in the Text Editor, you can see where changes were made. Edit Tracking has a more prevalent use as well.

In some software development it is not unusual to make several changes, begin debugging, and lose track of an earlier change. With Edit Tracking enabled, you can quickly scroll through your code to find a particular change and see if that change has been saved. This can be very helpful when a problem occurs while you are in debug mode.

If you are in debug mode and a problem arises, it may be hard to pinpoint exactly what line of code caused the initial problem. However, if you enable Edit Tracking, you can easily look for the last saved programming change and either identify it as a problem or rule it out. This gives you one added tool in fighting bugs.

To enable Edit Tracking in Visual Studio .NET 2005, follow these steps: First, select the Tool option from the Visual Studio .NET 2005 menu bar. Figure 6.15 illustrates the choices available to you when in the tool menu.

From the tool menu you can select Options to display the options window. This window contains all of the editable features of the Visual Studio .NET 2005 environment. Everything from the color of the text to saved settings during project creation can be set from here. The option for enabling Track Changes is available from the general section of the Text Editor node. Figure 6.16 illustrates the general section of the Text Editor options node.

From the editor options window pictured in Figure 6.16, you should check the Track Changes option. This will give you the ability to track those changes you make both before and after your last save. Track Changes is not the only useful option to have. Although some of these may not be new to Visual Studio .NET 2005, let us look at some other useful Visual Studio options before continuing.

> We will only be discussing those options that pertain to debugging. For a more comprehensive list of Visual Basic .NET 2005 options and their related meanings, check the Visual Studio 2005 Web site at www.microsoft.com.

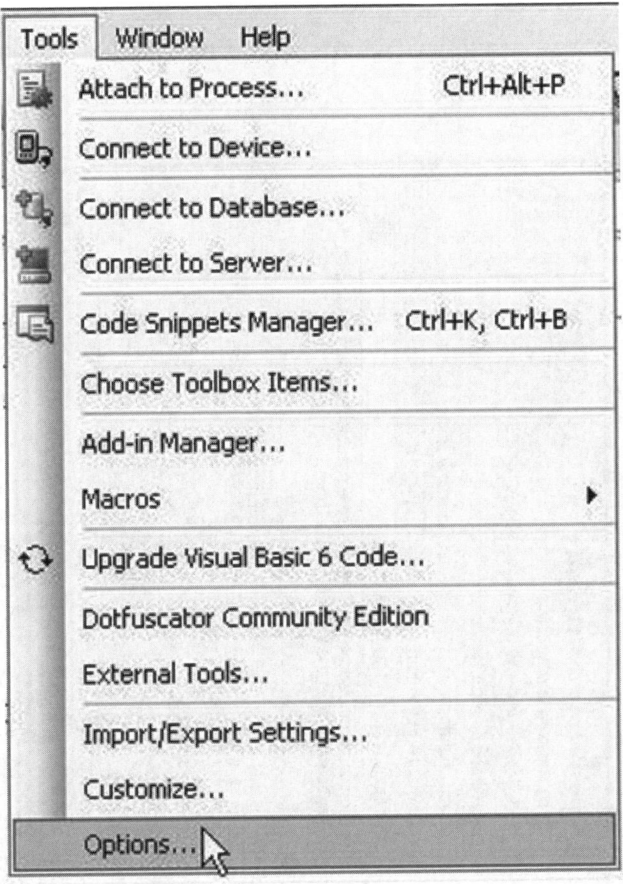


**Figure 6.15 The tool menu.**

## *Projects and Solutions*

The first option we will focus on in the Projects and Solutions section of the options window is the Show Output window when build starts. In Visual Studio .NET 2005 this is unchecked by default. Checking this option will allow you to see the build information in the output as your application is being built, either for release or debug. The following listing shows the contents of the output window when building `ComplicatedMath()` for debug:

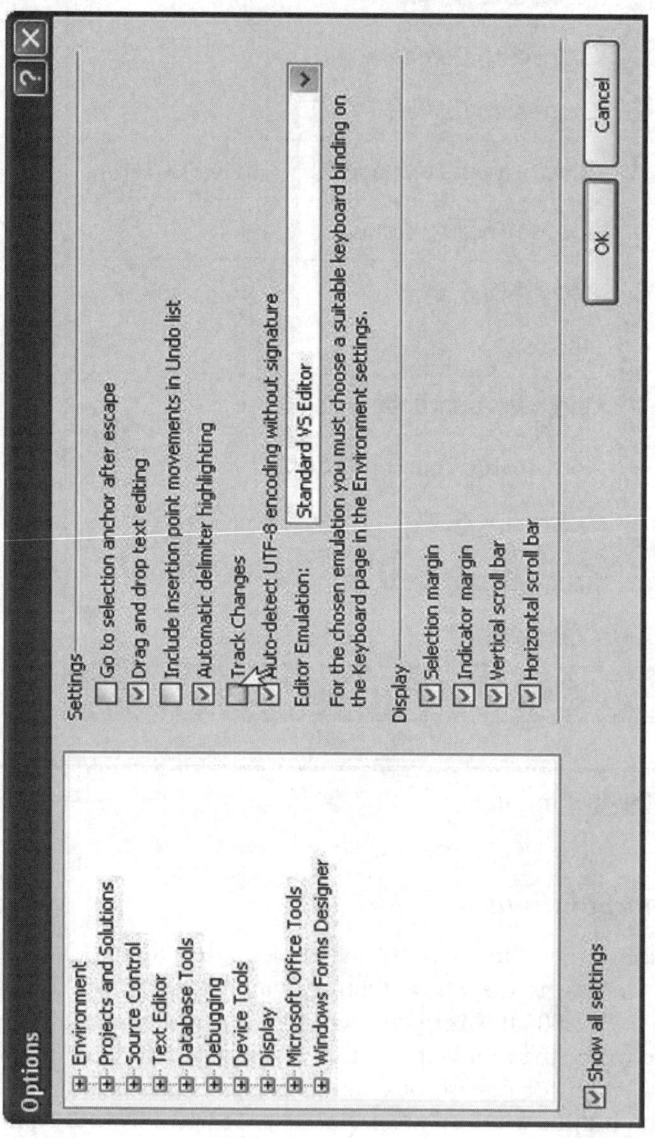


**Figure 6.16 General editor options.**

**Listing 6.11: Building Output for `ComplicatedMath()` Compile**

```
'.NET': Loaded 'C:\WINDOWS\assembly\GAC_32\mscorlib\
2.0.3600.0__b77a5c561934e089\mscorlib.dll', No
symbols loaded.
'.NET': Loaded 'C:\WINDOWS\assembly\GAC_MSIL\
vshostutil\8.0.1200.0__b03f5f7f11d50a3a\
vshostutil.dll', No symbols loaded.
'.NET': Loaded 'C:\WINDOWS\assembly\GAC_MSIL\
System.Windows.Forms\2.0.3600.0__b77a5c561934e089\
System.Windows.Forms.dll', No symbols loaded.
'.NET': Loaded 'C:\WINDOWS\assembly\GAC_MSIL\System\
2.0.3600.0__b77a5c561934e089\System.dll', No symbols
loaded.
'.NET': Loaded 'C:\WINDOWS\assembly\GAC_MSIL\
System.Drawing\2.0.3600.0__b03f5f7f11d50a3a\
System.Drawing.dll', No symbols loaded.
'.NET': Loaded 'C:\Documents and Settings\
Administrator\Desktop\TDH Projects\Test\bin\
Test.vshost.exe', No symbols loaded.
'.NET': Loaded 'C:\WINDOWS\assembly\GAC_32\
System.Data\2.0.3600.0__b77a5c561934e089\
System.Data.dll', No symbols loaded.
'.NET': Loaded 'C:\WINDOWS\assembly\GAC_MSIL\
System.Xml\2.0.3600.0__b77a5c561934e089\
System.Xml.dll', No symbols loaded.
The thread 0x2a4 has exited with code 0 (0x0).
The thread 0x2b0 has exited with code 0 (0x0).
'.NET': Loaded 'C:\Documents and Settings\
Administrator\Desktop\TDH Projects\Test\bin\
Test.exe', Symbols loaded.
The thread '<No Name>' (0x280) has exited with code
0 (0x0).
The thread 0x278 has exited with code 0 (0x0).
The program '[548] Test.vshost.exe: .NET' has exited
with code 0 (0x0).
```

If this option remains unchecked, the output window will only appear if there is a build or compile error. That is, of course, unless you uncheck the next option, "Always show Error List if build finishes with error," which is checked by default. However, with the exception of performing an automated build, I can think of no compelling reason to uncheck this option.

The next set of options you may want to look at are in the Build and Run section of the Projects and Solutions node. The first is a drop-down list of options that can take place before building. These options are:

- Save all changes
- Save changes to open documents only
- Prompt to save changes to open documents
- Don't save changes to open documents

By default, the Visual Studio .NET IDE is set to save all changes. In previous versions the default was prompt to save changes. However, I always like to save any changes I have made automatically when I build a project.

The next option helpful in debugging is On Run, when projects are out of date. Your options here are:

- Always build
- Never build
- Prompt to build

With this option, "Prompt to build" is selected by default. We can generally leave this like it is, but changing it will not necessarily hurt. In fact, many people, when prompted to build their project at run, select build anyway. Therefore, if you want to avoid another message box asking for your input, change this option to "Always build."

## Text Editor

This is the same section that contains the Edit Tracking options. However, there are some other very useful options here as well. For example, in the "All languages" section, under General, there are two very helpful settings for debuggers. The first is Word Wrap.

Word Wrap controls the length of your lines in the IDE. It is not uncommon, with the amount of parameters that some functions can take on, for lines to extend far beyond the borders of the visual page. Word Wrap will force those extended lines of code to wrap around the visual borders of the IDE. This allows programmers to see all of the code contained in an argument without having to scroll.

Word Wrap is unchecked by default. To enable Word Wrap, check this option.

Another useful option is line numbers. The line number options, like the name describes, displays the line number next to each line of code in the IDE. The line number itself appears in the left-hand margin of the IDE, in the same area as the Edit Tracking markers.

To enable line numbering, check the line numbers option. Figure 6.17 illustrates a block of code with the line numbers option enabled.

As you can see in Figure 6.17, each line of code is now numbered for easy reference. This is especially handy when debugging because Visual Studio .NET will always associate an error with a specific line of code. Having each line already numbered will let you find those errors quickly.

In the example we just worked through, we set Word Wrap and line numbering in the "All languages" node. This set those options for every programming language in Visual Studio .NET 2005. However, just after the "All languages" node are nodes for individual programming languages. If you only wanted to enable certain options for certain languages, you could take advantage of that here. The individual language options are:

- Basic
- C#
- C/C++
- HTML (Hypertext Markup Language)
- Plain Text
- SQL Script
- Visual J#
- XML (eXtensible Markup Language)

### *Database Tools*

One very useful option resides in the Data Connections node of Database Tools. The only option in here is "Limit SQL results sent to output window to:." This option is very useful if you are debugging an application with a lot of database queries in it. If you happen to run a function that returns a recordset from a query in the immediate window, or direct the output using debug.print, you may receive a lot of rows back. This option lets you specify the number of rows the functions are allowed to return before closing output.

Upon checking this option, an input box will open. This box will let you indicate the precise number of lines to input before stopping. The

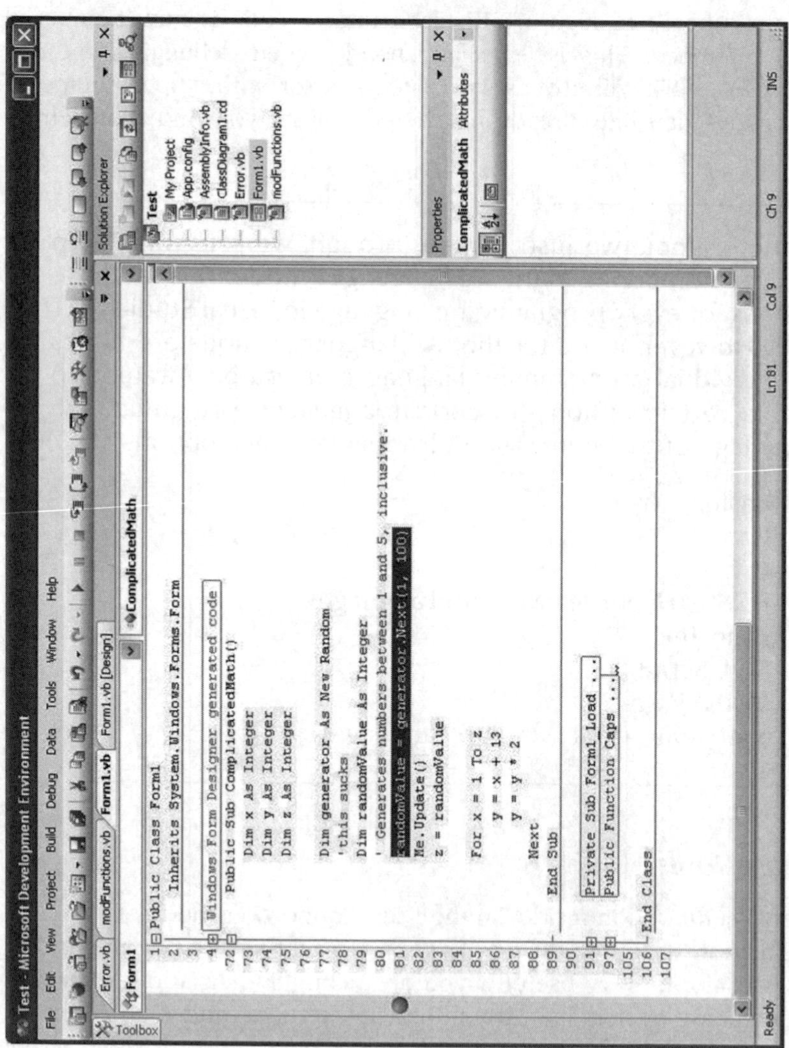


Figure 6.17 Line numbering.

options window will default this amount to 500 rows. However, unless you have a compelling reason, you should not have to go above 25 to 50 lines. Having just a handful of lines returned to you will still give you a good base of what the function returns and keep your output window manageable.

The next option node, Query/View Designer, contains another useful option. Although you probably will not be setting this option for any of your designing projects, it might be someplace to look if you are having unexplainable bugs. The first option in this node is `Cancel long running query:`. The modifiable option for this is `Cancel after [] seconds`. By default, this value is checked and set to 30 seconds. If you find that you are having trouble running longer queries, you may want to check this setting and either extend the time or disable it altogether.

## Debugging

The Debugging node of the options window contains the most useful set of options for debuggers. Figure 6.18 illustrates all of the options in the Debugging/General node.

As displayed in Figure 6.18, there are 23 different settings that you can check pertaining to debugging. Let us discuss a few of them. The first and sixth ones are related to another new feature of Visual Studio .NET 2005:

- When one process breaks, break all processes
- Breakpoints: Enable filtering by process and thread

In Visual Studio .NET 2005 you can configure your debugging environment to track your applications' execution by process or thread. If you have used breakpoint in your debugging, you can configure them to filter based on the criteria related to processes and threads.

The sixth option in the General node enables the ability to allow your breakpoints to filter by process or thread. As displayed in Figure 6.18, this option is enabled by default. Filtering your breakpoints is especially useful if you are programming any kind of media, such as video or audio. In many cases you will want to monitor how your media streams are interacting with the rest of the application by thread. This is also true of large-scale database work.

If you want to add breakpoints to your application but do not want them to be triggered by anything other than a particular thread or process, you can simply filter out anything running through a processor by filtering its ProcessID, ThreadID, or a number of other criteria. To configure a

- [ ] Warn if no symbols on launch (Native Only)
- [x] When one process breaks, break all other processes
- [ ] Color the text when breakpoints and the current statement span the entire line
- [x] Enable address-level debugging (Disassembly window, Registers window, address breakp
  - [ ] Show disassembly if source is not available
- [x] Breakpoints: Enable filtering by process and thread
- [x] Enable Just My Code
  - [x] Warn if no user code on launch
- [x] Output: print a message when an exception occurs
- [x] Output: print a message when a module is loaded
- [x] Output: print a message when a module is unloaded
- [x] Output: print a message when a program exits
- [x] Output: print a message when a thread exits
- [x] Output: print output from programs being debugged
- [x] Output: send output to the Immediate window instead of the Output window
- [x] Only use source code that exactly matches the original version
- [x] Use Console Window
- [x] Evaluation: Always allow property and other implicit function calls (Managed only).
  - [x] Automatically call ToString() when evaluating object values (C# Only).
- [ ] Evaluation: Show raw structure of objects
- [x] Evaluation: Show non-public members for non-user objects (Visual Basic Only)
- [ ] Confirm when deleting all breakpoints
- [ ] Treat exceptions crossing appdomain boundaries as unhandled (Managed Only)

**Figure 6.18 Debugging options.**

breakpoint filter, right-click on that breakpoint and select the Breakpoint > Filter option, as seen in Figure 6.19. This will open the breakpoint filter window. Figure 6.20 illustrates the breakpoint filter window. As seen in this figure, a breakpoint can be filtered on a number of criteria. These criteria are:

- MachineName
- ProcessID
- ProcessName
- ThreadID
- ThreadName

To activate the filter, simply enter in any of these criteria with the appropriate argument in the `Filter:` box. The other option within the Debugging/General node that relates to breakpoint filtering is:

`When one process breaks, break all other processes`

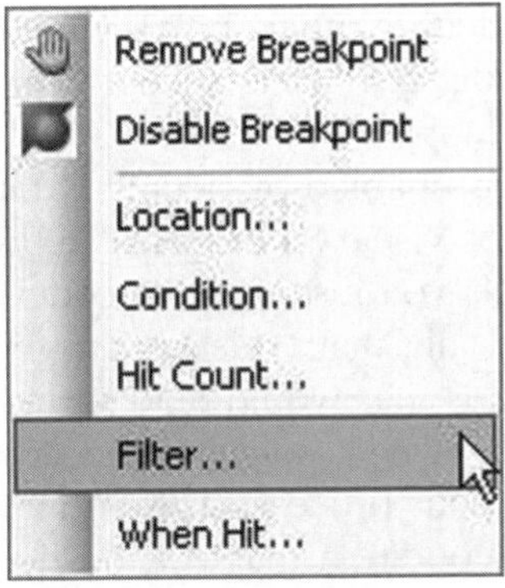
Remove Breakpoint
Disable Breakpoint
Location...
Condition...
Hit Count...
Filter...
When Hit...

**Figure 6.19 The breakpoint filter menu option.**

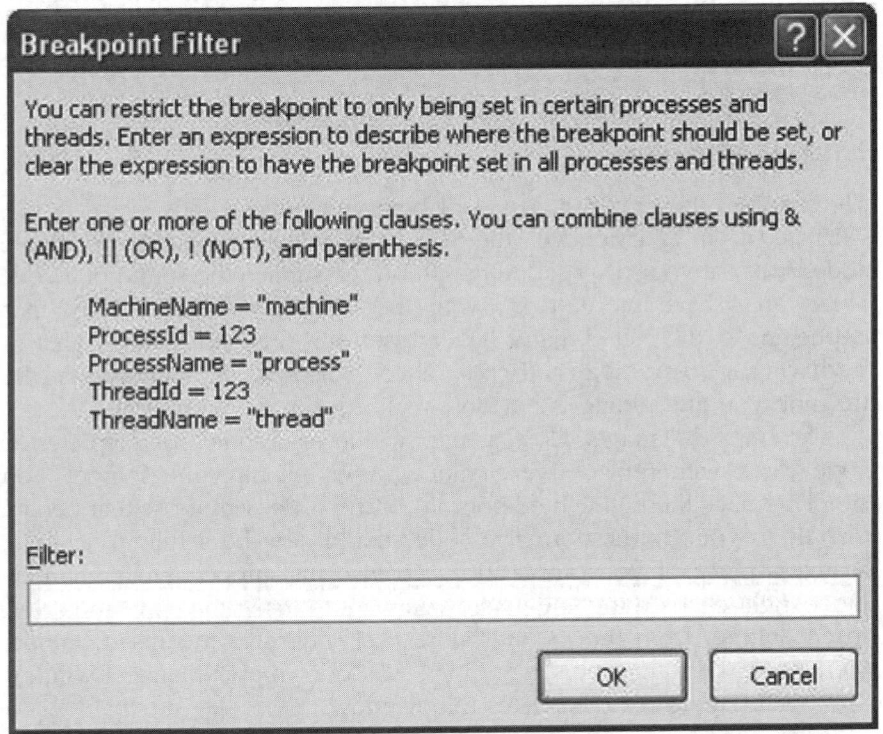
Breakpoint Filter
You can restrict the breakpoint to only being set in certain processes and threads. Enter an expression to describe where the breakpoint should be set, or clear the expression to have the breakpoint set in all processes and threads.
Enter one or more of the following clauses. You can combine clauses using & (AND), || (OR), ! (NOT), and parenthesis.
MachineName = "machine"
ProcessId = 123
ProcessName = "process"
ThreadId = 123
ThreadName = "thread"
Filter:
OK
Cancel

**Figure 6.20 The breakpoint filter window.**

This option is useful when you are working with breakpoint filters. By default, this option is checked, meaning that when one process breaks, they all will. However, you may want to know what is causing a specific process to break, while letting others break without your interaction. With this option disabled, you can track specific processes and only pause when those processes cause a break.

Another option that is enabled by default is Enable Just My Code. This is another new feature of Visual Studio .NET 2005. Just My Code is a new Microsoft feature that lets you just edit that code which you have worked on. By letting you edit only that code which you have worked on, you can avoid those situations that would lead to unrealized code.

You should experiment with some of the general debugging options to see how they effect your process. If there is an error that you do not care to report on, or a condition that you do not want to match in your debugger, chances are you can enable or disable it from the general debugging options window.

The next feature of Visual Studio .NET 2005 we will discuss is the Snippet Manager. The Snippet Manager is a new tool that helps programmers by supplying them with ready-to-use lines of code that address many common problems.

## *Snippet Manager*

The Snippet Manager is a new tool being introduced into Visual Studio .NET 2005. On a basic level, the Snippet Manager is a giant, modifiable code library at your disposal. Although on the surface the sound of a code library may have more to do with the act of writing code and not debugging it, the fact is that it is very useful in preventing bugs. That is, by having a library of tested code at your disposal, you know that the function you are adding is not only realized, but itself bug-free.

The Snippet Manager allows you to, within your code, insert a pretested code block with replaceable elements. After inserting the snippet, you simply replace the highlighted portions of the code with those that pertain directly to your application. The code should now be a fully functional, seamless piece of your application. To insert a snippet into your code block, right-click on the line where you want to insert the code and select Insert Snippet from the menu. Figure 6.21 illustrates the Insert Snippet menu. After clicking on Insert Snippet, the Code Snippet Manager window will open. Figure 6.22 illustrates this window.

From the Code Snippet Manager you can navigate to the particular solution you want to implement. Upon finding the snippet that you need, double-click that snippet to transfer it to your application. The elements of the snippet that you need to change to adapt it to your code will now be highlighted for you.

To demonstrate the Snippet Manager we will add a snippet to `ComplicatedMath()`. By selecting and opening the Code Snippet window,

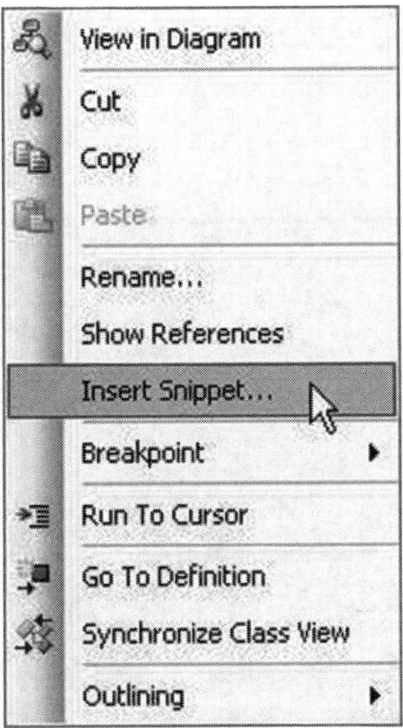


**Figure 6.21 The Insert Snippet menu.**

we will select the math snippets and insert the snippet for creating a random number. Figure 6.23 shows our code after adding the random number snippet.

Notice that in Figure 6.23 there are two parameters for the function `generator.Next()`. These two parameters are highlighted for you to let you know that you can adjust them to fit the needs of your particular situation. All of the code snippets have highlighted elements for you to adjust to your needs. However, some of the snippets can be quite long and may require more adjusting than others. The following is a list of the snippets that Microsoft provided with Visual Studio .NET 2005 as of the printing of this book.

## VB.NET

- Access user settings
- Activate a running application
- Add a comment to your code
- Add a Windows Forms control at runtime
- Add an element to XML data
- Add check marks and shortcut keys to Windows Form menu item
- Add context menus to Windows Forms
- Add menus and menu items to Windows Forms

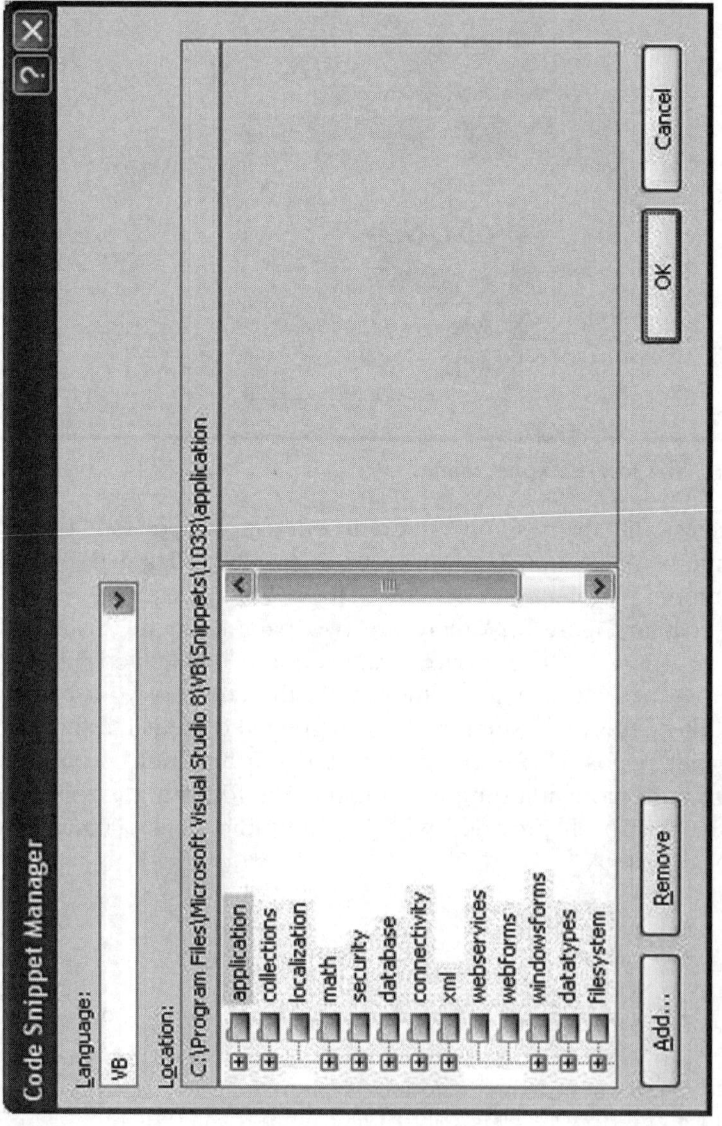


**Figure 6.22 The Code Snippet Manager window.**

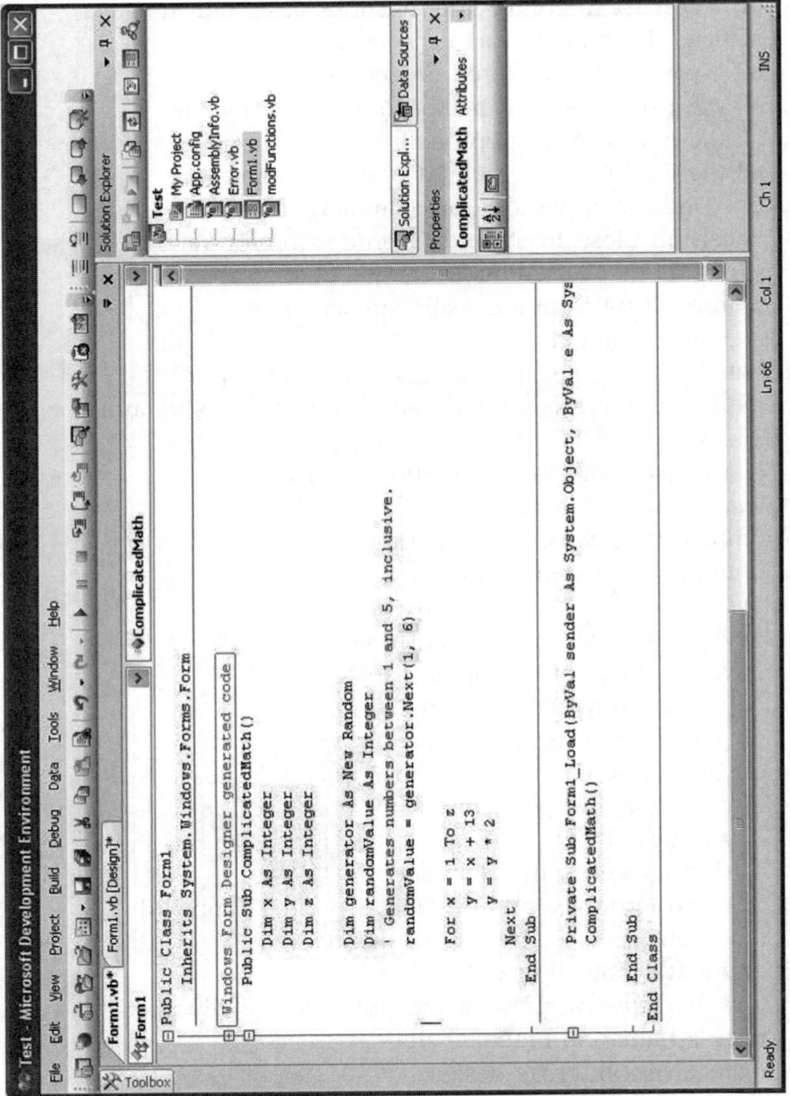


Figure 6.23 A piece of code inserted using the Snippet Manager.

- Add two related DataTables to a DataSet
- Arrange Multiple Document Interface (MDI) child forms
- Build only selected portions of the source code
- Calculate a principal and interest payment
- Calculate basic trigonometric functions using degree values
- Calculate basic trigonometric functions using radian values
- Calculate the sum-of-years depreciation
- Call a parameterized stored procedure
- Call the ExecuteReader method of a DataCommand
- Call the ExecuteNonQuery method of a DataCommand
- Call the ExecuteScalar method of a DataCommand
- Call Windows application programming interfaces (APIs)
- Cancel the Close Event and Override Control Validation when a user clicks the Close button
- Capture output from a console application
- Catch an exception
- Centralized response to changes in the desktop
- Change the foreground and background text colors in a console window
- Clear items from a bound ListBox control
- Clear the console window
- Compute the hash code of a string
- Continue a Windows service
- Convert a number to a hexadecimal string
- Convert a number to an octal string
- Convert a string into an array of bytes
- Convert an array of bytes into a string
- Convert an ArrayList to an array
- Convert mouse coordinates to screen coordinates
- Copy a bitmap image to the clipboard
- Copy a file
- Copy an integer to the clipboard
- Copy and retrieve a class instance from the clipboard
- Copy items on Windows Forms menus
- Copy text to the clipboard
- Copy the active window or the screen to the clipboard
- Create a bitmap at runtime
- Create a custom brush design
- Create a DataAdapter
- Create a DataColumn
- Create a DataCommand
- Create a DataRelation
- Create a DataSet

- Create a DataTable
- Create a DataTable with columns and a primary key
- Create a DateTime literal
- Create a file
- Create a folder
- Create a font
- Create a key method for a TreeView node
- Create a message queue
- Create a method that changes the values of the parameters
- Create a method that does not return a value
- Create a method that returns a value
- Create a method that takes a variable number of parameters
- Create a method that takes an optional parameter
- Create a new DataRow based on an existing DataTable
- Create a new exception class
- Create a pen
- Create a registry key and set its values
- Create a solid brush
- Create a structure definition
- Create a tempory file
- Create a transaction
- Create a triangle shape using a GraphicsPath object
- Create a typed dictionary class
- Create an e-mail message
- Create an enumeration with custom values
- Create an environment variable
- Create an expression column
- Create an XML file from data in a DataSet
- Create and send an HTML e-mail message
- Create DataCommands with a CommandBuilder
- Create decimal literals
- Create MDI child forms
- Create transparent windows Forms
- Declare a default property
- Decrypt a string
- Delete a file
- Delete items on Windows Forms menus
- Detect desktop display resolution
- Determine all selected items in a ListView
- Determine if a file exists
- Determine if a folder exists
- Determine if the network is available
- Determine the active MDI child

- Determine the selected item in a ListView
- Determine the selected node in a TreeView
- Determine the size of a file
- Determine the span between two dates
- Determine the span between two times
- Determine the Windows system directory
- Determine whether a registry key exists
- Determine which control on a Windows Form is selected
- Determine which modifier key was pressed
- Determine the current Windows version
- Display modal and modeless Windows Forms
- Display one Windows Form from another
- Do Until (Condition) … Loop
- Do While (Condition) … Loop
- Drag a window by dragging the client area of a form with a title bar
- Drag a window by dragging the client area of a form without a title bar
- Draw a filled ellipse on a Windows Form
- Draw a filled rectangle on a Windows Form
- Draw a line on a Windows Form
- Draw a pie chart
- Draw outlined shapes
- Draw text on a Windows Form
- Draw vertical text on a Windows Form
- Encrypt a string
- Enumerate attributes of an XML element
- Enumerate the lines of a file
- Evaluate an If…Else statement
- Execute a SELECT statement
- Execute a stored procedure
- Execute a stored procedure that returns a value
- Fill a Combobox with available fonts
- Fill a DataSet with the results of a parameterized stored procedure
- Fill a DataTable with data
- Filter data in a DataView
- Find the amount of disk space available
- Find the current user's name
- Find the names of resources in an assembly
- Find a node in XML data
- For Each…Next (Collection Loop)
- For…Next (Integer Loop)
- Format characters in bold in a RichTextBox control
- Generate multiline string literals

- Get a random number using the Rando class
- Get information about a file
- Handle unhandled Windows Forms exception
- Implement data try/catch blocks
- Implement input/output (I/O) try/catch blocks
- Initialize an array
- Iterate the nodes recursively in an XML file
- Iterate through records in a DataReader
- Keep a Windows Form on top
- List applications
- List environment variables
- Load a column from a database table into a Listbox control
- Load a cursor file from an assembly
- Load an assembly at runtime
- Load a RichTextFile (RTF) into a RichTextBox control
- Locate an element in an array
- Locate changed data in a DataSet
- Loop a sound playing on a Windows Form
- Macro code for inserting text into the code editor
- Macro code for setting a project property
- Make a file request with Hypertext Transfer Protocol (HTTP)
- Make a start-up Windows Form invisible
- Merge menu items programmatically
- Move files
- Move items on Windows Forms menus
- Parse column data in a text file
- Parse a file path
- Parse an e-mail address
- Pause a Windows service
- Peek at messages
- Ping another computer
- Play a beep from a Windows Form
- Play a sound
- Populate a ComboBox from a column of a database table
- Populate a ComboBox from an array
- Populate a Combobox from an ArrayList
- Populate a Tree Control with XML data
- Populate a TreeView control based on master-detail tables
- Print a Windows Form
- Purge queue contents
- Query a DataTable
- Read access data into a DataSet
- Read an XML file into a DataSet

- Read class data from an XML file
- Read entries created by a particular application from the event log
- Read entries from the event logs
- Read registry values
- Read text from a file
- Read XML from a file using the XmlTextReader
- Remove parts of a string
- Resize a button dynamically based on the text property
- Resize Windows Forms
- Retrieve a list of message queues on the local computer
- Retrieve a list of service
- Retrieve accessibility preferences
- Retrieve an environment variable
- Retrieve an image from the clipboard
- Retrieve an integer from the clipboard
- Retrieve information about battery life
- Retrieve information from the parent form of a dialog box
- Retrieve message labels
- Retrieve or change user preferences for menus
- Retrieve text from the clipboard
- Retrieve the drive names on the local computer
- Reverse the contents of an array
- Save records in a DataTable to a database
- Save the contents of a RichTextBox to an RTF
- Search for a record in a DataTable using a key field
- Search for a string in an array of strings
- Search for an item in a Windows Forms ListBox control
- Search within a string
- Select a range of dates in a Windows Forms calendar control
- Select an item in a Windows Forms ListBox control
- Select block with integers
- Select block with strings
- Send a message to a message queue
- Send an e-mail message
- Send and receive messages programmatically
- Send keystrokes to another application
- Set the color of a pen
- Sort an array
- Sort data in a DataView
- Specify the formatter for retrieved messages
- Start a Windows service
- Start an application
- Stop a Windows service

- Stop an application
- Stop playing sounds in the background
- Throw an exception
- Turn off constraints while filling a DataSet
- Update a data source with the contents of related DataTables
- Update a DataRow with the value from a variable
- Update the ProgressBar based on minimum, maximum, and current values
- Upload a file using My.Computer.Network
- Use the #If…Then…#Else directives
- Validate a date
- Validate that passwords are complex
- Validate the format of an e-mail address
- While (Condition)…End While
- Write class data to an XML file
- Write new text files
- Write registry values
- Write text to files
- Write to the application event log from a specified source
- Write to the My.Application LogC#/Visual J#
- Basic attribute implementation
- Checked
- Class
- A common constructor pattern
- Destructor
- Do statement
- Else statement
- Encapsulate Field
- Encapsulate Field Get
- Encapsulate Field Set
- Enum
- Override object.Equals
- Event stub
- Exception type
- For iteration by index
- If statement
- Indexer
- Interface
- Save way to invoke an event
- Implement a simple iterator
- Lock statement
- MessageBox.Show
- Method stub — body

- Method stub — no body
- "Named" iterator/indexer pair
- Namespace
- #If
- #Region
- Property
- Propertyg
- Property Stub
- Property Stub Get
- Property Stub Set
- Static int main
- Static void main
- Struct
- Switch statement
- Try catch
- Try finally
- Unchecked
- Unsafe statement
- Using statement
- While statement

You will find that using some of these snippets will likely reduce the amount of time you use in your debugging. Keep in mind that there is no reason to waste time and energy writing and debugging code that has already been written and debugged.

## Exception Assistant

The Exception Assistant is a new and valuable tool available to users of Visual Studio .NET 2005. The purpose of this tool is to enhance the capabilities of the old method of conveying exception information to the debugger. That is, the person debugging an application will now be given much more information about an exception when one is encountered.

In previous versions of Visual Studio, be they .NET or before, the method for conveying exception information back to the debugger was fairly simplistic. That is, the interface for such data was a simple message box that displayed the exception information. In many cases the information provided was very cryptic and required further research on the part of the debugger just to interpret the exception, not to mention finding a solution.

However, with the release of Visual Studio .NET 2005, the information provided when an exception is thrown is much more intuitive and helpful.

In fact, the Exception Assistant displays exception information to the debugger in a way that allows him or her to research a solution right from the exception window. Using smart tags, similar to the process employed in Microsoft Office, Visual Studio .NET will offer automated fixes for your exceptions. If the exception is more complicated, you may not get an automated fix, but you will still get a good deal of information about the exception and what could have caused it.

Let us throw an exception and have Visual Studio display the Exception Assistant. Figure 6.24 shows an edit that we have made to the `ComplicatedMath()` subroutine. One line of the subroutine has been edited to purposely generate a divide-by-zero exception.

When this code is executed in the debugger we see that an exception is immediately thrown. The Exception Assistant is displayed with some helpful information. Figure 6.25 shows the Exception Assistant. Looking at the Exception Assistant pictured in the figure, you can see that the assistant not only has identified the divide-by-zero error, but also has offered some help. Using hyperlinks, you can research different ways to correct the error.

## *Unused Variable Notification*

The Unused Variable Notification tool, while available for years to most Java IDE users, is fairly new to users of Visual Studio. The concept behind the tool is to help you fully realize your code and thus eliminate some otherwise avoidable bugs. When you write a section of code, the Visual Studio .NET 2005 IDE will track your usage of the variables that you declare. The IDE will then alert you to any and all variables that were declared but never used in your code. Conversely (especially as pertaining to Visual Basic .NET), the IDE will also inform you as to any variables that were used and never declared.

> Visual Basic programmers were spoiled for years before the .NET framework with the ability to use variables in certain situations without having to declare them. Visual Basic would simply internally declare the variable as a variant to fit most situations in which it could be used. However, with the release of .NET and a shift toward a more object-oriented Visual Basic, this rule has gradually changed. Now all variables must be declared and used.

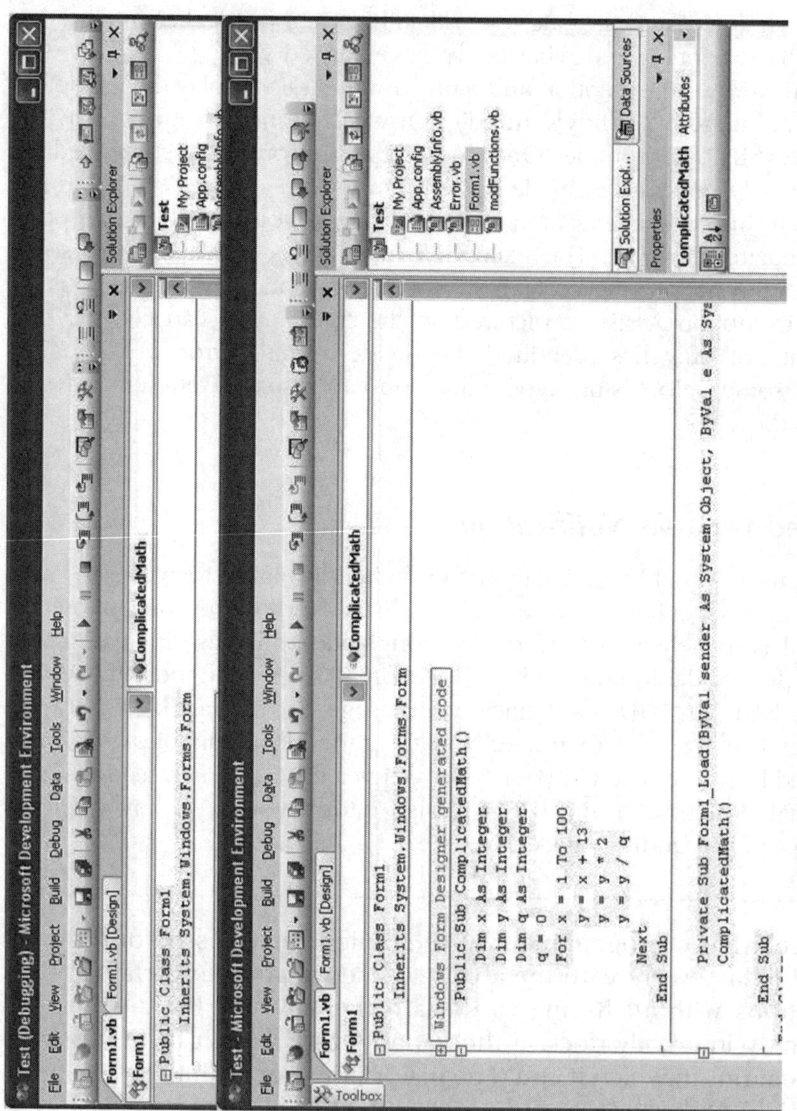


Figure 6.24 Code that will generate a divide-by-zero error.

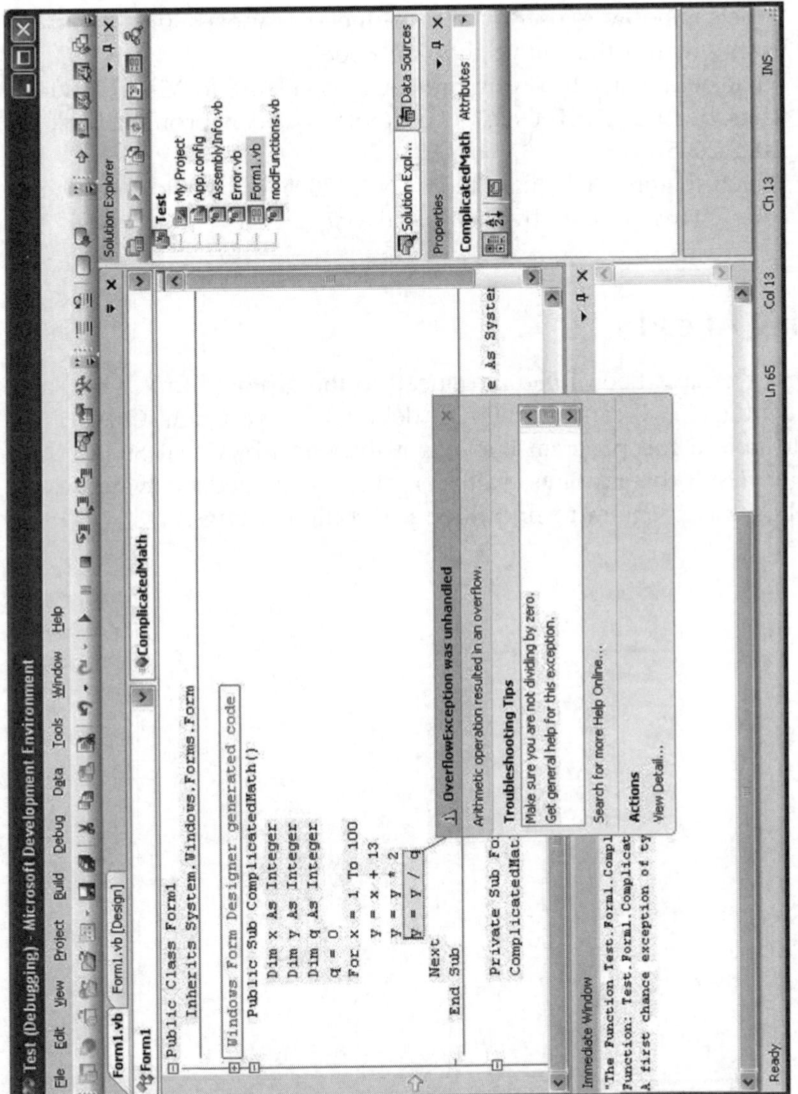


Figure 6.25 The Exception Assistant.

## Review Questions

1. Name three new features of Visual Studio .NET 2005.
2. Which new feature of Visual Studio .NET 2005 enhances the functionality provided by breakpoints?
3. Which window is used to test a function by executing it without having to run the full application code?
4. What debugging tool was previously available to Visual Studio 6 users but not .NET users? (The tool has been brought back for .NET 2005.)
5. Which feature of Visual Studio .NET 2005 will track and identify code changes made by multiple users?

## Looking Ahead

Now that we have been fully introduced to the arsenal of tools available in the debugger, we can use them to debug a full program. Chapter 7 is going to take a full program and run it through the Visual Studio .NET debugger. Using breakpoints, watches, and the immediate window, we will debug this program to find three pre-compiled bugs.

# Chapter 7

# Testing

To this point in the book, we have covered defining bugs, programming to avoid bugs, and using tools to find bugs. All of these subjects have one thing in common: they all involve, to a major extent, the services of the programmer. The programmer(s) of an application will be most heavily involved in all of these subjects, which is not necessarily a bad thing.

Without sounding obvious or redundant, the programmer will be the key person to program the application. By this, he or she will implement all of the techniques provided in Chapters 1 through 6 to help avoid bugs in the first place. Performing these functions is, again stating the obvious, the main job of the programmer.

In the process of performing their main function of creating the application and writing the necessary code, programmers should also use several testing tools in performing a cursory evaluation of their progress. The testing and debugging tools, like those described in Chapters 5 and 6, are also meant for use primarily by the programmer. The head programmer or developer will generally run his or her code in different stages through IDE debugging, that is, using the Visual Studio IDE in debug mode, and testing tools to check his or her progress. A standard Q&A developer or formal tester may not have access to, or knowledge of, tools such as the design time debugger to perform code-level debugging. Furthermore, anyone but the programmers may not have access to the source code itself. For these reasons, application testing is usually spilt into two distinct phases: design time testing and beta testing.

The design time phase of testing is normally performed by the programmer or the programming staff. Design time testing is often tightly woven into, and at times indistinguishable from, the design process itself. The earlier chapters of this book covered this phase of testing in detail.

The beta phase of testing is normally performed by people who were not directly involved in the programming process, but have knowledge of the application's intended functionality. These beta tested will typically not be technical in background, and possibly have used similar applications to the one being tested.

However, no matter how hard the programmer tries, and no matter how much time is spent in debug mode, nothing will compensate for a good test schedule. There will always be a bug that can inevitably slip through the cracks of the programmer's fingers. Therefore, a formalized debugging platform is needed to identify and locate the odd bug that may have worked its way into the compile.

This chapter will help you determine when it is time to formally test your application. Included in this discussion is an explanation of the steps needed to set up a test environment and proceed with your testing. By the end of this chapter you will have fully tested your new application, identified any existing bugs, and located the offending code.

## When Is It Time to Test?

One question that can be very difficult to answer, especially for programmers, is "When is it done?" In this case, where we are discussing applications, it can be rather difficult for a programmer to determine when an application is actually finished. Many application developers, coders, and programmers are, to some degree, perfectionists. As such, many developers and programmers can continue to work on projects almost indefinitely, constantly tweaking and refining their work.

> It is not uncommon, especially in the realm of shrink-wrapped applications (those developed primarily to be sold to the general public), to have applications referred to in the same way as living documents. That is, it can be generally accepted that applications are a form of living project, in that they are never truly finished, and constantly changing through upgrades, updates, revisions, and service patches.

Taking the term literally, an application is finished when it does everything that was originally established in the planning sessions for that application to do. Therefore, when going by the strict definition of the word, an application is done when it fulfills the descriptions of its capabilities as set aside in the planning for that application — assuming that you have a full plan in place that outlines the explicit goals of the application.

For example, if you or your team is writing an application that is supposed to import external spreadsheets, calculate the values embedded within those spreadsheets, and then send e-mails to specific people based on those calculations, then it would be fairly easy to determine when that application is finished. You could, with relative ease, check to see if the three main components of the application are in place. Having those elements, one to import, one to calculate, and one to e-mail, will signify that the application is complete per its design plan and can proceed to testing.

Not all applications can be as easy to finish. Most applications encounter multiple changes and multiple rewrites before the end of the development phase, also referred to as scope creep. These changes, even smaller ones, can make it very hard to determine when an application should be considered finished.

There is one part of the application building process that is inherently flawed. It is this flaw that allows for such ambiguity when determining the completeness of an application — a flaw that, for now, is unavoidable. Let us first discuss this flaw, and then we can use that knowledge to help in determining the completeness of an application. Simply knowing that a process is flawed, even if there is no fix for that flaw, can help you tremendously.

The first phases of the design process, which we have established are the most important, are where a fundamental flaw is embedded. That is, during the design process, the layout for the application is established. All of the functions, abilities, look, and feel of the program are fleshed out during these design sessions. Keep in mind that at this point, more than any other in the process, the application is very vulnerable. The entire direction of the coder's efforts is decided in these design sessions.

The flaw in this process is that the design process uses inherently nontechnical tools and more simple means to design a technical product. In other words, when designing an application and mapping out the expectations of what the application should do, the process begins in a nontechnical state, yet the product of that non-technology-based process is expected to be a technologic application.

So now we have a fundamental problem or flaw in our application development process: How do you design a technological wonder using a nontechnological process? To answer this, you have only but to look at the alternatives. The flaw in the process that forces this question is that without the use of a technologically advanced design process, you cannot design a fully cohesive technological product. There are aspects of the coding process, causes and effects of writing one particular piece of code one way as opposed to another, that simply cannot be anticipated, replicated, or repaired on a piece of paper.

The goal of the design process is to say that Application X should perform a particular task, for example, write a series of values to a database. It is now the task of the next phase of the project, the coding phase, to make that happen. However, the exposed flaw here is that the design process does not take into account the means of the end; its only concern (by design) is the end. So when Application X reaches the coding phase, it is the burden of the programmers to figure out, using the technical tools at their disposal (the programming IDE, debugging tools, etc.), what the best way to achieve the goal set forth by the design process is.

When Application X is being coded, the programmers may decide to use Remote Data Objects (RDO), ActiveX Data Objects (ADO), ADO.NET, or any one of a dozen ways to get information from the application to the database, which is the intended goal of the design. In doing so, the programmers may find that choosing one path to the goal over another, although producing an acceptable result, may cause more development and programming than first anticipated, or in a worse-case scenario, the choice may cause a ripple effect into other aspects of the application itself.

There are multiple ways to produce a desired result in any programming language, each with a possibly unique set of circumstances surrounding their implementation. Therefore, when implementing the thoughts and ideas of the designers, it may be necessary for the programmer to tweak or even redesign portions of the application to get other parts working. It is in this gray area, the area where programmers must choose between two paths to the same end, that applications can be worked and reworked, thus blurring the line between when an application is truly finished for testing and when more work needs to be done.

> The purpose of this discussion is not to say that our current, most popular methods of designing applications — where a group of people sit with pens, pencils, and even white boards, brainstorming a design — are wrong. In fact, I not only believe these methods to be an integral part of application building, but I also trust in them as a necessary device in creating programs that work. I fully believe that for technology to grow and meet the demands of the people who use it on a daily basis, nontechnical people need to be involved in the design of such applications. However, what this discussion should serve to do is simply point out that there is a flaw inherent in the process, and it needs to be recognized to understand its impact.

We have now established that there is a flaw in the design process where a forced ambiguity in the initial design concept can lead to impromptu changes being made by the programmers. This flaw, while having an obvious impact on the coding process, has an even greater impact on the testing process. The impact on the coding process is that the programmers are now making decisions and possibly doing extra coding. This added work affects the job flow and the overall workload.

The impact on the testing process is even greater, though. Because the design process is purely nontechnical, and should be that way, details tend to be overlooked. The omission of these details, causing extra work in the coding process, can greatly blur the line between an application that still needs coding and one that is finished. If, while an application is in the coding process, the design suddenly changes, how do you know when it is finished? This is the hurdle you need to overcome before you can move into the testing phase.

As programmers begin developing the application code, they may discover that there are multiple ways to achieve the goals set forth in the design. This will lead to interactions within the code that could not necessarily be foreseen during the design phase — interactions that may lengthen the amount of time it takes to develop an application before it goes into testing.

For example, earlier in this section we described a fictitious application that was designed to retrieve data from a spreadsheet and send that data to a database. With retrieving and posting data being the only goals set by the design team, the programmers begin coding. At this point the coders make a decision and choose one of any number of methods for connecting to a database. The choice they make here is paramount to the outcome of the application.

The unaccounted for factors in this example design are:

1. The format of the data in the spreadsheet:
   - Spreadsheet program such as Lotus or Microsoft Excel
   - Flat text file
   - Random access file
   - Web stream
   - Multiple files (mix of any of the above)
2. The location of the file being imported:
   - Network drive
   - Local drive
   - Web
   - E-mail

3. Any data manipulation that needs to be done to prepare the data for export:
   - Parsing stream data
   - Parsing file data
   - Combining/separating fields
   - Performing field calculations
4. The method for posting to the database:
   - Use ADO.NET
   - Use RDO
   - Execute Structure Query Language (SQL) stored procedures
   - Post to other database, such as Oracle or Access

This list, although not comprehensive, is fairly daunting, and this is only for an application with one simple goal. Imagine if this were a fairly large application with 10 or 20 goals each, with a set of variables that may or may not be accounted for. How does one choice affect the remaining goals? It is hard to tell. That is why such interactions cannot be accounted for in the design process. These situations can only be dealt with during the coding process. However, the way you deal with them will determine how easily you will be able to pass the application to the testing unit.

The biggest mistake that can be made by any programmer in a situation like this is to simply make decisions concerning what paths to take without exploring how those decisions impact the remainder of the project. Even the smallest decision born of an ambiguity of the design can lead to one or several developers not knowing in what direction the project is moving or what phases of development have been reached.

The confusion caused when more than one person make choices that affect the work flow and progress of several other people is what makes it hard to tell when an application is ready for testing. For this reason, several steps should be taken at all phases of the project to ensure the signs that an application is ready for testing are easy to see.

During the design process, try to make sure as many questions as possible are answered. To do this may require a certain level of technological insight at the design phase. When ensuring that as many questions as possible are answered, be careful that you do not go overboard; there is a fine line here, and getting too granular in the design process can be just as detrimental as not being granular enough. For example, if in the design process you attempt to map out every item used and how it should be done, you run the risk of inadvertently creating bugs through interactions that are unsound. Although this is a process that is perfected over time, try to map out enough of the project that the major elements are accounted for, but leave enough wiggle room that the programmers can manipulate the design if problems occur.

During the coding process try to keep close track of any design changes you may need to make to complete a section of code. If the changes are significant enough, make sure the updated information is propagated to the other programmers on the project so that any other code blocks affected by the changes can be modified. For example, using the sample already established in this section, if while programming the application you find that Remote Data Objects (RDO) is incompatible with the database you are writing to, that information should be distributed to any other team members to ensure any traces of RDO are cleaned up and changed.

As you progress through the coding phase of the project and you begin to think about when you may be able to move into testing, try asking yourself the following questions to see if you are ready for testing.

- Are the major goals of the application's design met?
- Can the application perform when run in an IDE debug environment?
- Have any changes to the initial design been accounted for?
- Will the application compile?

Let us assume that you are unsure about how to answer any of these questions. For example, the first question, while the most basic of the lot, may be the hardest to answer. There are times in software production where timelines and deadlines govern the development process. For example, when discussing shrink-wrapped software, presales schedules and consumer seasons may have a greater influence over the production schedule of a product. In is not uncommon, when dealing with this type of production, to hit a deadline and have some portions of the design not met. In this case, you either document your shortcomings for future enhancements or move the deadline to accommodate the extra work. The more common result is that the missed goals, if they do not greatly affect the overall functionality of the product, are documented and left for future development.

The second question addresses a basic form of testing. That is, the programmers doing the coding will periodically run all or portions of the program in debug mode to test their code. Running the code in debug mode is a good gauge of whether or not a program will hold up under compiled testing.

> Keep in mind that debug mode testing is by no means a perfect decision-making tool to judge an application's readiness for testing. If an application does not hold up under debug mode testing, then it is clearly not ready for compiled testing. However, if the same application does perform well while in debug mode, it may still run into problems when compiled.

Do not assume, however, that a pass through the debug mode editor is the only indication that an application is ready for the compiler. A good pass through only indicates one thing, the fact that the application can be compiled without throwing a compiler error. You must take into account all of the other indicators of testing preparedness to determine if you are ready for compiled testing.

Question 3 serves as a guide to ensure that all proper documentation has been done. The dissemination of information is paramount to the success of any project. From civil engineering to government to application development, the sharing of information is the most important aspect of any project. Getting the right information into the hands of the right people will go a long way in bringing you to success.

Therefore, when dealing with the coordination of larger projects, especially application development, the utmost priority should be placed on documenting the current state and course of the project. If anything in the project changes, especially a change that would affect more than one person on the team, the information pertaining to the change needs to be distributed to the remaining team members as soon as possible. Getting this information to the right people will allow any complementary changes to be made with the least amount of impact. For example, using our established sample project, if the programmer in charge of creating the "database uploading" piece of the program chooses to use ADO.NET, the information about the change should be sent to the other programmers as soon as possible to allow the remainder of the application to be built accordingly.

The simple process of informing the entire team about changes to the design or underlying structure of a program will help everyone stick as closely as possible to the intent of the design. The process of determining if an application is ready for testing will also be easier if everyone has access to the same documentation to account for design and direction changes in a timely manner.

With all of the information provided to you in this section you may have noticed one thing: there is no clear-cut formula to use in determining if an application is ready to be compiled and tested. The process of sending an application to the testing team is still largely based on personal opinion and experience. However, the information we have discussed herein should give you a good guideline as to the type of information you should be looking for, and the types of questions you should be asking yourself.

Once you have determined that an application is ready to be compiled and tested, it is time to set up the testing environment. The next section of this chapter will help you through the process of setting up a proper test environment.

## Setting Up the Test Environment

The proper test environment can mean the difference between achieving good test results and being forced to do hours of needless work. Without the proper test environment, your application may be testing against unrelated conditions that would provide false results and distract from the actual issues that exist, if any. Before we address how to set up the environment itself we need to clear up one common misconception about testing.

If you were asked what the primary purpose of compiled testing was, that is, testing outside of the programming interface itself, what would you say? Chances are your answer would be like that of many programmers or engineers: to make sure that compiled program works as designed. Although this answer may be correct on a certain level, it is very misleading and omits some very important information.

Keep in mind that the purpose of this book is debugging. Therefore, one of the purposes of testing is obviously related to debugging. However, looking back through our discussions, the major cause of bugs within applications is in the interaction between that application and its environment, including other applications. Therefore, compiled testing is really testing for how the application being tested relates and interacts within a predetermined and controlled environment. What is the difference?

Most, but not all, programming errors should be fleshed out during the programmer's testing in debug mode. This should be one of the criteria that are met before an application is compiled and tested. Therefore, when an application is sent to formal testing, what is really being tested is the way that application works within the environment that it is meant to work within. By testing in this manner, bugs will be easier to find and deal with, as will be explained later in this chapter.

This definition of compiled testing should not be taken to suggest that when you are testing an application the only problem you will find will not be directly related to the application being tested. This could not be further from the truth. The reality is that some programming errors do slip by the programmers and the compiler. However, some perfectly good, sound, and functional code can work fine in debug mode, seem to meet a design goal, but not take into account some X factor or unknown variable of the production environment.

For example, in the last section we described a very simple design for an application that would read information from a spreadsheet, perform some calculations, and output the resulting information to a database. Although this may seem like a very simple and straightforward set of three application goals, you will find that there are many environmental factors that can cause a bug or two. Let us assume that the programmers have completed the application and it tested fine in debug mode. That is, while the programmers were still coding the application, they tested it in the programming IDE and confirmed that the program does in fact read information from a spreadsheet, perform calculations on the data, and output the results to a database correctly. Now the program goes into compiled testing. What bug could be found?

In this application, two of the three target goals of the application depend on outside interaction to function correctly. The following is a short list of some of the things that can affect the functionality of this otherwise correctly functioning application:

- The spreadsheet being read from is of the correct type (i.e., the application is expecting a Microsoft Excel or CSV file, and in fact, that is what is being supplied).
- The fields in the spreadsheet are in the correct order.
- All of the expected information is being provided.
- The provided information is in the correct format (i.e., numeric fields are formatted as numbers).
- The spreadsheets are in the expected location.
- The values within the spreadsheet are able to be calculated (no dividing by zero or multiple alpha characters).
- The database is set up with the expected permissions.
- The database has the correct columns for output.
- The columns of the output databases are formatted as expected.

As you can see, even a program that has been developed correctly and functions exactly as expected at the time of compile can still produce bugs based on the environmental factors of the testing platform. This list of potential bugs is from one application that functions perfectly with three small goals. Imagine if this were a typical application with 10 or 20 goals and one or two programming errors that made it through the compile. Now you can see the importance and true purpose of compiled testing.

Before testing can begin, the testing environment must be built. The accuracy and integrity of the test environment will dictate the accuracy and integrity of the test results. Therefore, not only must the description of the test environment be complete, but also the programming environment must coincide with the testing environment, which in turn must be the same as the eventual production environment.

The testing environment itself, at least in part, should be determined during the design process. That is, using our previous example, a well-written (but concise) design statement for this application would be as follows:

```
"...an application that accepts input from a Microsoft
Excel spreadsheet residing in the path 'c:\
spreadsheet\input.xls'. The application performs
calculations on the fields 'Amount', 'Time', 'Labor',
'Parts', and 'Tax'. The resulting fields will be
written to the 'Total_Bills' database on the '\\
billingSQL' Microsoft SQL server..."
```

This statement represents, in part, a typical design statement. From this short description we can determine the following elements that should be in place in our testing environment:

1. The spreadsheet should be in the Microsoft Excel format.
2. The spreadsheet should include the fields Amount, Time, Labor, Parts, and Tax.
3. The test environment should contain a Microsoft SQL database server named billingSQL.
4. The SQL server should contain a database named Total_Bills.

Looking at this list there may be some problems when testing begins. When you are establishing a test environment, accuracy is very important. There are some key pieces of information about the testing environment that we still do not know.

First, we do not know what client or server operating system(s) this application should run under. We can assume that the application should run under that latest operating environment, in this case Microsoft Windows XP Professional for a client and Microsoft Windows Server 2003 for the server. However, what if the ultimate production environment of the application could include Windows XP Home, Windows 2000, or even Windows 98? This information will be important to know so that these operating scenarios can be accounted for.

Along the same discussion of operating systems, we do not know what versions of the involved software we need. Which versions of Microsoft Excel and Microsoft SQL server are needed to run the application correctly? Again, this information needs to be known before the testing can begin.

For the sake of moving our discussion along, let us say that we have determined the following components are needed to create an accurate testing environment:

- Microsoft Windows 98
- Microsoft Windows XP Professional
- Microsoft Windows Server 2003
- Microsoft Excel 2003
- Microsoft SQL Server 2000

Now that we have our requirements, we can proceed with the creation of the test environment. Earlier in this section we described a perfect test environment as embodying two concepts: accuracy and integrity. Ensuring that we have knowledge of all of the components needed has taken care of the accuracy part. Now we need to focus on integrity.

To create a testing environment that has integrity and will provide the most accurate results, it should be as removed from the programming and production environments as possible. Separating the test environment serves two main purposes. First, any production information will be safe from the contamination that may be caused by the application being tested. Because the application has yet to be tested, there is no way to say for certain what it will do to the environment surrounding it. Therefore, to keep any data, applications, and even machines safe from unexpected manipulation, the testing environment should be removed from these items.

The second purpose for keeping the testing environment separate from the production environment(s) is converse to the first. That is, you do not want production data or applications affecting the test results of the program being tested. Because it is an unaccounted for variable, there is no way of knowing how production information will affect the application being tested. The fact is that interference from production data and application may cause unexpected errors or anomalies in the test results.

To create a proper test environment, all of the networking, application, and data structures pertaining to the test environment should be completely separate from the production environment. The two environments should not share any resources. Figure 7.1 illustrates our current sample production environment.

In Figure 7.1 we can see that the production environment is fairly large. Let us now examine a map of the elements that we know are needed to complete our testing environment. Figure 7.2 illustrates the testing environment. Examining Figure 7.2, you can see that all of the elements needed to test our sample application are in place. Now take a look at both Figure 7.1 and Figure 7.2; you will notice that both networks contain the elements required to facilitate testing. However, the production environment pictured in Figure 7.1 contains not only added elements that could adversely affect the testing, but also production data that might be impacted by the testing. Therefore, it is necessary to build out the testing environment as a separate entity. Figure 7.3 illustrates what this combined, yet distinct, set of networks might look like.

Examining Figure 7.3, we can see that although all of the necessary components for testing exist in the production environment, using them would be very risky. Therefore, the second testing network must be established. The goal for having this test network is to establish it in a way

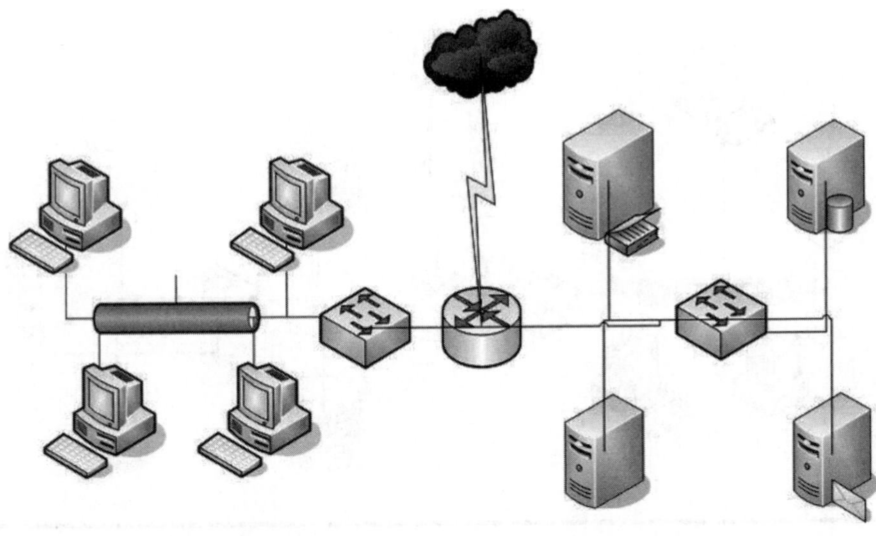

Figure 7.1 A network map of the current production environment.

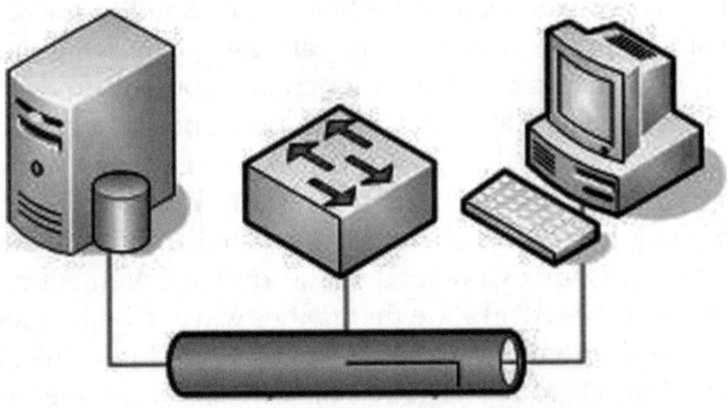

Figure 7.2 The elements required for the testing environment.

that allows for no data passing between the two networks. In Figure 7.3 it may look like the two networks are connected at a central device; however, that is not necessarily the case.

Both the production and test environments are connected to a central switch. However, just because the two networks share a common device does not mean that they are connected to each other or even share information. In this example, the central switch has been set up with two virtual networks. The production environment connects to one, while the test environment connects to another.

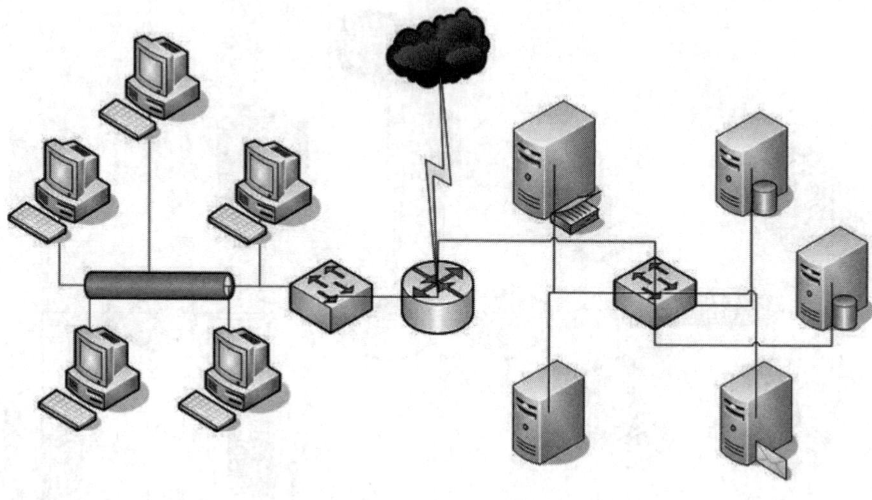

**Figure 7.3 The combined testing and production environments.**

Using a setup where two networks stem from a common device allows for a scenario such as that in Figure 7.4.

In Figure 7.4 we can see that by being connected to the same switch, both the test and production network can now share a common Internet connection. The sharing of an Internet connection will not directly allow for the transfer of data between the two networks, but it will allow you to share some resources that you would otherwise have to duplicate.

The application can now be tested on the separate test environment with no risk of contamination either to or from the production environment. All of the resources outlined in the design statement are available to testers in this test network. Are there other ways to build a test network? Absolutely. There are about as many ways to build test environments as there are applications to test. The reason why we chose the approach we did, using such a close tie between the production and test environments, is for several reasons.

First, if the testing is being performed in an environment where application development is not the standard order of business, the test environment can be more easily dissolved when testing is complete. Many companies, while not in the business of developing application, may have a need to develop one or two programs for their own use. Following proper testing protocols, these companies can still create a separate environment to properly test these applications.

When testing is complete, the resources of the test environment can be absorbed for use into the production environment more easily given that the two environments technically exist off a common device. This

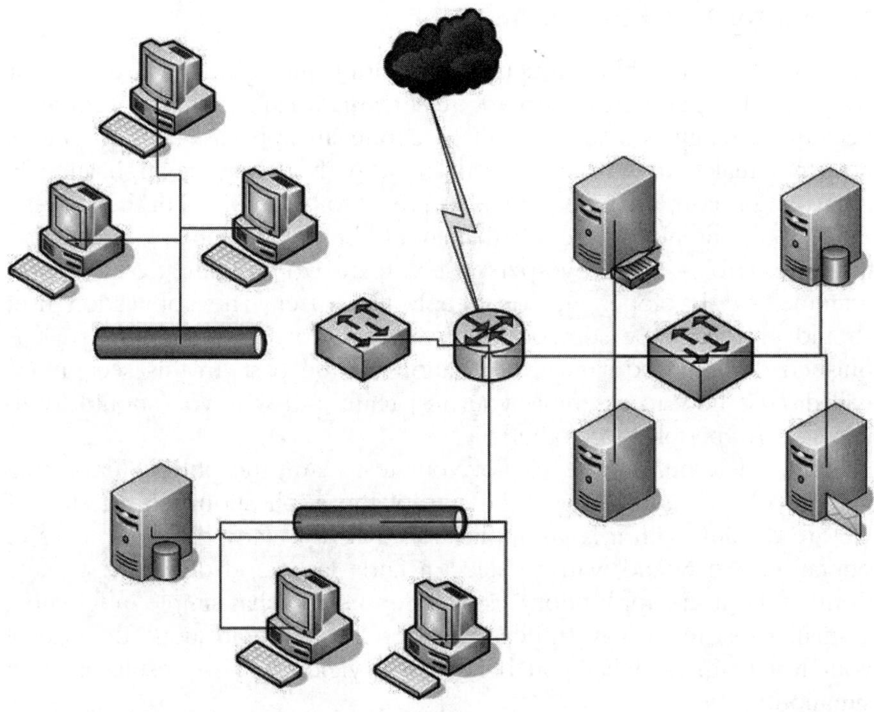

**Figure 7.4 Two virtual networks sharing a resource.**

will allow the company to not waste time on the maintenance of a network that it may not need again.

Another reason for having the two networks so closely related, yet separate, is that many companies may not have the resources available from the beginning to set up a long-term testing environment. Some resources, such as servers, workstations, or connectivity devices, may have to be borrowed from the production environment on a short-term basis. Having the networks closely related will facilitate the movement of these resources from one network to the other for the time needed.

This section should have given you a good overview of some of the issues that need to be approached when building your test environment. Because each environment has different needs, telling you exactly how to build a network that suits you would be difficult. However, if you follow the guidelines presented here, you should find it easy to create a good test environment.

The next section will give you some general information about how to choose your test team.

## Choosing the Test Team

The quality of the bugs you uncover during the testing phase of your project will depend greatly on your test team. We are using the term *team* because it really is a team effort to debug an application. One person does not make up a testing team. To properly debug an application in the testing phase, multiple people will need to be involved in the process.

The least number of people that should be involved in any application testing is two. A small two-person test team would consist of one programmer or developer and one application user. The application user should preferably be someone who will use the application when it is finished or has used similar applications in the past. In this section we will discuss how to assemble your test team and why you should try to use specific people over others.

When determining the size of your test team, the only criterion that may be of use as a factor is the size of the application being tested. If we are dealing with a large application that has many different facets of operation, we would want to select a fairly large and diverse test team. Conversely, if the application is smaller and somewhat simple in function, a smaller test team may suffice. Therefore, you should judge the size of your test team by what you believe will yield the best results in your situation.

Now, let us profile some different people you may want to include in your test team. Different people will be better in certain situations than others. The key to assembling the best team is knowing what the strengths of each team member should be.

> If you work in a larger corporation, especially one that specializes in application development, you may have the fortune of having a specialized test team already in place. It is not uncommon to have a quality assurance (QA) and testing department permanently in place for testing applications in larger companies. If this is the case, then you may have no choice but to use them. However, you may still want to read through this section of the chapter to help you understand what those testers' strong points are going to be.

The first and most obvious choice for many people when assembling an application test team is to choose one or more of the application's developers. Selecting a developer as a tester definitely has its good points. For one, the developers are going to be aware of any functions that the application should perform. Therefore, a developer may be quite thorough in his or her testing. The developer will also be able to recognize, with a higher degree of confidence, when the results of a function are not what they should be. Naturally one would select a developer when assembling a test team. However, there are some things to consider about developers that may make you want to have at least more than one person on your team.

The first problem with having a developer on your test team is that developers, by nature, think like developers. That being said, developers do not think like users. A developer knows how the application is supposed to work. Therefore, a developer will know what to do, and more importantly what not to do, when testing an application. This may impact the results you get in test.

If a developer knows how an application is supposed to work, chances are that he or she will not uncover as many bugs. What developers do in the testing phase may mimic very closely what they already do when running the application in debug mode. Although this does not apply to all developers who test applications, it can be a factor in determining your test team.

In looking back over the pros of having a developer on your test team, the benefits far outweigh the risks. This is why at the opening of this section the statement was made to include at least one developer in your test team.

More valuable members of your team may be the people who represent the users of the application. In assembling your test team you should include at least one person who would be a potential user of the application when it is finished. The reasoning behind having users test your application is to ensure that the application itself is functional and user-friendly.

Because the users have had little or no involvement in the design of the application, they can be great guides to tell if your program is up to par. Users know what they want out of an application, and they know what to expect in an interface. If an application is not intuitive, it may lead to problems and possibly even bugs. A good example of this can be seen in Figure 7.5.

Examining Figure 7.5, without any knowledge of the development of the application illustrated, which button would delete the open record? On the application there is a button named "Delete Record" and a button named "Delete History." Looking closely at Figure 7.5, you can see that the current open record is from the folder labeled "History." A developer, especially one who worked on the interface, would know exactly which button to press and quickly select that one. However, a user might not be as quick and may even select the wrong button.

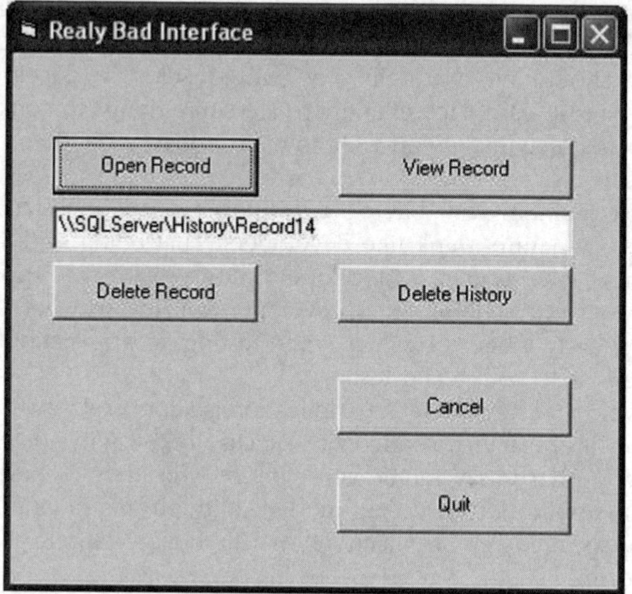


**Figure 7.5 An unintuitive interface.**

The one disadvantage to using nondevelopers in testing roles is that they may not immediately recognize a bug when they come across one. Conversely, they may also think that unfamiliar results are bugs when in fact they are not. For this reason, the users involved with the testing process should at least be familiar with the functionality of the application being tested to get an accurate result.

By this, the users should be the intended users of the finished application, i.e., people from the corporate department or demographic that will be using the application when it is finished. Their feedback will help you determine how well your application performs in comparison to what is currently being used. This group of people will offer the most value in terms of ensuring your application has met all of its requirements.

In assembling your test team, one more group of people should be represented. These should be average people who, for lack of a better term, can be counted on to break things, that is, a group of people who are not technically inclined, nor are they going to be the potential users of the finished product. They are just people who can be counted on to open every window and press every button trying to generate errors and uncover bugs. Now the question is, What do you do once you think you have found a bug?

## Finding Bugs

Bug reporting can be just as important as the process of finding the bugs in the first place. Once a bug is found during the testing phase, a process must be put in place to then convey that information to the appropriate person or team of people for correction. After all, finding a bug in a program does no good if the bug is never fixed.

Before you begin the testing phase of your project you need to have a process in place to allow for the efficient reporting of errors. Although some larger software houses have applications with large databases devoted to the logging, tracking, and remediation of bugs, a simple pen and paper can do the job just as well. The key is to ensure that you are gathering the correct information about the bug to be able to reproduce the anomaly in a development environment and correct it.

The best way to achieve this is to create a bug-reporting form. The bug-reporting form would then be given to all of the testers. Testers, upon finding a suspected bug, can then log their findings, hand in the form, and continue the testing process. The following list illustrates the type of information that can be gathered on a bug-reporting form:

General tester information: This allows the developer working on the bug remediation to contact the tester and clear up any ambiguities.

- Tester name
- Contact information

Bug information: This should contain enough information for a developer to recreate the data in a development environment.

- Bug description
- Title of form where bug was found
- List of steps that lead to the generation of the bug
- (Text of error generated)
- (Title of error box)
- (Dataset being accessed)
- (External file being accessed)

The items in the list that appear in parentheses are optional. That is, not every bug will be accompanied by an error box. Therefore, the text of the error should be optional, but very helpful, information.

Simple forms like this allow the testers to convey information about the application, whether it is a bug or not, to the developers in a reasonable amount of time and in a fairly efficient manner.

## Review Questions

1. What are the two distinct phases of application testing?
2. Who normally performs the beta phase?
3. What is the fundamental flaw in the design process?
4. What are the two main purposes served by separating the production environment from the test environment?
5. The quality of the bugs you uncover during the testing phase of your project will depend greatly on the quality of what?
6. What is the one disadvantage to using nontechnical users in a testing role?
7. Why must you ensure that you are collecting the correct information about a bug?
8. What is the best way to achieve the goal of collecting bug infomation?
9. Name one field that should be provided in the general tester information section.
10. Name two pieces of information that could help you recreate a bug.

## Looking Ahead

Chapter 8 focuses on documenting your final product. Writing efficient, bug-free applications is one thing, but what happens when you pass that application on to a new set of developers? Documenting your application and its revisions will help everyone who works on your code in the future. Chapter 8 will centralize its discussion on a new feature of Microsoft's Visual Studio 2005: the ability to add XML documentation tags into your code.

# Chapter 8

# Commenting Your Code with XML

By this point, using all of the information provided in this book, your code is clean, well documented, free of bugs, and tested. This brief chapter covers one final piece of information. In this chapter we will discuss the use of eXtensible Markup Language (XML) tags in your code to produce documentation based on that code.

Although this information is closely related to code commenting, it was placed near the end of the book simply because it is not as closely related to debugging as commenting is. However, this information is extremely helpful, to programmers, debuggers, and testers. The correct and consistent use of these XML tags can help you to easily create useful documentation based on your code libraries.

XML code documentation tags have been available to Java programmers for quite some time, and C# users gained the functionality during the last release of Visual Studio. However, if you are strictly a Microsoft Visual Basic person, you may not be aware of the addition or usefulness of these tags in Microsoft's Visual Studio 2005.

> There are some who would argue that XML documentation tags were available in 2003 for Visual Basic. NET users. However, this was accomplished with third-party add-ins and not native support, as it will be in .NET 2005.

XML documentation tags allow you to mark up your code libraries, compile them, and then produce Microsoft-style help files (.chm).

Each field in this help file can be created using an XML tag. These tags are added into the library in the same way comments are. Then, after the file is compiled, a documentation compiler can be run against the newly created library. The documentation compiler will read the parse information from the code library and assemble it into a CHM document.

There are a few free XML documentation compilers available. Some compilers, although recognizing the full set of standard tags, may also recognize a few proprietary ones, so check your compiler's documentation before selecting. One of the more popular XML documentation compilers is a free tool known as NDoc (available at ndoc.sourceforge.net).

> At the time this book was written, a native XML documentation compiler was not included with the distribution of the Visual Studio .NET 2005 Beta. This is, of course, with the exception of the /doc code compiler command line option. This may change with the full release.
>
> Also, at the time this book was written, NDoc did not yet support the .NET framework 2.0.

Let us now take a look at the XML tags used to document code.

## XML Tags

The following listing is a library, ClassLibrary1, written in C#:

**Listing 8.1: ClassLibrary1**

```
using System;
namespace ClassLibrary1
{
   public class Class1
   {
      private bool Calc = false;
      public Class1()
      {
      }
```

```
        public void GetTenthCalc()
        {
        }
        public int GetTenth(int GetTenthValue)
        {
            return GetTenthValue / 10;
        }
        public bool Finished
        {
            get
            {
                return Calc;
            }
            set
            {
                Calc = Finished;
            }
        }
    }
}
```

Here we can see that this is just a simple .dll file, extremely basic in nature. However, how would we get the methods within this code documented for future developers? Of course we could do it manually, but why do that when there are several XML tags at our disposal for this very purpose.

The standard tags that are available to you for documenting your libraries are as follows:

- <c> — Embedded code font in other text
- <code> — Multiple lines of source code as examples
- <example> — An example of using a member
- <exception> — An exception thrown by the current member
- <include> — Includes an external documentation file
- <list> — The heading row of a list
- <para> — A paragraph of text
- <param> — A method parameter
- <paramref> — A reference to a parameter in other text
- <permission> — The security permission required by a member

- <remarks> — Supplemental information about the library or member
- <returns> — Return value of a method
- <see> — An embedded cross-reference to another member
- <seealso> — A reference in a "See Also" list
- <summary> — A summary of the object
- <value> — The value of a property

These tags are used in the standard XML manner with an opening and closing tag, as shown here:

```
<summary>
</summary>
```

However, to force the compiler into recognizing the tags as XML documentation tags (you are not just trying to pass them off as code), you need to precede the tags with three comment marks. For example, in C# three / marks would precede the XML tags:

```
///<summary>
///
///</summary>
```

In Visual Studio .NET 2005, three `'''` marks are used to prefix comments in Visual Basic:

```
'''<summary>
'''
'''</summary>
'''<remarks></remarks>
```

Most programming languages that support XML tags do so in this format, using three comment marks before each.

Using this knowledge allows the commenting of the simple code library from Listing 8.1 to provide some key information for other programmers. We will focus on using as many of the tags as possible to provide the most information.

> Please note that all comments, other than those needed for the XML documentation tags, have been removed to make the code more readable for this chapter. Normally the XML documentation tags would complement your normal commenting structure, not replace it.

Listing 8.2 shows our sample code library with a few `<Summary>` tags added.

**Listing 8.2: ClassLibrary1 with XML Tags**

```
using System;
namespace ClassLibrary1
{
/// <summary>
/// This is a Sample Code Library for The Debugger's
Handbook.
/// </summary>
/// <remarks> This sample was written by J. F.
DiMarzio</remarks>
    public class Class1
    {
        /// <summary>
        /// This Class1 provides all of the
functionality of the library
        /// </summary>
        private bool Calc = false;
        public Class1()
        {

        }
/// <summary>
/// GetTenthCalc returns the 10th of any number
supplied
/// </summary>
/// <example><c>GetTenthCalc</c>20</example>
        public void GetTenthCalc()
        {
        }
        public int GetTenth(int GetTenthValue)
        {
            return GetTenthValue / 10;

        }

        public bool Finished
        {
```

```
            get
            {
                return Calc;
            }
            set
            {
                Calc = Finished;
            }
        }
    }
}
```

Given the way they are separated visually from the code, even if you do not know C#, you can easily see the comments that should be added to the "Summary" section of the help file. If you are using NDoc, this library can now be compiled and run through NDoc to create the help file. For instructions on using NDoc, or any other XML to CHM generator, please refer to that product's documentation.

> To correctly form a CHM file, you must configure Visual Studio to create an XML sheet that will accompany the library through the generator. To do this, go to your project's properties page and enter a name for the XML file. By default, this value is blank, and therefore not created.

Look for the `<Summary>` tags and compare that information to the "Summary" fields shown in Figure 8.1. Looking at the help file in Figure 8.1, you can compare the locations of the "Summary" field text to the `<Summary>` tags included in the file. This will give you a good idea as to where this information is populated within the help file. An option within NDoc to display missing field data has been turned on to show you where there is still data to be entered. (Normally these fields will simply show as blank.)

Using this information, you can now easily comment, mark up, and document all of your code libraries.

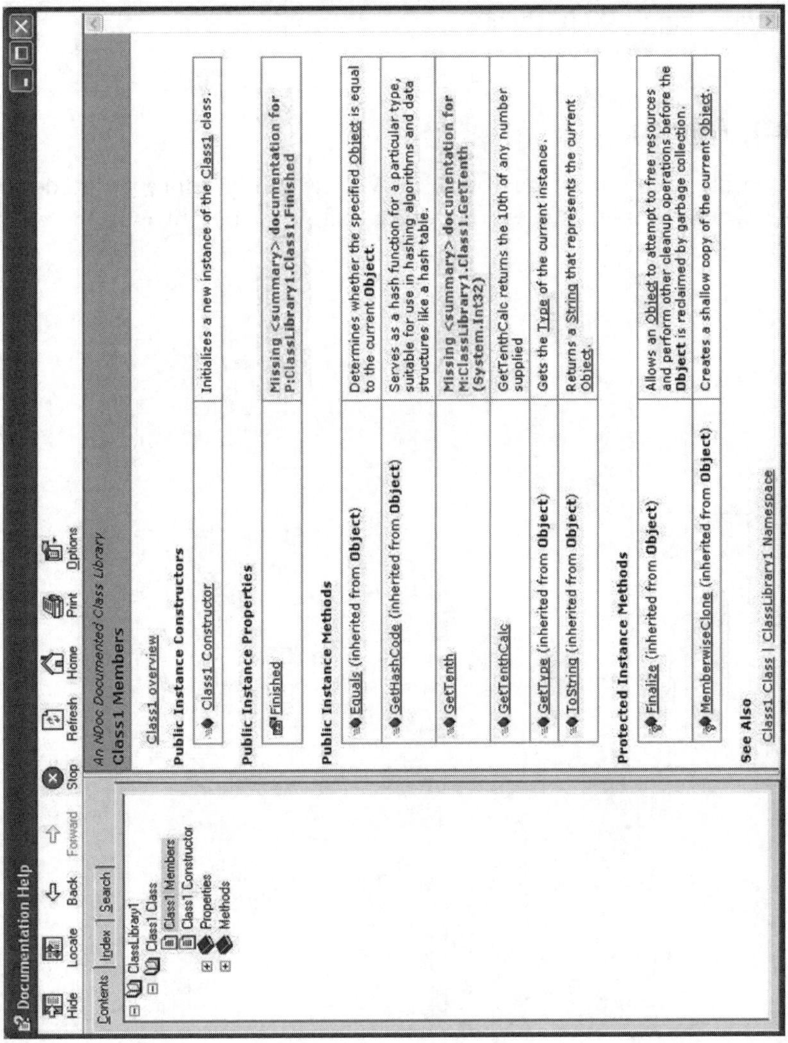

**Figure 8.1 A populated help file.**

## Review Questions

1. What functionality do XML tags provide for programmers?
2. What file extension is created by XML documentation compilers?
3. Which XML tag is use to create the "Summary" field of the help file?
4. What parameter needs to be specified in Visual Studio before generating an XML sheet?

## Looking Ahead

The remaining chapters of this book provide a handy reference guide to be used when looking up error codes that may be thrown by your applications.

# Chapter 9

# Real-World Scenarios: Opening Files

The remainder of this book will focus on a number of real-world cases that are commonly plagued by bugs. There are instances where a programmer can be caught up in the code and easily miss a command, setting, or variable, or simply use a process incorrectly. Although learning a new process or theory from a book is a great way to introduce yourself to the concept, it will never really sink in until you see it in practice.

We will take nine common situations where bugs can present themselves and point out the areas of concern, the misconceptions, and the solutions. This is the best way to put the knowledge gained in the first part of this book into action. The scenarios, each of which will be the subject of this and the following chapters (e.g., this chapter will discuss Scenario 1, Chapter 10 will discuss Scenario 2, and so on), will cover the following topics:

- Opening files: This section examines the common bugs that can present themselves in code used for opening files that are external to the application.
- Reading from and writing to files: Now that the files are open, data can be read from and written to them. Both of these processes offer unique ways to miss a bug.
- Saving program settings: Saving program settings on the surface is very similar to writing to a file. However, it can prove to be a bit

more destructive in that any bugs may affect the data that you plan on using to run your application.

- Working with objects: One of the problems that can arise when working with object-oriented programming languages is working with objects. It can be difficult to keep track of and correctly define objects, especially when you are under the pressure of a deadline.
- Editing the registry: If there is one topic that instantly gives programmers a fright, it is editing the registry; one bug can ruin an entire machine.
- Adding and removing functionality to the window's termination button: One way to spice up any application is to add custom code to the standard terminate button. Bugs here are tough to capture because this is one of the few places where, if your code works correctly, the application shuts down.
- Opening a database: Opening databases is similar in concept to opening and reading files, but now there are credentials that need to be passed. This offers another layer of coding that a bug can hide in.
- Reading a database: One thing that has changed dramatically from version to version of Visual Studio is the process of reading databases. Not keeping up with these changes can create some confusing bugs.
- Searching a database: Searching through a database offers unique ways of creating bugs because your query code can be executed outside of the application.

In using these cases we are going to examine the code behind performing these procedures in C# and VB.NET. The code will first be presented in a common first-pass appearance that many programmers may use in their own development. This first pass of the code will then be run and the resulting bug will be displayed.

> You should take the time in each scenario to then look over the code and try to determine from where the bug may be generated. Looking over the code and running it in your own compiler will give you a better understanding for how these errors can occur.

Finally, the source of the bug will be revealed and several solutions will be offered to solve the problem. The new source code will then be displayed in its entirety to give you a basis for comparison against the original first-pass code. Such scenarios are the best way for you to practice using the techniques covered in the first half of this book.

As you read through the scenarios, it may be beneficial for you to try executing the sample code in your own compiler. Most of the examples will compile correctly and generate errors on their execution, or in the execution of certain functions. This will reinforce to you that you cannot rely on the compiler to catch every bug.

With this covered, let us move on to the first example, opening files.

## Opening Files

The first example that we will examine in this chapter is the fairly common task of opening files. Most business applications will involve some form of file interaction. Whether reading from, writing to, or creating from nothing, files need to be opened to become functional elements within your program.

Although working with files is fairly commonplace, that does not mean it is equally as easy. That is, for as many times as you will likely use file tools in your applications, each time can be just as complicated and frustrating as the last. In older languages, multiple lines of code can be required to define, locate, and open files.

> This section includes examples from Microsoft Visual Basic 6, Visual Basic .NET, and Visual C#. However, because file tools have vastly improved from Visual Studio 6 to Visual Studio .NET, some topics, such as executing the close method in the wrong place, may only apply to Microsoft Visual Basic 6.

There are several scenarios where the processes of, and related to, opening a file can cause you some headaches. In this example we will look at two of those scenarios. The first is executing the close method in the wrong place. The second will look at miscellaneous syntactical errors that are easy to overlook but can generate errors in your application code.

Bugs formed from code that interacts with files create a unique problem for programmers and debuggers. Working with files can involve several steps, many of which rely on actions controlled external to the actual application. In a typical application that interacts with a file, the following processes are usually followed:

- Locate file
- Open file
- Understand format of file
- Interact with file
- Close file

Four of these five processes can be directly altered or impacted by elements outside your application. Therefore, when debugging applications that interact with files, it can be difficult to identify if the bug is code related or if the problem lies in the files. For this reason, take some time when you review the following scenarios and familiarize yourself with the problem code.

## Executing the Close Method in the Wrong Place

Microsoft Visual Basic 6 remains one of the most popular programming languages in business environments. More than six years after its initial release, thousands of programmers continue to author applications using the product.

Many of the advancements seen in Visual Studio. NET products were not available in Visual Basic 6. Therefore, performing functions such as opening files can involve a few extra steps, such as closing the file when you are finished. The process of closing a file, although on the surface is quite benign, can cause many headaches if not handled correctly.

The following code block is from a Visual Basic 6 application that generates a bug. The application is a simple form with a button. When the form is loaded, a file is opened. The button on the form has been coded to write a line of text to the file.

### VB6

```
Private Sub Form_Load()
'**********************
'Sample VB6 program
'   jfd
'   5/5/2005
'**********************
'Begin:
'**********************
```

```
'Opens the file Example.txt
Open "c:\example.txt" For Output As #1
Close #1
'**********************
'End
'**********************
End Sub
Private Sub Command1_Click()
'**************************
'Writes the word "Test" to Example.txt
'**************************
'Begin
'**************************
Write #1, "Test"
'**************************
'End
'**************************
End Sub
```

This application compiles correctly and will start without error. However, there is a bug within the code. The bug cannot be seen until the user clicks on the form's button. Once the button is clicked, the following error is thrown:

```
Run-time error '52':
Bad file name or number
```

Take time now to look over the code once again and try to locate the bug. There are only three lines of code in the program, and one contains the bug.

The bug lies in the `Form_Load` section of the code. If you follow the program's logic in your head, it should follow these steps in order:

- Load
- Open the file
- <User clicks on button>
- Write to file
- Close file

Now look again at the code. The example provided loads, opens the file, and then closes it before the user can interact with the button.

Therefore, by the time the user clicks on the button, the file is closed and parameter `#1` in the line `Write #1, "Test"` makes no sense. The program throws an "unknown file" exception.

The following is the corrected code, in VB6 format:

**VB6**

```
Private Sub Form_Load()
'**********************
'Sample VB6 program
'   jfd
'   5/5/05
'**********************
'Begin:
'**********************
'Opens the file Example.txt
Open "c:\example.txt" For Output As #1
'**********************
'End
'**********************
End Sub

Private Sub Command1_Click()
'**************************
'Writes the word "Test" to Example.txt
`   and closes the file
'**************************
Write #1, "Test"
Close #1
'**************************
'End
'**************************
End Sub
```

In the next section we will examine other syntactical errors that can lead to bugs when dealing with files. These errors will focus more on syntax in relationship to file location and navigation. Pay careful attention to these examples.

## Other Syntactical/File Navigation Errors

Once again, our example will center on the text file `c:\example.txt`. Here we have two smaller examples in VB.NET and C# that illustrate common syntactical errors. Look at the following blocks of code. They contain language for opening the text file `Example.txt`.

The samples contain bugs that will generate an error when run. As is the case with most of the examples we will be covering, the code samples may compile correctly. This is to further enforce the mentality that one cannot rely solely on the compile when debugging code. The run error is listed after the code blocks.

### VB.NET

```
Private Sub Button1_Click(ByVal sender As
System.Object, ByVal e As System.EventArgs) Handles
Button1.Click
'****************************
'Opens the file Example.txt
'   jfd
'   05/05/2005
'****************************
'Declarations:
'****************************
Dim FileToOpen As System.IO.File
'****************************
'Begin
'****************************
FileToOpen.Open("c:\example.text",IO.FileMode.Open)
'****************************
'End
'****************************
End Sub
```

The following is a block of C# code that performs the same function as the VB.NET code we just examined:

### C#

```
static void Main()
//**********************
```

```
//Opens the file Example.txt
//  jfd
//  05/05/2005
//***********************
{
Application.Run(new Form1());
}

private void button1_Click(object sender,
System.EventArgs e)
{
//*************************
//Declarations:
//*************************
string path = "c:\\example.text";
//*************************
//Begin
//*************************
File.Open (path,System.IO.FileMode.Open);
//*************************
//End
//*************************
}
```

> If you are not familiar with Microsoft C#, note the double backslashes in the path definition `c:\\example.text`. This is not a syntactical error. In fact, had this been written in the more familiar `c:\example.text` format, the compiler would have thrown a compile error. C# requires this extra backslash to correctly process the path string.

As stated, these two code samples will generate errors when run. The fact that they can pass the compiler does not help us here. When run, the following error condition is generated by the code:

### Error

```
An unhandled exception of type
'System.IO.FileNotFoundException' occurred in
mscorlib.dll

Additional information: Could not find file "c:\
example.text".
```

> This error is a dynamic error message. Therefore, depending on the environment that you are running in, this message can change. Keep that in mind as you compile and run your own applications, particularly the section of the error labeled as `Additional information:`. This section of the error code will change depending on the path and name of the file specified in the code you are running.

Take the time now to look back over the code and find the problem. Even if you are not terribly familiar with VB.NET or C# code, you should still be able to spot the error. However, the bug that you are looking for is fairly common and easily overlooked.

In these examples, the VB.NET line `FileToOpen.Open("c:\example.text",IO.FileMode.Open)` and the C# line `string path = "c:\\example.text";` are the offending lines of code. The extension of the file we have been working with is `.txt`, not `.text`. This is a fairly common mistake and one that is easy to overlook. This scenario brings to light the importance of paying attention to the little details. It is not always the large complicated formulas that cause all of the headaches and bugs.

Programmers, and people who work with files on a daily basis, will tend to read the extension .txt as the word *text* in their head. This habit, associating one word for another in one's head, can make finding such a bug just a little bit harder.

The following two samples represent the corrected VB.NET and C# code blocks, respectively. The simple correction to this problem was to replace `c:\example.text` with `c:\example.txt`.

### VB.NET

```
Private Sub Button1_Click(ByVal sender As
System.Object, ByVal e As System.EventArgs) Handles
Button1.Click
```

```
' ****************************
'Opens the file Example.txt
'   jfd
'   05/05/2005
'*****************************
'Declarations:
'*****************************
Dim FileToOpen As System.IO.File
'*****************************
'Begin
'*****************************
FileToOpen.Open("c:\example.txt",IO.FileMode.Open)
'*****************************
'End
'*****************************
End Sub
```

**C#**

```
static void Main()
//************************
//Opens the file Example.txt
//************************
{
Application.Run(new Form1());
}
//*************************
private void button1_Click(object sender,
System.EventArgs e)
{
//*************************
//Declarations:
//*************************
string path = "c:\\example.txt";
//*************************
```

```
//Begin
//************************
File.Open (path,System.IO.FileMode.Open);
//************************
//End
//************************
}
```

With the filename `c:\example.txt` now spelled correctly, you can be content in sending your new bug-free project out into the world. However, there is a situation where, even when running the now corrected code, you may still see the following error:

### Error

```
An unhandled exception of type
'System.IO.FileNotFoundException' occurred in
mscorlib.dll

Additional information: Could not find file "c:\
example.txt".
```

This is the same error that is thrown when the filename is misspelled within the code. How can the code still throw this error if the code has been corrected? There is actually a logical explanation for this. Whether the filename is misspelled or the file does not physically exist, the program cannot see it.

On a basic level, without more code than what we have supplied in the previous examples, the program does not care *why* the file does not exist, only that the requested file cannot be located. Therefore, the same error is thrown when the name of the file has been misspelled and when the file does not physically exist. We will call this a problem containing a common error code.

> A common error code is a single error code that can be thrown under multiple conditions and by multiple bugs.

Combating a common error code when it can be generated by many different bugs can be a very difficult and confusing task. To minimize some of the confusion, the logical conclusion would be to minimize the number of bugs that can be associated with a specific error condition. By eliminating or ruling out one or more of the conditions that could throw a particular error, your job will be easier.

In the last examples we covered, we have two bugs that can generate the same error — the misspelling of a filename and the potential that the file may not physically exist when it is requested. To maximize our debugging efforts, and minimize our risk, we should try to eliminate as many of the conditions that can throw this error as possible.

For our scenario we have two possible conditions that can throw the error. Therefore, we have two possible conditions to eliminate. Although we cannot practically fight against programmers who make spelling errors, we can test that a file exists before the program attempts to open it.

The following two blocks of code are corrected VB.NET and C# samples with the addition of routines that will test for the existence of the requested file. If the requested file, in this case `c:\example.txt`, does not exist, a message box is displayed informing the user. This will help clarify which bug generated the error.

There is also an added benefit to testing for the existence of a file before opening it. When you programmatically attempt to open a file that does not exist, the operating system will throw an error back to the application. Without some form of handling, the error will cause the application to crash. By testing for the existence of a file before you open it, you can catch any errors that may get thrown and keep the program from crashing. Even if the program is not built to function if the requested file is not available, at least it will shut down cleanly.

The following code samples illustrate a very simplistic form of testing for the existence of a file. Notice that the code is placed before any interactions with the files are called.

> Keep in mind that there are many ways to accomplish almost any goal in programming. Although the solution outlined here may not be the sleekest or most optimized, its purpose is to simply illustrate a concept.

> It is always a good idea to combine error handling and other proactive debugging tools in all your coding projects. You should always try to minimize the number of issues that may cause an application to crash.

**VB6**

```
Private Sub Form_Load()
'*********************
'Sample VB6 program
'
'5/5/05 jfd
'*********************
'Begin:
'*********************
'Checks for the existence of and
`   Opens the file Example.txt
If Dir("c:\example.txt", vbNormal) <> "" Then
    Open "c:\example.txt" For Output As #1
Else
    MsgBox "The requested file does not exist."
End If
'*********************
'End
'*********************
End Sub

Private Sub Command1_Click()
'*************************
'Writes the word "Test" to Example.txt
'*************************
Write #1, "Test"
Close #1
'*************************
'End
'*************************
End Sub
```

**VB.NET**

```
Public Class Form1
    Inherits System.Windows.Forms.Form
```

```
    Private Sub Button1_Click(ByVal sender As
System.Object, ByVal e As System.EventArgs) Handles
Button1.Click
'*********************************
'Checks for the existence of and opens
'   the file Example.txt
'
'   jfd
'   05/05/2005
'*********************************
'Declarations:
'*********************************
    Dim FileToOpen As System.IO.File
'*********************************
'Begin
'*********************************
    If FileToOpen.Exists("c:\example.txt") Then
       FileToOpen.Open("c:\example.txt",
IO.FileMode.Open)
    Else
       MsgBox("The requested file does not exist.")
    End If
'***********************************
'End
'***********************************
    End Sub
End Class
```

**C#**

```
static void Main()
//****************************
// Checks for the existence of and opens
//     the file Example.txt
//****************************
{
```

```
    Application.Run(new Form1());
}

private void button1_Click(object sender,
System.EventArgs e)
{
//****************************
//Declarations:
//****************************
string path = "c:\\example.txt";
//****************************
//Begin
//****************************
    if (File.Exists(path))
    {
       File.Open (path,System.IO.FileMode.Open);
    }
    else
    {
       MessageBox.Show ("The requested file does not
exist.");
    }
//****************************
//End
//****************************
}
```

Although not every possible issue dealing with the act of opening a file could be addressed in such a short space, Chapter 9 covered the more common problems. In Chapter 10 we will be looking at some bugs that may come up while reading data from the files once they are open.

# Chapter 10

# Real-World Scenarios: Reading Files

In Scenario 1, we examined the process of opening files. However, now that the files are open, what should you do with them? Do not assume that once you get past opening the file you are in the clear. In fact, just as many problems can occur once the file is successfully opened as can occur during the process of opening the file.

The major problem we will examine related to this scenario is opening a file as the incorrect type. If you have been programming for any length of time, you have no doubt had a need to open and work with a file. In doing so, you may have realized, especially in some older languages, *how* you open the desired file is just as important as the file itself.

## Opening a File as the Incorrect Type

When working with files you must decide how you are going to use the file before you open it. That is, a determination must be made as to the type of the file. You can open a file for `Append`, `Input`, `Output`, or `Random Access`. Each has a unique set of characteristics and a corresponding set of reasons why you would call them.

Before looking at the bugs presented in this section, let us review what each option for file type encompasses.

## Append

When opening a file as the type `Append`, all text added to the file will be appended to the end of the last addition. For example, if you have a file that contains the single text line

```
"No more rhymes now, I mean it."
```

and you add the line

```
"Anybody want a peanut!"
```

the resulting file would look as follows:

```
"No more rhymes now, I mean it."
"Anybody want a peanut!"
```

## Input

Opening a file as the type `Input` means that information from the file will be used as input for the application. Files of the type `Input` cannot be written to. This is important to recognize, as is it easy to get confused. The confusion comes because input is supplied as a parameter to the call that opens the file. Therefore, one could assume that you are marking the file as "Open for input," meaning information could be written to the file. However, this is not the case and files of type `Input` cannot be written to.

## Output

Files open as type `Output` can be written to, but not read from. However, where `Output` and `Append` differ is in the fact that `Output` will rewrite the current contents of the file every time the file is written to. Therefore, if your file contains the line

```
"Then rang the bells both loud and deep..."
```

and you write to it the line

```
"...God is not dead nor doth he sleep."
```

your file will appear as follows:

```
"...God is not dead nor doth he sleep."
```

## Random

A file opened for `Random Access` can be both read from and written to. However, the read and write procedures for `Random Access` files work a bit differently. `Random Access` files function almost like simple databases, in that all of the information needs be placed at — and read from — predetermined intervals. The following could be considered a `Random Access` file, as a new entry starts every 10 characters:

```
123 321 random access files do not contain just
numbers 1234567890
```

As explained in these examples, planning on how a file is going to be used, then opening the file as the correct type, is critical in avoiding bugs. The following samples show how bugs can be generated by opening a file as an incorrect type. Read through the samples and try to spot the bug. Keep in mind that the code can be compiled and run if you want to generate your own bugs.

The following examples are provided in Visual Basic 6 only. Four examples are provided, each structured slightly different from the one before; however, they all throw the same error code. The first example involves opening a file as `Input`; the second, `Random`; the third, `Output`; and the final, `Append`. Again, all of these examples will compile and run. The error code is given at the end of the third example.

Take a few minutes to see if you can spot the bugs.

## VB6

```
Private Sub Form_Load()
'*********************
'Sample VB6 program
'
'5/5/05 jfd
'*********************
'Begin:
'Opens the file Example.txt
'*********************
If Dir("c:\example.txt", vbNormal) <> "" Then
    Open "c:\example.txt" For Input As #1
Else
    MsgBox "The requested file does not exist."
End If
'*********************
'End
'*********************
End Sub
```

```
Private Sub Command1_Click()
'*************************
'Writes the word "Test" to Example.txt
'*************************
Write #1, "Test"
Close #1
'*************************
'End
'*************************
End Sub
```

**VB6**

```
Private Sub Form_Load()
'*********************
'Sample VB6 program
'
'5/5/05 jfd
'*********************
'Begin:
'Opens the file Example.txt
'*********************
If Dir("c:\example.txt", vbNormal) <> "" Then
    Open "c:\example.txt" For Random As #1
Else
    MsgBox "The requested file does not exist."
End If
'*********************
'End
'*********************
End Sub

Private Sub Command1_Click()
'*************************
'Writes the word "Test" to Example.txt
'*************************
```

```
Write #1, "Test", Now
Close #1
'*************************
'End
'*************************
End Sub
```

**VB6**

```
Private Sub Form_Load()
'*********************
'Sample VB6 program
'
'5/5/05 jfd
'*********************
'Begin:
'Opens the file Example.txt
'*********************
If Dir("c:\example.txt", vbNormal) <> "" Then
    Open "c:\example.txt" For Output As #1
Else
    MsgBox "The requested file does not exist."
End If
'*********************
'End
'*********************
End Sub

Private Sub Command1_Click()
'*************************
'Writes the word "Test" to Example.txt
'*************************
'Declarations:
'*************************
Dim inputString As String
'*************************
```

```
'Begin
'**************************
Input #1, inputString
Close #1
'**************************
'End
'**************************
End Sub
```

**VB6**

```
Private Sub Form_Load()
'**********************
'Sample VB6 program
'
'5/5/05 jfd
'**********************
'Begin:
'Opens the file Example.txt
'**********************
If Dir("c:\example.txt", vbNormal) <> "" Then
    Open "c:\example.txt" For Append As #1
Else
    MsgBox "The requested file does not exist."
End If
'**********************
'End
'**********************
End Sub

Private Sub Command1_Click()
'**************************
'Writes the word "Test" to Example.txt
'**************************
Dim appendedInput as String
Input #1, appendedInput
```

```
Close #1
'*************************
'End
'*************************
End Sub
```

The following error condition is thrown from all three of the previous examples:

```
Error:
Run-time error '54':

Bad file mode
```

There is nothing cryptic about this error message. Simply stated, it lets you know that you have tried to work with a file as if it were a type other than the type you opened it as. Let us discuss where the bugs in our examples were by examining the solutions.

In the first example we opened a file as the type `Input`. Looking further through the code you will see that when the user clicks on the form's button, the code then tries to write information to the file. This is an easy mistake to make because of the syntax used in VB6.

When opening the file, the syntax used is

```
Open "c:\example.txt" For Input As #1
```

Reading this line in English it appears that the intention is to open the file for input. Therefore, the natural conclusion would be to write to the file. In fact, what this line says is that you are opening the file and using its contents as input for the application. If you want to work with a file opened as the type `Input`, the correct action would be to read from the file. The corrected example is as follows:

## VB6

```
Private Sub Form_Load()
'*********************
'Sample VB6 program
'
'5/5/05 jfd
'*********************
'Begin:
'Opens the file Example.txt
'*********************
```

```
If Dir("c:\example.txt", vbNormal) <> "" Then
    Open "c:\example.txt" For Input As #1
Else
    MsgBox "The requested file does not exist."
End If
'**********************
'End
'**********************
End Sub

Private Sub Command1_Click()
'**************************
'Writes the word "Test" to Example.txt
'**************************
'Declarations:
'**************************
Dim inputString As String
'**************************
'Begin:
'**************************
Input #1, inputString
Close #1
'**************************
'End
'**************************
End Sub
```

In the second example we dealt with, a file was being opened as type `Random`. By definition, files of type `Random` can be both written to and read from. Logic then dictates that you can use `Write`, `Input`, or any of the other VB6 methods for working with file data. However, as we have found so far, programming is not always logical.

Using `Random Access` files as either input or output requires a couple of steps. Think of `Random Access` files as databases. These files are comprised of an infinite number of records. Each record is nothing more than a predefined number of characters. Therefore, you must define the number of characters in each record. After defining the record size, anything you read from or write to that file must be no more than that number of characters. The following line of code shows how to define a record length of 20 for a `Random Access` file in VB6:

```
Open "c:\example.txt" For Random As 1 Len = 20
```

Now that the file type is defined and the record length is set, we can either read from or write to our file. This is done using `Get` and `Put`. `Get` will get information out of the file and place it in a variable, while `Put` will put information into the file.

Let us now examine the solution example. Looking through the code you will notice a few things. First, we have defined a variable type called rRecord to hold the data being put in the file. This is not a necessary part of the procedure, but it helps if one file record contains more than one piece of information. For example, let us say you have a `Random Access` file that has a record size of 20 characters. You can use those 20 characters to hold two 10-character pieces of information. This is what we have done in the corrected example:

**VB6**

```
'**********************
'Declarations:
'  Types
'**********************
Private Type rRecord
    fName As String * 10
    lName As String * 10
End Type

Private Sub Form_Load()
'**********************
'Sample VB6 program
'
'5/5/05 jfd
'**********************
'**********************
'Begin:
'Opens the file Example.txt
'**********************
If Dir("c:\example.txt", vbNormal) <> "" Then
    Open "c:\example.txt" For Random As 1 Len = 20
```

```
Else
    MsgBox "The requested file does not exist."
End If
'**********************
'End
'**********************
End Sub

Private Sub Command1_Click()
'**************************
'Writes the word "Test" to Example.txt
'**************************
'Declarations:
'**************************
Dim authorInfo As rRecord
authorInfo.fName = "J"
authorInfo.lName = "DiMarzio"
'**************************
'Begin
'**************************

Put #1, 1, authorInfo
Close #1
'**************************
'End
'**************************
End Sub
```

After running the code in this example, the contents of the text file will appear as follows:

```
J DiMarzio
```

This is one 20-character record holding two 10-character fields.

Our third example depicted a file opened as `Output`. Once again, the incorrect operation was used in trying to work with the file. Files opened as type `Output` are used to write information to, not read information from. The bug in our example had the user trying to read data from an `Output` file. The corrected code, shown as follows, writes to the file rather than reading from it:

### VB6

```
Private Sub Form_Load()
'*********************
'Sample VB6 program
'
'5/5/05 jfd
'*********************
'Begin:
'Opens the file Example.txt
'*********************
If Dir("c:\example.txt", vbNormal) <> "" Then
    Open "c:\example.txt" For Output As #1
Else
    MsgBox "The requested file does not exist."
End If
'*********************
'End
'*********************
End Sub

Private Sub Command1_Click()
'*************************
'Writes the word "Test" to Example.txt
'*************************
'Begin
'*************************
Write #1, "Test"
Close #1
'*************************
'End
'*************************
End Sub
```

Finally, our Append example suffered from the same input/output misdirection as the others. When using a file as the type Append, you must write to the file. Keep in mind once again that anything you write to a file of the type Append will be placed on the last line of the file.

This is different from files defined as `Output`, which will overwrite the entire contents of the file every time it is written to.

The corrected code is as follows:

### VB6

```
Private Sub Form_Load()
'*********************
'Sample VB6 program
'
'5/5/05 jfd
'*********************
'Begin:
'Opens the file Example.txt
'*********************
If Dir("c:\example.txt", vbNormal) <> "" Then
    Open "c:\example.txt" For Append As #1
Else
    MsgBox "The requested file does not exist."
End If
'*********************
'End
'*********************
End Sub

Private Sub Command1_Click()
'*************************
'Writes the word "Test" to Example.txt
'*************************
Write #1, "Test", Now
Close #1
'*************************
'End
'*************************
End Sub
```

Visual Basic 6 is not the only programming language susceptible to file-type bugs. Although the syntax may not be nearly as confusing as that of Visual Basic 6, mistakes can be made. The following examples are provided in Visual Basic .NET and C#. The syntax for opening files in each language is quite similar.

Examine the following examples and find the bug in each.

## VB.NET

```
Private Sub Button1_Click(ByVal sender As
System.Object, ByVal e As System.EventArgs) Handles
Button1.Click
'***************************
'Sample VB .NET Program
' jfd
' 10/10/05
'***************************
'Declarations:
'***************************
Dim path As String
'***************************
'Begin
'***************************
path = "c:\example.txt"
If Dir(path) = "example.txt" Then
    Dim file As System.IO.FileStream = New
System.IO.FileStream(path, IO.FileMode.Open,
IO.FileAccess.Read)
    Dim writeToFile As System.IO.StreamWriter = New
System.IO.StreamWriter(file)
    writeToFile.Write("This is a test")
End If
'***************************
'End
'***************************

End Sub
```

## C#

```
static void Main()
//****************************
```

```
// Checks for the existence of and opens
//  the file Example.txt
//*****************************
{

   Application.Run(new Form1());
}

private void button1_Click(object sender,
System.EventArgs e)
{
//*****************************
//Declarations:
//*****************************
string path = "c:\\example.txt";
//*****************************
//Begin
//*****************************
   if (File.Exists(path))
   {
      FileStream file = new FileStream(path,
System.IO.FileMode.Open,System.IO.FileAccess.Read );
      StreamWriter writeToFile = new
StreamWriter(file);
      writeToFile.Write("This is a test.");
   }
   else
   {
      MessageBox.Show ("The requested file does not
exist.");
   }

//*****************************
//End
//*****************************
}
```

These samples compile correctly. When the user executes the code to write to the files, the following error is thrown. This same error is thrown by both examples.

### Error

```
An unhandled exception of type
'System.ArgumentException' occurred in mscorlib.dll

Additional information: Stream was not writable.
```

In both examples, the files are opened as readable streams. This is what throws the error as the code attempts to write to the files. Programming languages are picky about what you try to do with a file after you open it. You need to open a file correctly for the type of operation you want to perform on it.

The corrected code for each example is as follows. We have changed the readable stream into a writable stream. Keep in mind that using a ReadWrite stream would work as well.

### VB.NET

```
Private Sub Button1_Click(ByVal sender As
System.Object, ByVal e As System.EventArgs) Handles
Button1.Click
'***************************
'Sample VB .NET Program
' jfd
' 10/10/05
'***************************
'Declarations:
'***************************
Dim path As String
'***************************
'Begin
'***************************
path = "c:\example.txt"
If Dir(path) = "example.txt" Then
    Dim file As System.IO.FileStream = New
System.IO.FileStream(path, IO.FileMode.Open,
IO.FileAccess.Write)
```

```
    Dim writeToFile As System.IO.StreamWriter = New
System.IO.StreamWriter(file)
    writeToFile.Write("This is a test")
End If
'*****************************
'End
'*****************************

End Sub
```

**C#**

```
static void Main()
//*****************************
// Checks for the existence of and opens
//  the file Example.txt
//*****************************
{

    Application.Run(new Form1());
}

private void button1_Click(object sender,
System.EventArgs e)
{
//*****************************
//Declarations:
//*****************************
string path = "c:\\example.txt";
//*****************************
//Begin
//*****************************
    if (File.Exists(path))
    {
        FileStream file = new FileStream(path,
System.IO.FileMode.Open,System.IO.FileAccess.Write
);
```

```
        StreamWriter writeToFile = new
StreamWriter(file);
        writeToFile.Write("This is a test.");
    }
    else
    {
        MessageBox.Show ("The requested file does not
exist.");
    }

//*****************************
//End
//*****************************
}
```

In the next section we will look at some of the bugs that can come up when you attempt to create a program that requires you to save settings. There are many ways to save settings within an application, and just as many bugs that can be found.

## *Chapter 11*

# Real-World Scenarios: Saving Program Settings

Before the use of Microsoft's .NET platform, most developers chose to save application settings in one of nearly half a dozen places. Application settings could be saved in Random Access files, .ini files, flat files, or, if you were daring enough, the registry. There is nothing inherently wrong with any of these methods. Each offered a legitimate solution to the need of storing application-related settings and information.

With the advent of the .NET programming languages, and the wider acceptance of eXtensible Markup Language (XML) in the business landscape, a new option for saving application settings is available. A common solution is to keep settings in a file known as the App.config. The App.config is an XML-formatted file that is created with your .NET application. Let us examine some of the challenges of working with this file.

### *Reading from the `App.config` Incorrectly*

If you are unfamiliar with the `App.config` file, this section will be of particular interest for you. In Visual Basic .NET or C#, the `App.config` can be added to the work space and edited with the other project files. The structure of the file is nothing more than XML.

When you initially add the `App.config` to your project, it will be an empty "shell." The file will contain only the basic tags used by Microsoft's

.NET platform to understand the structure. The contents of the initial `App.config` file are illustrated below:

```
<?xml version="1.0" encoding="utf-8" ?>
<configuration>
    <appSettings>

    </appSettings>
</configuration>
```

A standard XML header begins the file, followed by two tags. The `<configuration>` tag defines the underlying structure as an `App.config` file. The `<appSettings>` tag holds all of the application key values, which are the settings that you will want to read into your program.

For the examples in this scenario, we will be adding two keys to our `App.config` file. We will then attempt to read these key values into both a Visual Basic .NET and C# application. The keys we will add to the `App.config` are `LogLocation` and `AlertType`, with the values of `"c:\logfiles"` and `"0"`, respectively. The working `App.config` file is as follows:

```
<?xml version="1.0" encoding="utf-8" ?>
<configuration>
    <appSettings>
        <add key="LogLocation" value="c:\logfiles" />
        <add key="AlertType" value="0" />
    </appSettings>
</configuration>
```

With the `App.config` complete, we will attempt to read the two key values from it. Because Visual Basic .NET and C# handle the `App.config` in different ways, we will be exploring two slightly different bugs based on the same concept. The first bug will relate to the type of values we are reading from the file.

Take a look at the Visual Basic .NET code that follows. Although this code compiles correctly, there is a problem with the way it reads values from the `App.config`. Take some time and try to find the bug.

**VB.NET**

```
Private Sub Button1_Click(ByVal sender As
System.Object, ByVal e As System.EventArgs) Handles
Button1.Click
```

```
'****************************
'Reads values in the App.Config
' jfd
' 10/10/05
'****************************
'Declarations:
'****************************
Dim alertType As Integer
Dim logPath As Integer
Dim configSettings As
System.Configuration.AppSettingsReader = New
System.Configuration.AppSettingsReader()
'****************************
'Begin
'****************************
alertType = configSettings.GetValue("AlertType",
GetType(Integer))
logPath = configSettings.GetValue("LogLocation",
GetType(Integer))
'****************************
'End
'****************************
End Sub
```

Although this code sample will compile correctly, as with all of the samples in this chapter, it does throw an error. This time we are in luck. Unlike most of the error codes we have seen so far, the one thrown by this error is fairly descriptive. Let us take a look at the error.

## Error

```
An unhandled exception of type
'System.InvalidOperationException' occurred in
system.dll

Additional information: The value 'c:\logfiles' was
found in the appSettings configuration section for
key 'LogLocation', and this value is not a valid
System.Int32.
```

This is an example of a very well written descriptive error code. Reading it, you can see that our code correctly attempted to retrieve the value `'c:\logfiles'` from the key `'LogLocation'`. However, the core of the error states that the value `'c:\logfiles'` is not an integer. Because we already know that `'c:\logfiles'` is not an integer value, there must be a problem in the code.

Examining the code again, we find that the line that grabs the value `'c:\logfiles'` from `'LogLocation'` is as follows:

```
logPath = configSettings.GetValue("LogLocation",
GetType(Integer))
```

In fact, the code does request that the value be taken as an `Integer` and placed into the variable `logPath`.

A problem like this is easy to correct now, but imagine if this was a program with 30,000 lines of code. In a situation like that, it may be a bit harder to find and correct a problem like this. The reason why this can be so hard to remediate is because we are dealing with a two-part bug. We have already identified the second part of the bug as the following line:

```
logPath = configSettings.GetValue("LogLocation",
GetType(Integer))
```

Correcting just this line may not fix the bug. Somewhere within the code, the variable `logPath` may also be dimensioned as an integer. We must now locate the dimensioning statement for `logPath` and correct it to match the remainder of the code. The following line is the dimensioning statement for `logPath` from our example:

```
Dim logPath As Integer
```

It clearly does create the variable `logPath` as an integer. The full corrected code is as follows:

### VB.NET

```
Private Sub Button1_Click(ByVal sender As
System.Object, ByVal e As System.EventArgs) Handles
Button1.Click
'*****************************
'Reads values in the App.Config
' jfd
' 10/10/05
'*****************************
```

```
'Declarations:
'****************************
Dim alertType As Integer
Dim logPath As String
Dim configSettings As
System.Configuration.AppSettingsReader = New
System.Configuration.AppSettingsReader()
'****************************
'Begin
'****************************
alertType = configSettings.GetValue("AlertType",
GetType(Integer))
logPath = configSettings.GetValue("LogLocation",
GetType(String))
'****************************
'End
'****************************

End Sub
```

In the next example we will look at come C# code that also attempts to obtain the value "c:\logfiles" from the key LogLocation. However, there is a reason why we have this example separated from the previous one. Take a look at the following block of C# code:

**C#**

```
static void Main()
//****************************
// Reads values in the App.config
//****************************
{

    Application.Run(new Form1());
}

private void button1_Click(object sender,
System.EventArgs e)
{
```

```
//******************************
//Declarations:
//******************************
int path;
path =
ConfigurationSettings.AppSettings["LogLocation"];
//******************************
//Begin
//******************************
MessageBox.Show(path);
//******************************
//End
//******************************
}
```

With a keen eye you should have noticed that this code block suffers from the same bug as the previously discussed Visual Basic .NET code. The variable path is defined as an int:

```
int path;
path =
ConfigurationSettings.AppSettings["LogLocation"];
```

Although the bug is the same, the difference between this example and the Visual Basic .NET example is that the C# compiler will throw an error here. This example will not compile. The following error is thrown by the compiler:

```
C: \Visual Studio Projects\BookExampleFileC\
Form1.cs(112): Cannot implicitly convert type
'string' to 'int'
```

To correct this problem, make the following change:

```
string path;
path =
ConfigurationSettings.AppSettings["LogLocation"];
```

This one change will allow the code to compile and execute correctly. The full, corrected code, which will compile correctly, is as follows:

**C#**

```
static void Main()
//******************************
// Checks for the existence of and opens
```

```
//  the file Example.txt
//*****************************
{

    Application.Run(new Form1());
}
private void button1_Click(object sender,
System.EventArgs e)
{
//******************************
//Declarations:
//******************************
string path;
path =
ConfigurationSettings.AppSettings["LogLocation"];
//******************************
//Begin
//******************************
MessageBox.Show(path);
//******************************
//End
//******************************
}
```

This section covered the use of the `App.config` file and some common bugs that can arise when reading values into your application. If you are a user of Microsoft's Visual Studio .NET, the `App.config` file is an important tool that can make quick work of your application setting needs. However, when working with such a file, be sure that you double-check all of your definitions and dimensions.

The next scenario we will discuss involves working with objects. We will look at common bugs that can surface when working with objects. This scenario will be of particular interest to anyone who has recently moved from Visual Studio 6 to the Visual Studio .NET platform.

# Chapter 12

# Real-World Scenarios: Working with Objects

Scenario 4 deals with a fairly broad range of potential bugs: objects. Visual objects such as buttons, text boxes, and combos are some of the most common elements in applications today. It is the use of objects such as these that give an application its personality and makes it user-friendly.

Through this scenario we will cover two examples. The first examines bugs that will arise when objects are not defined correctly. This example will be of particular interest to programmers who either do not have a lot of experience on Visual Studio .NET or recently moved from Visual Studio 6 to Visual Studio .NET. This is because under many circumstances, the context help or the compiler will catch mistakes in the definition of an object. However, many programmers may either not notice the context help or put the incorrect code in a place where the compiler may not throw an error.

The second example we will cover deals with the problem of wanting to access objects from one form or class in another form or class. Applications often require that information from objects in one form be shared, moved, or manipulated by information or objects in a second form or class. Although this may sound like an easy task, there are some complications in performing such a procedure.

## Not Defining the Object Correctly

It is not uncommon to define an object without having a corresponding form object. The first scenario we will examine looks at a syntax bug that can occur with programmers who are rather inexperienced with Visual Studio .NET. If one writes code in haste, or ignores the context help, he or she may make syntax mistakes.

The following Visual Basic .NET example contains a syntax bug that is easy to fall into. Examine the sample and try to find the syntax error.

### VB.NET

```
Private Sub Button1_Click(ByVal sender As
System.Object, ByVal e As System.EventArgs) Handles
Button1.Click
'****************************
'Sample VB .NET Program
' jfd
' 10/10/05
'****************************
'Declarations:
'****************************
Dim sampleObject As TextBox1
Dim boxContents As String
'****************************
'Begin
'****************************
boxContents = sampleObject.Text
'****************************
'End
'****************************

End Sub
```

The preceding sample will not compile correctly. The bug is in the dimensioning statement:

```
Dim sampleObject As TextBox1
```

In most programming languages, when an object is added to a form, the IDE will automatically rename each new instance of the object. This allows the users to continue adding new objects without running into a naming conflict, until the programmer has a chance to give each object a logical name. For example, if you were to add three ComboBoxes to a Visual Basic form, Visual Basic would automatically rename the objects ComboBox1, ComboBox2, and ComboBox3.

The problem that can come from such a convenience is that programmers rarely rename the new objects. Therefore, it becomes second nature to work with objects as TextBox1, ComboBox1, or Label1.

Although the error is somewhat easy to make, the compiler will catch it immediately. The error thrown by the compiler is actually quite straightforward.

### Error

```
C:\BookScenarioFile\Form1.vb(65): Type 'TextBox1' is
not defined.
```

The correction is again quite simple; define the object as a TextBox and not TextBox1, as is shown in the corrected code:

### VB.NET

```
Private Sub Button1_Click(ByVal sender As
System.Object, ByVal e As System.EventArgs) Handles
Button1.Click
'****************************
'Sample VB .NET Program
' jfd
' 10/10/05
'****************************
'Declarations:
'****************************
Dim sampleObject As TextBox
Dim boxContents As String
'****************************
'Begin
'****************************
boxContents = sampleObject.Text
'****************************
'End
'****************************

End Sub
```

The next example is based on the same concept as the previous one. In this case we will create a piece of code that can accept an object as a parameter. Let us look through both Visual Basic .NET and C# samples, which illustrate the same bug.

## VB.NET

```
Private Sub Button1_Click(ByVal sender As
System.Object, ByVal e As System.EventArgs) Handles
Button1.Click
'****************************
'Sample VB .NET Program
' jfd
' 10/10/05
'****************************
'Declarations:
'****************************

'****************************
'Begin
'****************************
StoreData(ListBox1)
'****************************
'End
'****************************
End Sub

Private Sub StoreData(ByVal selectedData As ComboBox)
'****************************
'Sample VB .NET Program
' jfd
' 10/10/05
'****************************
'Declarations:
'****************************
Dim dataCollector As String
'****************************
'Begin
```

```
'***************************
dataCollector = selectedData.SelectedText
'***************************
'End
'***************************
End Sub
```

**C#**

```
static void Main()
//***************************
// Checks for the existence of and opens
//  the file Example.txt
//***************************
{
    Application.Run(new Form1());
}

private void button1_Click(object sender,
System.EventArgs e)
{
//*****************************
//Declarations:
//*****************************

//*****************************
//Begin
//*****************************
StoreData(listBox1);
//*****************************
//End
//*****************************
}

private void StoreData(System.Windows.Forms.ComboBox
selectedData)
{
```

```
//*****************************
//Declarations:
//*****************************
string dataCollector;
//*****************************
//Begin
//*****************************
dataCollector = selectedData.SelectedText;
//*****************************
//End
//*****************************
}
```

The two preceding code samples both illustrate the same bug. In them we see a small application with a secondary subroutine. This subroutine takes one parameter, a `ComboBox`. The main section of the code then calls the subroutine and passes it one object from the form as the parameter. The bug is in the calling of the subroutine. The call does not pass the routine the correct object.

Take the time to look back at the two code samples. Notice that the calls do not pass the correct object. Although, like the first example we looked at, this error will be caught by the compiler, it can be avoided by paying attention to the details.

The error code thrown by the samples is as follows:

### Error

```
C:\BookScenarioFile\Form1.vb(78): Value of type
'System.Windows.Forms.ListBox' cannot be converted
to 'System.Windows.Forms.ComboBox'.
```

Correcting these samples is as easy as passing it the proper object. The corrected samples are as follows:

### VB.NET

```
Private Sub Button1_Click(ByVal sender As
System.Object, ByVal e As System.EventArgs) Handles
Button1.Click
'****************************
'Sample VB .NET Program
' jfd
```

```
' 10/10/05
'****************************
'Declarations:
'****************************

'****************************
'Begin
'****************************
StoreData(ComboBox1)
'****************************
'End
'****************************
End Sub

Private Sub StoreData(ByVal selectedData As ComboBox)
'****************************
'Sample VB .NET Program
' jfd
' 10/10/05
'****************************
'Declarations:
'****************************
Dim dataCollector As String
'****************************
'Begin
'****************************
dataCollector = selectedData.SelectedText
'****************************
'End
'****************************
End Sub
```

**C#**

```
static void Main()
//****************************
// Checks for the existence of and opens
```

```
//  the file Example.txt
//******************************
{

    Application.Run(new Form1());
}

private void button1_Click(object sender,
System.EventArgs e)
{
//******************************
//Declarations:
//******************************

//******************************
//Begin
//******************************
StoreData(comboBox1);
//******************************
//End
//******************************
}
private void StoreData(System.Windows.Forms.ComboBox
selectedData)
{
//******************************
//Declarations:
//******************************
string dataCollector;
//******************************
//Begin
//******************************
dataCollector = selectedData.SelectedText;
//******************************
//End
//******************************
}
```

In the next example of Scenario 4, working with objects, we will look at a more common problem, one that affects programmers on a daily basis — the problem of trying to share objects and object information between forms and classes.

## Not Being Able to See an Object from All Forms

As discussed, it is a common practice to share objects among forms, classes, and modules within an application. With the size, complexity, and robustness of today's applications, it is almost impossible not to share information between forms.

That being said, it is not always as simple as it seems. Take a look at the following samples of Visual Basic .NET and C# code; try to spot the bug.

### VB.NET

```
Private Sub Button1_Click(ByVal sender As
System.Object, ByVal e As System.EventArgs) Handles
Button1.Click
'****************************
'Sample VB .NET Program
' jfd
' 10/10/05
'****************************
'Declarations:
'****************************

'****************************
'Begin
'****************************

'****************************
'End
'****************************
End Sub

Module Sample
    Public Function SetComboBox()
```

```
    '***************************
    'Sample VB .NET Mod. Function
    ' jfd
    ' 10/10/05
    '***************************
    'Declarations:
    '***************************

    '***************************
    'Begin
    '***************************
    Form1.ComboBox1.Text = "Hello World!"
    '***************************
    'End
    '***************************
  End Function
End Module
```

**C#**

```
static void Main()
//*****************************
// Sample C# program
//  jfd
//  10/10/05
//*****************************
{

    Application.Run(new Form1());
}

private void button1_Click(object sender,
System.EventArgs e)
{
//*****************************
//Declarations:
//*****************************
```

```
//*****************************
//Begin
//*****************************

//*****************************
//End
//*****************************
}

public Class1()
{
    //*****************************
    //Declarations:
    //*****************************

    //*****************************
    //Begin
    //*****************************
    Form1.comboBox1.Text = "Hello World!";
    //*****************************
    //End
    //*****************************
}
```

These samples both contain a bug. The line of code that contains the bug and throws the error should not be that hard to spot; it is one of the only lines of user-written code in the samples. The easiest way to spot this one is to run the code through the compiler. This is one bug that will not pass the compiler.

The error thrown by the compiler is as follows:

### Error

```
C:\ BookExampleFile\Sample.vb(3): Reference to a non-
shared member requires an object reference.
```

This may seem like one of the more cryptic errors we have seen come from the compiler. What it is saying is that it recognizes that we are trying to get information out of an object that is not on the same form; however, it does not recognize *how* we are trying to do it.

The key to correcting this is to properly address the form that contains the object we are trying to access. A new object must be created as the type of the form containing the object to be shared. That is, if the object being shared is on a form with the standard IDE given the name of Form1, then the new object must be dimensioned or defined as a type `Form1`.

The corrected code is as follows. Take a look through the code and examine where the changes have been made. Note how the form has been used as an object type. You will no doubt see this type of bug again in your day-to-day programming.

### VB.NET

```
Private Sub Button1_Click(ByVal sender As
System.Object, ByVal e As System.EventArgs) Handles
Button1.Click
'****************************
'Sample VB .NET Program
' jfd
' 10/10/05
'****************************
'Declarations:
'****************************

'****************************
'Begin
'****************************

'****************************
'End
'****************************
End Sub
Module Sample
    Public Function SetComboBox()
        '****************************
        'Sample VB .NET Mod. Function
        ' jfd
        ' 10/10/05
        '****************************
        'Declarations:
```

```
        '***************************
        Dim MainForm As New Form1()
        '***************************
        'Begin
        '***************************
        MainForm.ComboBox1.Text = "Hello World!"
        '***************************
        'End
        '***************************
    End Function
End Module
```

**C#**

```
static void Main()
//****************************
// Sample C# program
//jfd
//10/10/05
//****************************
{

    Application.Run(new Form1());
}

private void button1_Click(object sender,
System.EventArgs e)
    {
//*****************************
//Declarations:
//*****************************

//*****************************
//Begin
//*****************************

//*****************************
//End
```

```
//******************************
}

public Class1()
{
    //******************************
    //Declarations:
    //******************************
    Form1 formMain = new Form1();
    //******************************
    //Begin
    //******************************
    formMain.comboBox1.Text = "Hello World!";
    //******************************
    //End
    //******************************
}
```

In this scenario we looked at common bugs that can come from working with objects. Although there are many object-related bugs that you will encounter in your day-to-day programming, this scenario should have offered you a good base of knowledge on which you can build a better understanding of object debugging.

Scenario 5 will examine the somewhat destructive bugs that can come from working with the registry.

# Chapter 13

# Real-World Scenarios: Editing the Registry

> *Warning*: If you have been following along with the examples in this book by executing the code in your own compiler, you will want to think twice for this chapter. The code contained in this scenario deals with the computer's registry. Making changes to the registry can cause irreparable damage to your PC and may even render it useless.

In this scenario we will examine some of the bugs that can come from working with the system's registry. It is not a completely uncommon practice to write to and read from the registry of a PC. The registry is, at its most basic level, a composite of application settings. Therefore, it is a great place to deposit and retrieve any information you may need when working with your application.

One of the reasons why the registry is still a somewhat taboo subject is due to the reputation the registry has for wreaking havoc on computers. This is not entirely an unfounded reputation. Once you have access to the registry, you have access to everything in the registry; this includes the operating system's key settings, and those of any other software on the machine. Altering or manipulating any of these settings could cause the system to react unexpectedly or cease working entirely.

With a little training, some good quality assurance techniques, and a list of best practices to follow, the taboo nature of the registry should be a nonissue. Microsoft has been using the registry for over 10 years now, and plenty of developers have overcome their fear of working with the collection of settings. There is, however, another reason why some less experienced developers tend to be shy around the system registry: the misconception that doing so requires complicated application programming interface (API) calls. Depending on what you are doing in the registry, and what language you are working in, you may need to make API calls to accomplish certain tasks. However, there are a couple of predesigned functions that can be used to gather basic information from — and send information to — the registry.

These functions are `SaveSetting` and `GetSetting`. Let us examine what you should look out for when attempting to edit the registry using `SaveSetting` and `GetSetting`.

## Using `SaveSetting` and `GetSetting`

The Visual Basic 6 and Visual Basic .NET products offer a set of predefined functions called `SaveSetting` and `GetSetting`. As the names suggest, these functions write information to and read information from the registry. Using one simple function call is admittedly easier than going through the trouble of defining a few API registry functions to achieve the same set of results, especially if you are not experienced or comfortable making such calls.

`SaveSetting` and `GetSetting` will automatically work with data from the `"HKEY_CURRENT_USER\Software\VB and VBA Program Settings\<application name>"` registry key. In one respect this limits the amount of damage that the functions can do if misused. The functions will only see one section of the registry and are not able to reach many of the operating system keys. On the other hand, it also reduces their usefulness. Some programmers need to interact with settings unrelated to their application. For those situations, API calls may be best. However, if you are solely looking to work with settings related to the application you are building, `SaveSetting` and `GetSetting` should do the trick.

Take a look at the following blocks of sample code. They are both very simple applications that write the value `7` to the `Hello World` entry of the `"HKEY_CURRENT_USER\Software\VB and VBA Program Settings\Test\Sample Data"` key. Examine the samples and try to spot the bug.

### VB6

```
Private Sub Form_Load()
'**********************
'Sample VB6 Registry program
'
'5/5/05 jfd
'**********************
'Declarations:
'****************************

'****************************
'Begin:
'Opens the file Example.txt
'**********************

SaveSetting "Test", "Sample Data", "Hello World", "7"

'**********************
'End
'**********************
End Sub
```

### VB.NET

```
Private Sub Button1_Click(ByVal sender As
System.Object, ByVal e As System.EventArgs) Handles
Button1.Click
'****************************
'Sample VB .NET Registry Program
' jfd
' 10/10/05
'****************************
'Declarations:
'****************************

'****************************
'Begin
'****************************
```

```
SaveSetting("Test", "Sample Data", "Hello World", 1)

'****************************
'End
'****************************

End Sub
```

This set of examples is almost the equivalent of a trick question. The previous blocks of code do not throw any errors. However, this is not necessarily the sign of something good or bad. In fact, the reason why this function does not throw an error is that it serves two purposes.

Whether you are writing to an existing registry key or creating a new one for the first time, you would use the same `SaveSetting` function. That is, if you wanted to write data to the \Software Data\My Application key, you could use the following line of code.

```
SaveSetting("Test", "Sample Data", "Hello World", 1)
```

The problem here is that if you make a mistake, either in your code or in the use of your application after, you will not receive an error. Therefore, you could write to a completely incorrect registry key, solely because of a mistyped letter, and not realize it.

Behind the function `SaveSetting` is the API function call `RegCreateKey`. The call for `RegCreateKey` — illustrated as follows — will both create new keys and interact with existing ones. Therefore, there is no way for `RegCreateKey` or `SaveSetting` to know that you want to access an existing key as opposed to creating a new one.

```
Public Declare Function RegCreateKey Lib
"advapi32.dll" Alias "RegCreateKeyA" (ByVal Hkey As
Long, ByVal lpSubKey As String, phkResult As Long)
As Long
```

The best way to avoid an unexpected mishap when using `SaveSetting` is to test for the existence of the key you want to work with. This can be accomplished using the similar function `GetSetting`. By taking advantage of `GetSetting`, you can check that a key exists before you attempt to write to it.

The corrected code is as follows. In the following two examples we pass `GetSetting` the key we want to edit before we call `SaveSetting`. Take some time to look over this code and familiarize yourself with it. There is definitely room for improvement, but this is a big start. If you feel confident enough to copy this code into an IDE compile run it, try to create a notifier that lets you know when the code skipped a registry entry.

### VB6

```
Private Sub Form_Load()
'*********************
'Sample VB6 Registry program
'
'5/5/05 jfd
'*********************
'*********************
'Begin:
'Opens the file Example.txt
'*********************
If (GetSetting("Test", "Sample Data", "Hello World"))
Then
SaveSetting "Test", "Sample Data", "Hello World", "1"
End If
'*********************
'End
'*********************
End Sub
```

### VB.NET

```
Private Sub Button1_Click(ByVal sender As
System.Object, ByVal e As System.EventArgs) Handles
Button1.Click
'***************************
'Sample VB .NET Registry Program
' jfd
' 10/10/05
'***************************
'Declarations:
'***************************
'***************************
'Begin
'***************************
```

```
If (GetSetting("Test", "Sample Data", "Hello World"))
Then
SaveSetting("Test", "Sample Data", "Hello World", 1)
End If
'****************************
'End
'****************************

End Sub
```

In this short scenario we examined writing data to and reading data from the system registry using `SaveSetting` and `GetSetting`. These are two very useful functions that may work best when working together. If you are working with the registry and want to avoid the potential of making a disastrous mistake, try using `SaveSetting` and `GetSetting`.

In the next scenario we will work with producing custom code for the Windows terminate button. Writing code that is executed when a window is closed can be complicated if it is not something that you are used to doing.

# Chapter 14

# Real-World Scenarios: Window's Termination Functionality

There are as many different applications in the world as there are application developers. Each of these applications performs different functions; many perform multiple functions. Applications can open files, work with databases, adjust registry settings, and call remote procedures. With all of this activity, it is important to make sure your application closes as well as it opens. To ensure an application closes gracefully, many developers modify the code that terminates the application window.

I generally consider programs that do not modify, to some extent, the Window's termination code, to have a bug. The reason for this is that all applications should at least confirm your intent to exit. That is, if you have selected to close an application, especially if there is open live data in the application's work space, you should always prompt the user to confirm he or she wants to exit.

In many circumstances you should also prompt users to save their live data. The samples that follow demonstrate this. Take a look at these examples. The examples are flawed in that there is coding behind a form button, which we can assume for this scenario is an exit button. This code asks the user if he or she wants to exit and save his or her work.

The examples are flawed and should be considered to contain a bug, because the coder neglected to add the same code to the windows terminate button.

## VB6

```
Private Sub Form_Load()
'*********************
'Sample VB6 Program
'   prompts before exit
'5/5/05 jfd
'*********************
'*********************
'Begin:
'*********************

'*********************
'End
'*********************
End Sub

Private Sub Command1_Click()
'*************************
'prompts user before closing
'*************************
'Declarations:
'*************************
Dim openData As Boolean
'*************************
'Begin
'*************************
'   for this example we will set openData to true
'   to indicate that there is live data in the app
'*************************
openData = True

Select Case MsgBox("Are you sure you want to exit?",
vbYesNoCancel)
```

```
Case vbYes
    If (openData) Then
        If (MsgBox("Should I save your data?",
vbYesNo)) = vbYes Then
            End
        End If
    End If
Case vbNo

Case vbCancel

End Select

'*************************
'End
'*************************
End Sub
```

**VB.NET**

```
Private Sub Button1_Click(ByVal sender As
System.Object, ByVal e As System.EventArgs) Handles
Button1.Click
'***************************
'Sample VB .NET Program
'   jfd
'   10/10/05
'***************************
'Declarations:
'***************************
Dim openData As Boolean
'***************************
'Begin
'***************************
openData = True

Select Case MsgBox("Are you sure you want to exit?",
vbYesNoCancel)
```

```
Case vbYes
    If (openData) Then
       If (MsgBox("Should I save your data?",
vbYesNo)) = vbYes Then 'saves data
          Me.Close()
       End If
          Me.Close()
       End If
Case vbNo

Case vbCancel

End Select

'***************************
'End
'***************************

End Sub
```

**C#**

```
static void Main()
//*****************************
// Prompts user before
//     closing the application
// jfd
// 10/10/05
//*****************************
{

Application.Run(new Form1());
}

private void button1_Click(object sender,
System.EventArgs e)
{
//******************************
//Declarations:
```

```
//******************************
bool openData = true;
//******************************
//Begin
//******************************
switch (MessageBox.Show("Are you sure you want to
exit?","Exit Application",MessageBoxButtons.
YesNoCancel) )
    {
        case DialogResult.Yes:
            this.Close();
            break;
        case DialogResult.No:
            break;
        case DialogResult.Cancel:
            break;
        default:
            break;
    }
//******************************
//End
//******************************
}
```

To truly debug this small code and prohibit the user from potentially corrupting data by clicking on the windows terminate button, you must override the code behind this button. In VB.NET the windows terminate button code is fairly easy to locate and is illustrated as follows. You must add functionality to the `OnClosing` subroutine.

### VB.NET

```
Protected Overrides Sub OnClosing(ByVal e As
System.ComponentModel.CancelEventArgs)
'***************************
'Sample VB .NET Program
'   jfd
'   10/10/05
```

```
'***************************
'Declarations:
'***************************

'***************************
'Begin
'***************************

'***************************
'End
'***************************
End Sub
```

The equivalent of the `onClosing` code in Visual Basic 6 is the `Form_Terminate` subroutine. The corrected examples follow. They depict the code that prompts the user for a confirmation in the correct section of code.

## VB6

```
Private Sub Form_Terminate()
'**************************
'Writes the word "Test" to Example.txt
'**************************
'Declarations:
'**************************
Dim openData As Boolean
'**************************
'Begin
'**************************
'   for this example we will set openData to true
'   to indicate that there is live data in the app
'**************************
openData = True

Select Case MsgBox("Are you sure you want to exit?",
vbYesNoCancel)
Case vbYes
    If (openData) Then
```

```
        If (MsgBox("Do you want to save your data?",
vbYesNo)) = vbYes Then Unload (Me)
        End If
    End If
Case vbNo

Case vbCancel

End Select

'*************************

'End
'*************************

End Sub
```

## VB.NET

```
Private Sub Button1_Click(ByVal sender As
System.Object, ByVal e As System.EventArgs) Handles
Button1.Click
'***************************
'Sample VB .NET Program
'   jfd
'   10/10/05
'***************************
'Declarations:
'***************************
Dim openData As Boolean
'***************************
'Begin
'***************************
openData = True

Select Case MsgBox("Are you sure you want to exit?",
vbYesNoCancel)
    Case vbYes
        If (openData) Then
            If (MsgBox("Should I save your data?",
vbYesNo)) = vbYes Then Unload(Me)
```

```
            End If
         End If
      Case vbNo

      Case vbCancel

End Select

'****************************
'End
'****************************

End Sub

Protected Overrides Sub OnClosing(ByVal e As
System.ComponentModel.CancelEventArgs)
'****************************
'Sample VB .NET Program
'   jfd
'   10/10/05
'****************************
'Declarations:
'****************************
Dim openData As Boolean
'****************************
'Begin
'****************************
openData = True
Select Case MsgBox("Are you sure you want to exit?",
vbYesNoCancel)
    Case vbYes
       If (openData) Then
          If (MsgBox("Should I save your data?",
vbYesNo)) = vbYes Then e.Cancel = False
       End If
    End If
    Case vbNo
       e.Cancel = True
```

```
    Case vbCancel
       e.Cancel = True
End Select

'****************************
'End
'****************************
End Sub
```

**C#**

```
static void Main()
//****************************
// Confirms Exit
//  jfd
//  10/10/05
//****************************
{

    Application.Run(new Form1());
}
private void Form1_Closing(object sender,
system.ComponentModel.CancelEventArgs e)
{
    //****************************
    //Declarations:
    //****************************
    bool openData = true;
    //****************************
    //Begin
    //****************************
    switch (MessageBox.Show("Are you sure you want
to exit?","Exit Application",MessageBoxButtons.
YesNoCancel) )
    {
       case DialogResult.Yes:
          if (openData)
```

```
        {
            switch (MessageBox.Show("Should I save
your settings?","Save Settings",MessageBoxButtons.
YesNo) )
            {
                        case DialogResult.Yes:
                            e.Cancel=true;
                            break;
                        case DialogResult.No:
                            e.Cancel = false;
                            break;
                        default:
                            break;
            }
        }
        break;
    case DialogResult.No:
        e.Cancel=false;
        break;
    case DialogResult.Cancel:
        e.Cancel=false;
        break;
    default:
        break;
  }
  //******************************
  //End
  //******************************

}
private void button1_Click(object sender,
System.EventArgs e)
{
//******************************
//Declarations:
//******************************
```

```
bool openData = true;
//******************************
//Begin
//******************************

    switch (MessageBox.Show("Are you sure you want
to exit?","Exit Application",MessageBoxButtons.
YesNoCancel) )
    {
       case DialogResult.Yes:
          if (openData)
          {
             switch (MessageBox.Show("Should I save
your settings?","Save Settings",MessageBoxButtons.
YesNo) )
             {
                    case DialogResult.Yes:
                        e.Cancel=true;
                        break;
                    case DialogResult.No:
                        e.Cancel = false;
                        break;
                    default:
                        break;
             }
          }
          break;
       case DialogResult.No:
          e.Cancel=false;
          break;
       case DialogResult.Cancel:
          e.Cancel=false;
          break;
       default:
          break;
    }
```

```
//*****************************
//End
//*****************************
}
```

Most business applications deal, in one way or another, with databases. There are an infinite number of books on the market that deal with applications and their interactions with databases. This alone should be a testament to how treacherous the road to databases can be. In Scenario 7 we will discuss bugs that can be present while you attempt to open a database.

# Chapter 15

# Real-World Scenarios: Opening a Database

> For consistency, all of the examples in this scenario will assume that the databases you are connecting to are Microsoft Structure Query Language (SQL) databases. Even if you work with databases other than SQL, such as Oracle, much of the syntax — and the bugs — will remain the same. Therefore, read through the examples and try to apply the concepts to your own code.

It stands to reason that before you can work with the information contained within a database, you must first open the target database. The next few scenarios we cover in this book will be devoted to the bugs that are present in applications dealing with databases. This particular scenario will cover opening databases.

If you have never worked with databases, or are slightly unfamiliar with the process, we will cover the steps required to open a database. First, the target database must be located. This means that the databases you are attempting to connect to must be physically available. Because this process is similar enough to testing for the existence of files, we will not cover it here.

The second step, once the database is located, is to attempt to open the database. This is accomplished by passing the database credentials. Credentials are the keys to opening a database. The credentials include data location, username, and password. The three most common ways to pass credentials to a database are a simple string, a .udl file, and an Open Database Connectivity (ODBC) connection. Although each method gets the needed information into the application and opens the database, each also has a unique set of bugs that can bring the whole thing down.

Let us take a look at the first sample in our scenario, passing credentials as a simple string.

## Passing String Credentials

In the first example for this scenario we will be passing string credentials to a database application. There is a lot of information that can be passed to the database connector, and this can create more than a bug or two. Take a look at the following code samples and try to spot the bugs.

### VB6

```
Private Sub Command1_Click()
'*************************
'Defines and opens a local
' SQL database
'   jfd
'   10/10/05
'*************************
'Declarations:
'*************************
Dim cn As ADODB.Connection
'*************************
'Begin
'*************************
'   for this example we will set openData to true
'   to indicate that there is live data in the app
'*************************
Set cn = New ADODB.Connection
```

```
cn.ConnectionString = "Provider=sqloledb;Initial
Catalog=pubs;User Id=sa;Password="";"
cn.Open
cn.Close
'************************
'End
'************************
End Sub
```

## VB.NET

```
Private Sub Button1_Click(ByVal sender As
System.Object, ByVal e As System.EventArgs) Handles
Button1.Click
'***************************
'Sample VB .NET Program
'   jfd
'   10/10/05
'***************************
'Declarations:
'***************************
Dim cn As New
SqlClient.SqlConnection("database=pubs;uid=sa;
pwd="";")
'***************************
'Begin
'***************************
cn.Open()
cn.Close()
'***************************
'End
'***************************

End Sub
```

The preceding code samples will pass through the compiler correctly. This can leave you with a false sense of security, given that there is a bug in each sample.

Each application in our set of samples contains a button. When the user clicks on this button, the string credentials are passed to the database connector and the database is opened. However, when our samples are run and the user clicks on the button, he or she receives the following respective errors:

## VB6

```
Run-time error '3001':
Arguments are of the wrong type, are out of acceptable
range, or are in conflict with one another.
```

The error message thrown in from the VB.NET application is slightly different. Although the error is being thrown for the same condition, the .NET error message is slightly more descriptive. Let us take a look at the second error message.

## VB.NET

```
An unhandled exception of type
'System.ArgumentException' occurred in
system.data.dll

Additional information: Matching end delimiter " not
found in connection option value.
```

The problem is that each of the previous code blocks for this example suffer from the same bug: the password field is not defined. Before we can connect to the database, we must define a password. If you are familiar with Microsoft SQL Server, you may realize that the default password for the user `sa` is in fact blank. In looking at the connection string being passed, the user does attempt to define a blank password. However, it is passed incorrectly.

For instances where you need to pass a blank password, you can leave the password parameter out of the string or leave the field blank. No matter which option you choose, you should not use a blank string of "".

For example, you can use a blank password:

```
"Provider=sqloledb;Initial Catalog=pubs;User
Id=sa;Password=;"
"database=pubs;uid=sa;pwd=;"
```

Or you can leave the password parameter out:

```
"database=pubs;uid=sa;"
"Provider=sqloledb;Initial Catalog=pubs;User Id=sa;"
```

The corrected code is as follows. In the correction we have assumed that the username should have been sa and no password. Take time to look over the corrected code and compare it to the bug code.

## VB6

```
Private Sub Command1_Click()
'**************************
'Defines and opens a local
' SQL database
'   jfd
'   10/10/05
'**************************
'Declarations:
'**************************
Dim cn As ADODB.Connection
'**************************
'Begin
'**************************
'   for this example we will set openData to true
'   to indicate that there is live data in the app
'**************************
Set cn = New ADODB.Connection
cn.ConnectionString = "Provider=sqloledb;Initial
Catalog=pubs;User Id=sa;Password=;"
'**************************
'the user can also use the
'   following connection string
'   to pass a blank password
'
'cn.ConnectionString = "Provider=sqloledb;Initial
Catalog=pubs;User 'Id=sa;"
'
'**************************
cn.Open
cn.Close
'**************************
```

```
'End
'**************************
End Sub
```

**VB.NET**

```
Private Sub Button1_Click(ByVal sender As
System.Object, ByVal e As System.EventArgs) Handles
Button1.Click
'****************************
'Sample VB .NET Program
'   jfd
'   10/10/05
'****************************
'Declarations:
'****************************
Dim cn As New
SqlClient.SqlConnection("database=pubs;uid=sa;pwd=;")
'**************************
'the user can also use the
'   following connection string
'   to pass a blank password
'
'Dim cn As New
SqlClient.SqlConnection("database=pubs;uid=sa;")
'
'**************************
'****************************
'Begin
'****************************
cn.Open()
cn.Close()
'****************************
'End
'****************************

End Sub
```

C# handles the problem of a "" string a bit differently. In the following code sample we will attempt to define a connection string with a blank password using "" to represent the password. The key to understanding why C# handles this error differently than VB6 and VB.NET is to understand how the C# language is structured. Take a look at the following code:

## C#

```
private void button1_Click(object sender,
System.EventArgs e)
{
//*****************************
//Sample C# database code
//  jfd
//  10/10/05
//*****************************
//Declarations:
//*****************************
System.Data.SqlClient.SqlConnection cn = new
System.Data.SqlClient.SqlConnection("database=pubs;
uid=sa;pwd="";");
//*****************************
//Begin
//*****************************
    cn.Open();
    cn.Close();
//*****************************
//End
//*****************************
}
```

When this code is run through the compiler, an error is thrown. Because C# uses the semicolon as its line delimiter, and the quotation mark is the end of a string, the compiler will not understand the final six characters of the declaration line:

```
System.Data.SqlClient.SqlConnection cn = new
System.Data.SqlClient.SqlConnection("database=pubs;
uid=sa;pwd="";");
```

The compiler thinks that the string should end at the first quotation mark after the pwd=. Therefore, there should be a semicolon to follow it. When a semicolon or a closing parenthesis does not follow what C# believes is the end of the string, the compiler will not understand the code. Therefore, the compiler assumes it is incorrect.

The obvious correction is to remove the double quotations, which signify the blank password. The corrected C# code should appear as follows:

### C#

```
private void button1_Click(object sender,
System.EventArgs e)
{
//******************************
//Sample C# database code
//  jfd
//  10/10/05
//******************************
//Declarations:
//******************************
System.Data.SqlClient.SqlConnection cn = new
System.Data.SqlClient.SqlConnection("database=pubs;
uid=sa;pwd=;");
//******************************
//Begin
//******************************
    cn.Open();
    cn.Close();
//******************************
//End
//******************************
}
```

Now that we have cleared up that little bug, let us take a look at another one. The code that follows should look very similar to the corrected code above. So what can the problem be? Take a look through the following samples and try to locate the bug. Again, keep in mind that we are working with connection strings.

## VB6

```
Private Sub Command1_Click()
'*************************
'Defines and opens a local
' SQL database
'   jfd
'   10/10/05
'*************************
'Declarations:
'*************************
Dim cn As ADODB.Connection
'*************************
'Begin
'*************************
'   for this example we will set openData to true
'   to indicate that there is live data in the app
'*************************
Set cn = New ADODB.Connection
cn.ConnectionString =
"Provider=sqloledb;Server=MyServer;Initial
Catalog=pubs;User Id=sa;Password=;"
cn.Open
cn.Close
'*************************
'End
'*************************
End Sub
```

## VB.NET

```
Private Sub Button1_Click(ByVal sender As
System.Object, ByVal e As System.EventArgs) Handles
Button1.Click
'***************************
'Sample VB .NET Program
'   jfd
'   10/10/05
```

```
'****************************
'Declarations:
'****************************
Dim cn As New
SqlClient.SqlConnection("server=(MyServer);database=
pubs;uid=sa;pwd=;")
'****************************
'Begin
'****************************
    cn.Open()
    cn.Close()
'****************************
'End
'****************************

End Sub
```

**C#**

```
private void button1_Click(object sender,
System.EventArgs e)
{
//****************************
//Declarations:
//****************************
System.Data.SqlClient.SqlConnection cn = new
System.Data.SqlClient.SqlConnection("server=
Myserver);database=pubs;uid=sa;pwd=;");
//****************************
//Begin
//****************************
    cn.Open();
    cn.Close();
//****************************
//End
//****************************
}
```

Although this is not a glaring syntax-related bug, you should have noticed the issue. At this point in the book, it should be almost second nature for you to be looking at your code through the eyes of a debugger. If you are still unclear as to what the bug is, the errors that are thrown are as follows:

### VB6

```
Run-time error '-2147467259 (80004005)':
[DBNETLIB][ConnectionOpen (Connect()).]SQL Server
does not exist or access denied.
```

In this case, the VB6 error message is actually more descriptive than that of VB.NET and C#. You can tell right from looking at the VB6 error what the problem is. However, the VB.NET and C# message may leave you guessing. Take a look at the VB.NET and C# message for the same error:

### VB.NET and C#

```
An unhandled exception of type
'System.Data.SqlClient.SqlException' occurred in
system.data.dll

Additional information: System error.
```

Keep in mind that it is recommended that you use a `Try...Catch` statement in executing a .NET function like this. The .NET error message is actually telling us that we are not handling the actual error that is being thrown. Therefore, to see the correct error message — a .NET oxymoron — we need to handle this exception in a `Try...Catch` statement. From the `Try...Catch` statement we can throw the actual error that is being generated.

The following code represents the VB.NET and C# samples:

### VB.NET

```
Private Sub Button1_Click(ByVal sender As
System.Object, ByVal e As System.EventArgs) Handles
Button1.Click
'*****************************
'Sample VB .NET Program
'   jfd
```

```
'   10/10/05
'*****************************
'Declarations:
'*****************************
Dim cn As New
SqlClient.SqlConnection("server=(MyServer);database=
pubs;uid=sa;pwd=;")
'*****************************
'Begin
'*****************************
Try
    cn.Open()
Catch sqlExcpt As System.Data.SqlClient.SqlException
    Debug.Write(sqlExcpt.ToString)
End Try
cn.Close()
'*****************************
'End
'*****************************

End Sub
```

**C#**

```
private void button1_Click(object sender,
System.EventArgs e)
{
//*****************************
//Declarations:
//*****************************
System.Data.SqlClient.SqlConnection cn = new
System.Data.SqlClient.SqlConnection("server=(Myserve
r);database=pubs;uid=sa;pwd=;");
//*****************************
//Begin
//*****************************
    try
```

```
    {
       cn.Open();

    }
    catch (System.Data.SqlClient.SqlException
sqlExcpt)
    {
       Console.Write (sqlExcpt.ToString() );
    }
cn.Close();
//*****************************
//End
//*****************************
}
```

With the examples now using `Try...Catch` to handle the `SqlException`, we can see the error that is really being thrown by the code. The error codes are as follows:

### VB.NET

```
System.Data.SqlClient.SqlException: SQL Server does
not exist or access denied.
    at System.Data.SqlClient.SqlConnection.Open()
    at BookExampleFile.Form1.Button1_Click(Object
sender, EventArgs e) in C:\Documents and Settings\
Visual Studio Projects\ BookExampleFile\Form1.vb:line
108
```

### C#

```
System.Data.SqlClient.SqlException: SQL Server does
not exist or access denied.
    at System.Data.SqlClient.SqlConnection.Open()
    at BookExampleFileC.Form1.button1_Click(Object
sender, EventArgs e) in c:\documents and settings\
my documents\visual studio projects\
bookexamplefilec\form1.cs:line 158The program '[3396]
BookExampleFileC.exe' has exited with code 0 (0x0).
```

The database server in these examples does not exist. As discussed many times throughout this book, you should always be looking at places in your code where you should be testing for the existence of objects before interacting with them. Convention leads us to believe that if something can be deleted, moved, or renamed, it will be, but this should not make your application crash and burn. By testing for these objects first, you can prevent what could be a serious catastrophe.

> It is much better to notify a user that an object does not exist, or that for any reason your application simply cannot interact with the object, than to allow your program to crash. Crashing risks the loss of data and can affect other systems on the device that is running the code.

Let us add a quick, rough piece of code to our samples to check for the existence of a database before we try to interact with it. The following code samples are the corrected applications. The code now confirms the database exists before writing to it.

> Keep in mind that there are many different ways to perform different functions. Although one possible way to approach a solution is provided, it may not be the best or the best for your given situation.

In the following examples we use SQLDMO (Distributed Management Objective) to obtain a list of the current SQL server references. The SQLDMO information is set to a string array. We then cycle through that array looking for a match on the SQL server we are specifying.

To use SQLDMO, you have to add a Microsoft SQLDMO Object Library reference to your project. If you are using Visual Studio .NET, the reference is a COM object.

**VB6**

```
Private Sub Command1_Click()
'**************************
'Defines and opens a local
' SQL database
```

```
'   jfd
'   10/10/05
'**************************
'Declarations:
'**************************
Dim cn As ADODB.Connection
'**************************
'Begin
'**************************

Dim sqlApp As New SQLDMO.Application
Dim NameList As SQLDMO.NameList
Dim index As Long

Set NameList = sqlApp.ListAvailableSQLServers
For index = 0 To NameList.Count
    If NameList.Item(index) = "MyServer" Then
       Set cn = New ADODB.Connection
       cn.ConnectionString = "Provider=sqloledb;
Server=MyServer;Initial Catalog=pubs;User Id=sa;
Password=;"
       cn.Open
       cn.Close
    End If
Next

Exit Sub

'**************************
'End
'**************************
End Sub
```

## VB.NET

```
Private Sub Button1_Click(ByVal sender As
System.Object, ByVal e As System.EventArgs) Handles
Button1.Click
```

```
'*****************************
'Sample VB .NET Program
'   jfd
'   10/10/05
'*****************************
'Declarations:
'*****************************
Dim sqlApp As SQLDMO.Application
Dim namelist As SQLDMO.NameList
Dim i As Integer
'*****************************
'Begin
'*****************************
sqlApp = New SQLDMO.Application()
namelist = sqlApp.ListAvailableSQLServers()
For i = 1 To namelist.Count
    If namelist.Item(i) = "MyServer" Then
       Dim cn As New
SqlClient.SqlConnection("server=(MyServer);database=
pubs;uid=sa;pwd=;")
       cn.Open()
       cn.Close()
    End If
 Next i

 '*****************************
 'End
 '*****************************

End Sub
```

**C#**

```
private void button1_Click(object sender,
System.EventArgs e)
{
```

```
//******************************
//Declarations:
//******************************
//******************************
//Begin
//******************************
SQLDMO.Application sqlApp = new
SQLDMO.ApplicationClass();
SQLDMO.NameList nameList =
sqlApp.ListAvailableSQLServers();
    for(int i=0;i<nameList.Count;i++)
    {
        if(nameList.Item(i) == "MyServer")
        {
            System.Data.SqlClient.SqlConnection cn =
new System.Data.SqlClient.SqlConnection("server=
(Myserver);database=pubs;uid=sa;pwd=;");
            cn.Open();
            cn.Close();
        }
    }
//******************************
//End
//******************************
}
```

This code does the job of testing that the connection exists. However, in a full application, you may want to give the user a choice as to which server to connect to. In this case, you can use SQLDMO to populate a list box. The user can then select the server from the box and connect.

## VB6

```
Private Sub Form_Load()
'*********************
'Sample VB6 Program
'   populates SQL server combo box
```

```
'10/10/05 jfd
'*********************
'*********************
'Begin:
'*********************
Dim sqlApp As New SQLDMO.Application
Dim nameList As SQLDMO.nameList
Dim index As Long

Set nameList = sqlApp.ListAvailableSQLServers
For index = 0 To nameList.Count
    Combo1.AddItem (nameList.Item(index))
Next index
'*********************
'End
'*********************
End Sub

Private Sub Command1_Click()
'*************************
'Defines and opens a local
' SQL database
'   jfd
'   10/10/05
'*************************
'Declarations:
'*************************
Dim cn As ADODB.Connection
'*************************
'Begin
'*************************
Set cn = New ADODB.Connection
cn.ConnectionString = "Provider=sqloledb;Server=" &
Combo1.SelText & ";Initial Catalog=pubs;User Id=sa;
Password=;"
cn.Open
cn.Close
```

```
'**************************
'End
'**************************
End Sub
```

## VB.NET

```
Private Sub Form1_Load(ByVal sender As System.Object,
ByVal e As System.EventArgs) Handles MyBase.Load
'****************************
'Sample VB .NET Program
'   jfd
'   10/10/05
'****************************
'Declarations:
'****************************
Dim sqlApp As SQLDMO.Application
Dim namelist As SQLDMO.NameList
Dim i As Integer
'****************************
'Begin
'****************************
sqlApp = New SQLDMO.Application()
namelist = sqlApp.ListAvailableSQLServers()
For i = 1 To namelist.Count
    ComboBox1.Items.Add(namelist.Item(i))
Next i
'****************************
'End
'****************************
End Sub

Private Sub Button1_Click(ByVal sender As
System.Object, ByVal e As System.EventArgs) Handles
Button1.Click
'****************************
'Sample VB .NET Program
```

```
'    jfd
'    10/10/05
'***************************
'Declarations:
'***************************
Dim cn As New SqlClient.SqlConnection("server=" &
ComboBox1.SelectedItem &
";database=pubs;uid=sa;pwd=;")
'***************************
'Begin
'***************************
cn.Open()
cn.Close()
'***************************
'End
'***************************

End Sub
```

**C#**

```
private void Form1_Load(object sender,
System.EventArgs e)
{
//*****************************
//C# application for selecting
// SQL servers from a
// Combobox
//
// jfd
// 10/10/05
//
//*****************************
//*****************************
//Declarations:
//*****************************
//*****************************
```

```
//Begin
//******************************
SQLDMO.Application sqlApp = new
SQLDMO.ApplicationClass();
SQLDMO.NameList nameList =
sqlApp.ListAvailableSQLServers();
for(int i=0;i<nameList.Count;i++)
{
    cboServers.Items.Add(nameList.Item(i));
}
//******************************
//End
//******************************

}
private void button1_Click(object sender,
System.EventArgs e)
{
//******************************
//Declarations:
//******************************
 System.Data.SqlClient.SqlConnection cn = new
System.Data.SqlClient.SqlConnection("server=" &
cboServers.SelectedItem &
";database=pubs;uid=sa;pwd=;");
//******************************
//Begin
//******************************
    cn.Open();
    cn.Close();

//******************************
//End
//******************************
}
```

Take some time to develop a solution or two on your own. When developing a solution to the bugs that can found in connection strings, you should be sure to validate as much of the information as possible.

For information such as usernames and passwords, which cannot be validated with any easy before it is passed to the database server, handle the errors in a way that your application will not crash if the information is incorrect.

In our next example we will look at how database connections can be made with a .udl file.

## Obtaining Connection Settings from a .udl File

A .udl file (Universal Data Link) is a great way to read connection settings into an application. One of the better points of using .udl files is that they can be edited independent of the application that uses them. This is important if you are in an environment that changes often. Another important trait of .udl files is that they can also be distributed independent of the application that uses them. This is important because you do not have to change your application every time something happens in your data environment.

With all of this independence, it should come as no surprise that there is an equally impressive amount of bugs that accompany .udl files.

If you have never worked with a .udl file, we will go over a very basic one now. Let us look at an example of the .udl file that we will use for the examples in this section. The following instructions set up a .udl file pointing to a local SQL database.

The first step is to create the blank .udl file. To do this, create a new text document within your Windows environment. Figure 15.1 illustrates the creation of a new text document.

After the file is created, change the file's name to `<anything>`.udl. In our example we will use Test.udl, as seen in Figure 15.2.

Windows will warn you before you finish changing the file's name. This is a standard Windows warning, as seen in Figure 15.3, and you should reply yes.

After you reply yes, confirming the name change, you should see that the thumbnail icon used for the .txt file has changed. This confirms that you have now created a .udl file. The icon should appear as in Figure 15.4.

Now that the original text document has been renamed to have a .udl extension, it is a black .udl file. Double-clicking in this file will open the .udl Data Link properties dialog. From this dialog we can configure our .udl file to connect to our local database.

Open the Data Link properties dialog and select the Provider tab. This tab lists all of the database drivers available for us to use when creating a connection. Figure 15.5 illustrates the options in the Provider tab.

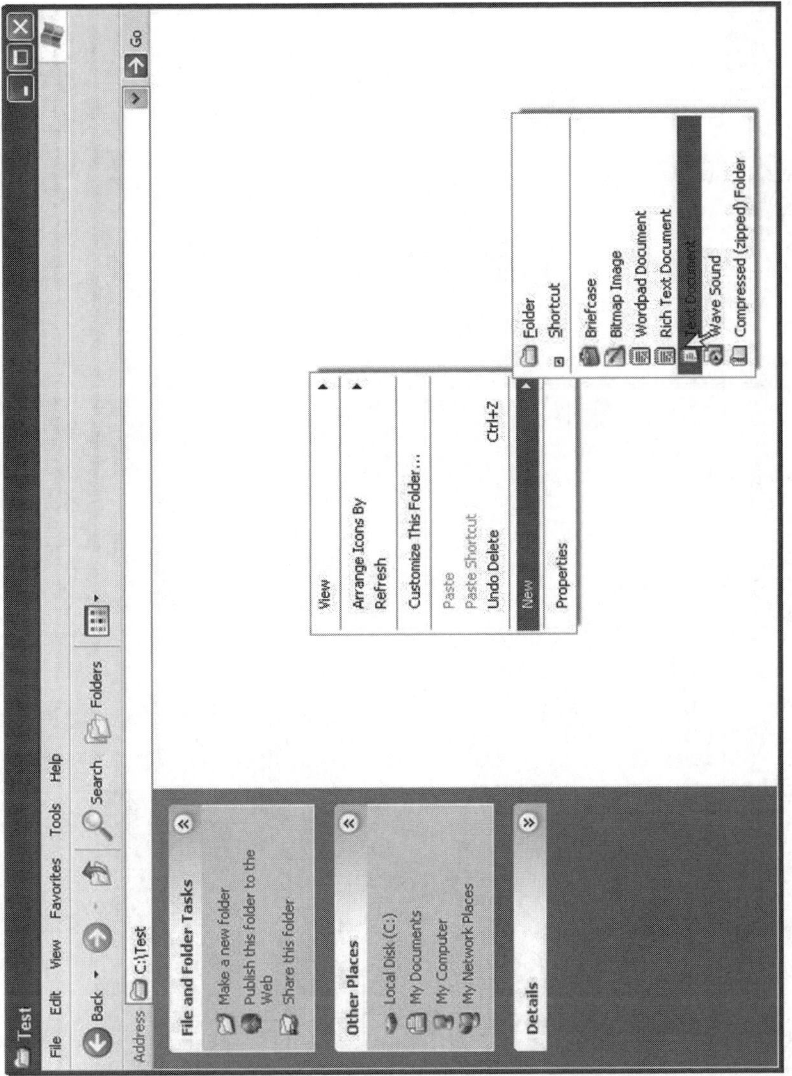


**Figure 15.1 Creating a new text document.**

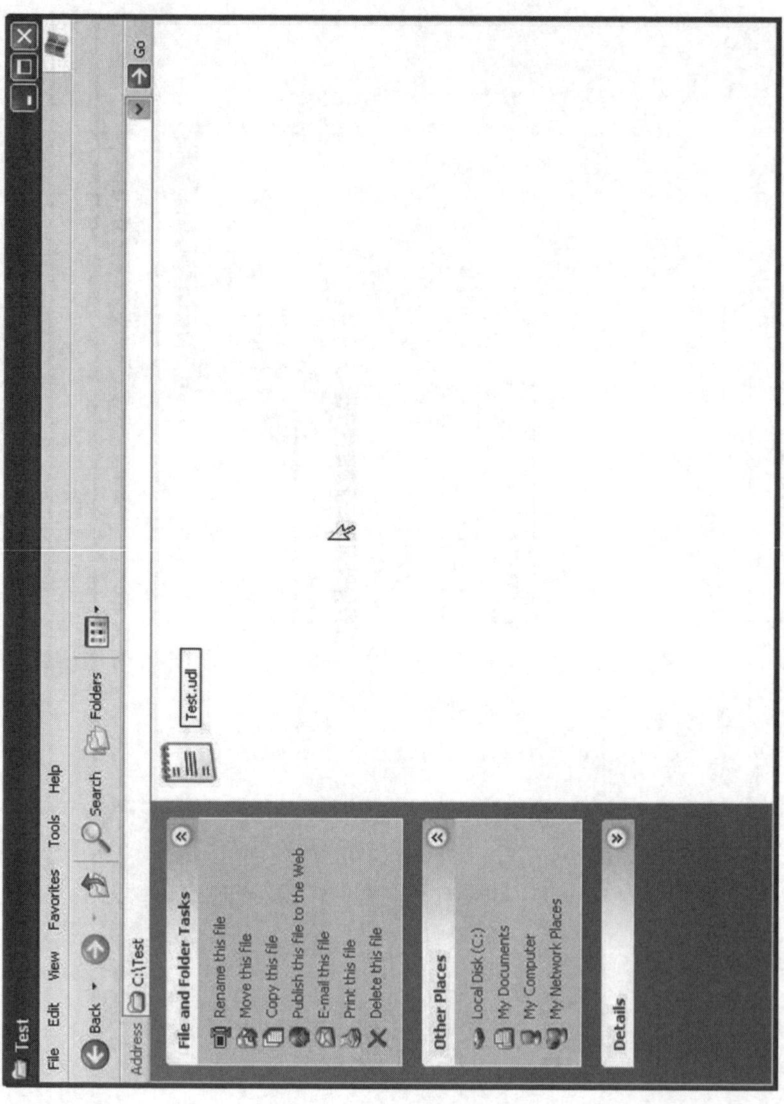


Figure 15.2 Renaming the .udl file.

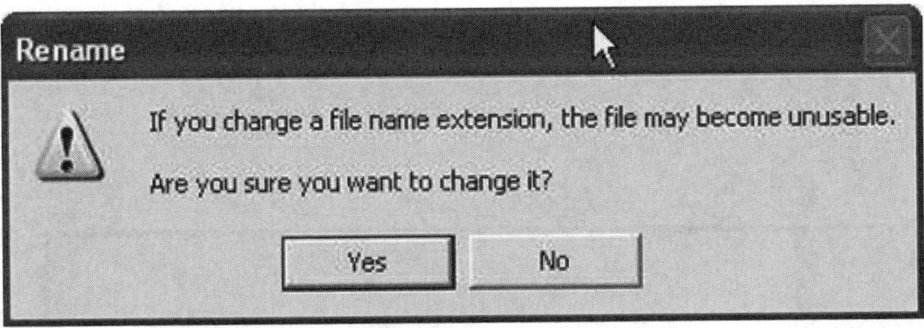


**Figure 15.3 Microsoft Warning dialog.**

Because the local database used in these examples is a Microsoft SQL database, we will be choosing the Microsoft OLE DB Provider for SQL Server. This will provide us with the necessary framework to build our connection external to our application. Selecting Microsoft OLE DB Provider for SQL Server will take us to the connection settings information area, or the Connection tab. The Connection tab is shown in Figure 15.6.

The information on the Connection tab should look familiar; it is the same information that is furnished from a connection string. The .udl file simply automates the passing of the connection information and keeps this data external to your application. Clicking on the Test Connection button will also provide you with a quick check of the availability of the database and the integrity of the credentials.

Now that our .udl file is created, let us take a look at the following code samples and try to spot the bugs. Each sample uses our Test.udl file.

## VB6

```
Private Sub Command1_Click()
'**************************
'Defines and opens a local
'  SQL database using .udl
'    jfd
'    10/10/05
'**************************
'Declarations:
'**************************
Dim cn As ADODB.Connection
'**************************
'Begin
'**************************
```

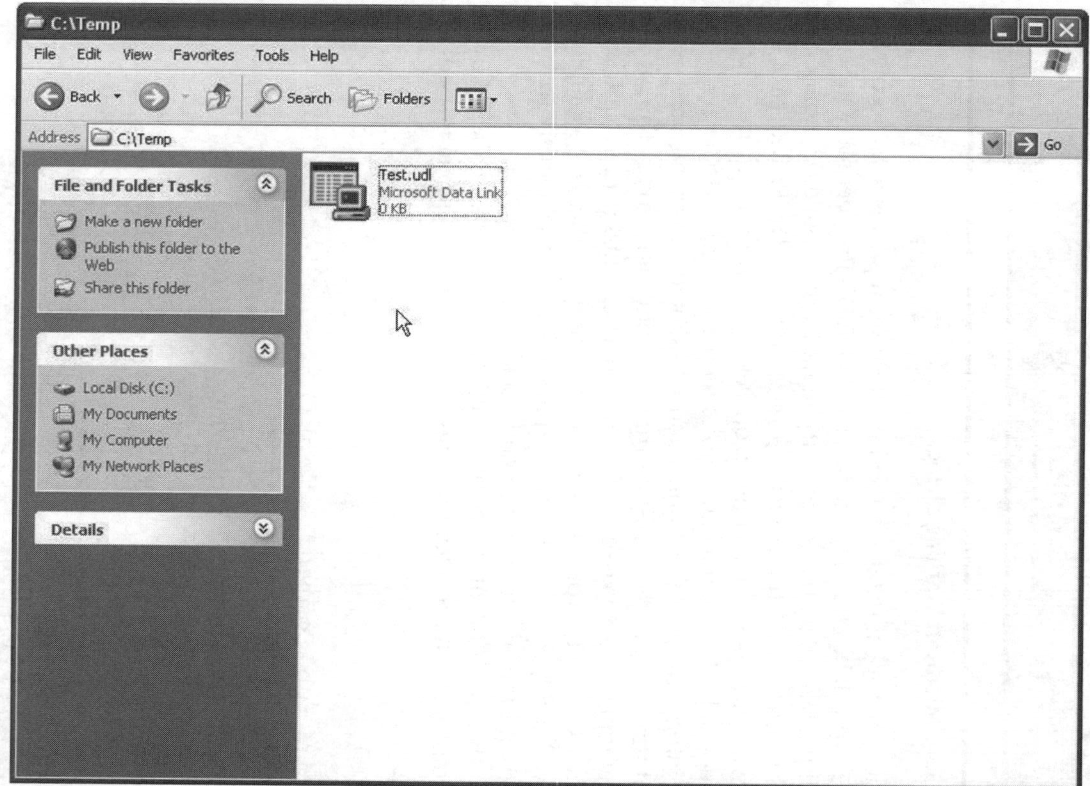


**Figure 15.4 The .udl icon.**

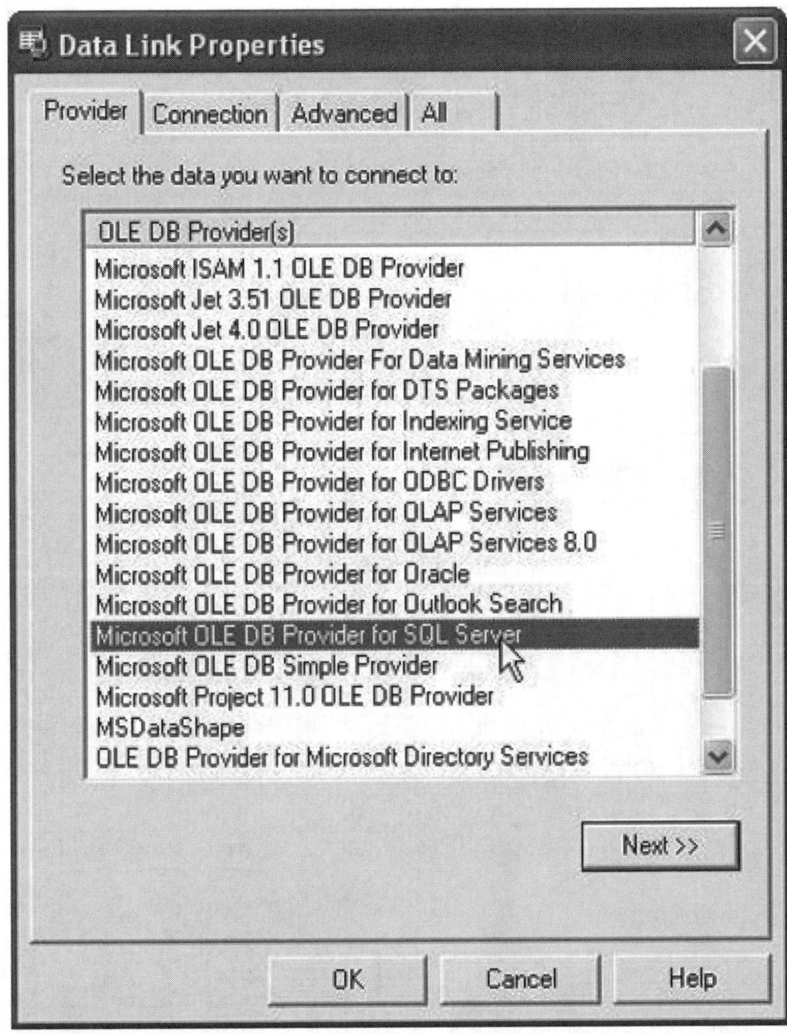


**Figure 15.5 The Provider tab.**

```
    Set cn = New ADODB.Connection
    cn.Open "File Name=c:\test.udl"
    cn.Close
Exit Sub
'***************************
'End
'***************************
End Sub
```

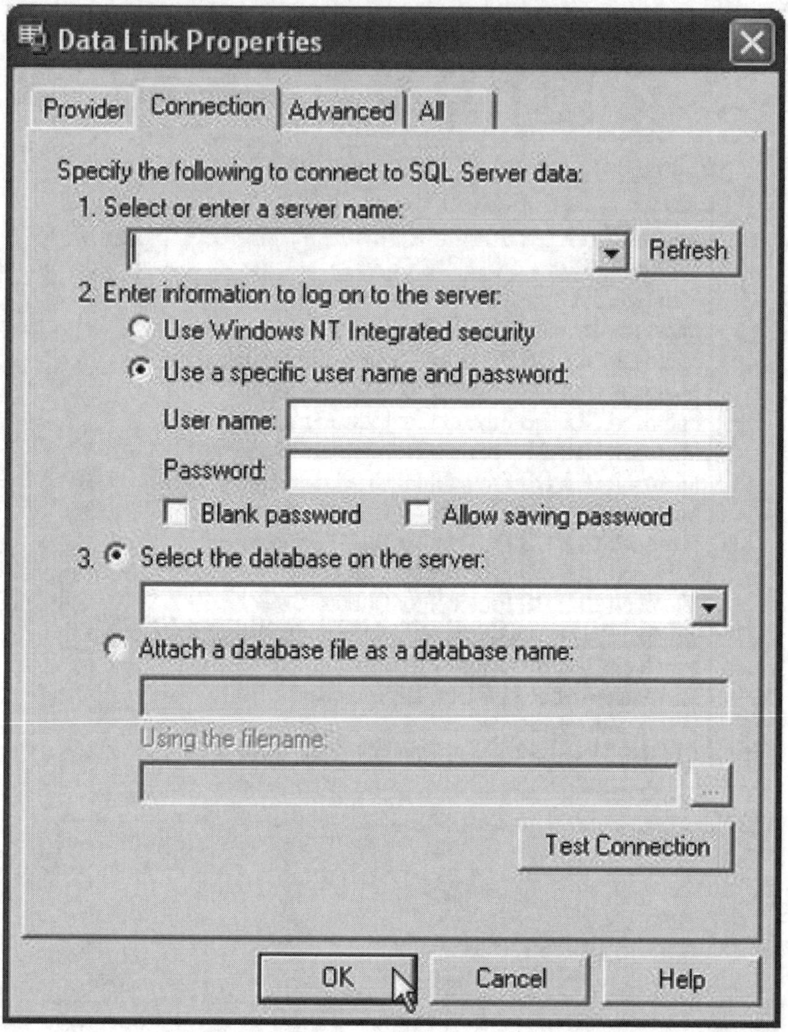

Figure 15.6 The Connection tab.

## VB.NET

```
Private Sub Button1_Click(ByVal sender As
System.Object, ByVal e As System.EventArgs) Handles
Button1.Click
'****************************
'Sample VB .NET Program
'   jfd
```

```
'   10/10/05
'****************************
'Declarations:
'****************************
Dim cn As New System.Data.OleDb.OleDbConnection("File
Name=c:\test.udl")
'****************************
'Begin
'****************************
cn.Open()
cn.Close()
'****************************
'End
'****************************
End Sub
```

**C#**

```
private void button1_Click(object sender,
System.EventArgs e)
{
//******************************
//C# application using a .udl file
//
//  jfd
//  10/10/05
//
//******************************
//******************************
//Declarations:
//******************************
    System.Data.OleDb.OleDbConnection cn = new
System.Data.OleDb.OleDbConnection ("File Name=
c:\\Test.udl");
//******************************
//Begin
//******************************
```

```
    cn.Open();
    cn.Close();

//******************************
//End
//******************************
}
```

The preceding blocks of code pass the compiler without error. However, when the user attempts to execute the connection code and attach to the .udl file, the following error is thrown:

> If you are not familiar with C#, keep in mind that the string `c:\\Test.udl` is the correct format for passing a directory path in C#.

### VB6

```
Run-time error '432'

File name or class name not found during Automation
operation
```

### VB.NET and C#

```
An unhandled exception of type
'System.ArgumentException' occurred in
system.data.dll

Additional information: Unable to load the UDL file
'c:\test.udl' listed in the ConnectionString.
```

This error is a product of the .udl file not existing, or not being physically present in the location your application is expecting it to be. Again, our best practice here is going to be to test for the existence of our .udl file before we attempt to use it.

The corrected code is as follows:

### VB6

```
'**********************
'Declarations:
```

```
'
'**********************
Dim udlExist as Boolean
'**********************

Private Sub Form_Load()
'**********************
'Sample VB6 program
'Checks for the existence of and
'   Opens a .udl file
'
'5/5/05 jfd
'**********************
'Begin:
'**********************
udlExist = False
If Dir("c:\test.udl", vbNormal) <> "" Then
    udlExist = True
Else
    UdlExist = False
    MsgBox "The requested .udl file does not exist."
End If
'**********************
'End
'**********************
End Sub

Private Sub Command1_Click()
'**************************
'Opens the database
'**************************
    If (udlExist) then
Set cn = New ADODB.Connection
       cn.Open "File Name=c:\test.udl"
       cn.Close
    End If
```

```
'*************************
'End
'*************************
End Sub
```

**VB.NET**

```
Private Sub Button1_Click(ByVal sender As
System.Object, ByVal e As System.EventArgs) Handles
Button1.Click
'*********************************
'Checks for the existence of and opens
'   a .udl file
'
'   jfd
'   05/05/2005
'*********************************
'Declarations:
'*********************************
      Dim FileToOpen As System.IO.File
'*********************************
'Begin
'*********************************
      If FileToOpen.Exists("c:\test.udl") Then
         Dim cn As New
System.Data.OleDb.OleDbConnection("File Name=
c:\test.udl")
         cn.Open()
         cn.Close()
      Else
         MsgBox("The requested .udl file does not
exist.")
      End If
'***********************************
'End
'***********************************
   End Sub
End Class
```

**C#**

```
static void Main()
//***************************
// Checks for the existence of and opens
//          the file Example.txt
//***************************
{

      Application.Run(new Form1());
}

private void button1_Click(object sender,
System.EventArgs e)
{
//****************************
//Sample C# application that tests for
// the existence of a .udl file
//    jfd
//    10/10/05
//****************************
//****************************
//Declarations:
//****************************
string path = "c:\\Test.udl";
//****************************
//Begin
//****************************
    if (File.Exists(path))
    {
        System.Data.OleDb.OleDbConnection cn = new
System.Data.OleDb.OleDbConnection ("File Name=
c:\\Test.udl");
        cn.Open();
        cn.Close();
    }
    else
    {
```

```
        MessageBox.Show ("The requested .udl file does
not exist.");
     }
//******************************
//End
//******************************
}
```

Here we use some of the same code from an earlier example. We are testing for the existence of a file before we begin to use it. One way you could take this code to the next level is to prompt the user for the name of the .udl file to use. This keeps you from having to hard code any settings.

Take some time now to develop your own solution to these examples. Write new code that prompts the user for a file name, then tests for the existence of that file and uses it to supply some connection settings. One method you can try is to use the FileListBox or similar control object to provide the user with a list of available .udl files from which to select.

> Do not forget that if you do a search for existing files to populate a FileListBox, it should not preclude you from also testing for the selected file's existence before opening.

In the next sample for this scenario we will look at one of the more common database connections methods, ODBC.

## Using ODBC Connections

ODBC connections, being an older application of database connection technology, have fallen out of favor with many programmers. However, for many small businesses, especially those running older platforms and older technology, it is still a prevalent connection method.

ODBC connections are clumsy compared to some of the newer methods of database connectivity. One reason is that they are not extremely portable. An ODBC connection needs to be created as a setting on each machine. This being the case, there are two kinds of ODBC connections that can be created: file and system.

Second, the use of ODBC connections often requires updating, or even writing, ODBC drivers to fit the database architecture you are programming for. This proves to be the major downside of using this technology. Many times programmers have to write packages to test for and distribute updated ODBC drivers to the PC that they are writing for.

> Chances are, if you are working with an ODBC connection, you are doing so with Visual Basic 6. Therefore, all of the samples in this example will be given using Visual Basic 6.

Let us take a look at some of the bugs that can be found in using ODBC connections. Because there is a running theme in this section of the book, the first bug should not be hard for you to find. Take a look through the first section of code. Take the time to find the bug and begin to ask yourself how you would fix it.

**VB6**

```
Private Sub Command1_Click()
'*************************
'Defines and opens a local
' SQL database using ODBC
'  jfd
'  10/10/05
'*************************
'Declarations:
'*************************
Dim cn As ADODB.Connection
'*************************
'Begin
'*************************

      Set cn = New ADODB.Connection
      cn.Open "DSN=LocalServer"
      cn.Close

'*************************
'End
'*************************
End Sub
```

In this small sample we call an ODBC connection to supply us with the information we need to reach our desired database. This sample compiles correctly. However, when it is run the following error is thrown:

**VB6**

```
Run-time error '-2147467259 (80004005)':

[Microsoft][ODBC Driver Manager] Data source name
not found and no default driver specified
```

As you should be aware of by now, you must test for all external components that can negatively affect your application. The aforementioned error condition clearly indicates that the ODBC connection we are calling does not exist.

The following corrected code tests for the existence of the connection before calling it:

**VB6**

```
'**********************
'Declarations:
' Types
'**********************
Option Explicit

Private Const SQL_SUCCESS As Long = 0
Private Const SQL_ERROR As Long = -1
Private Const SQL_FETCH_NEXT As Long = 1

Private Declare Function SQLDataSources Lib
"ODBC32.DLL" _
         (ByVal hEnv As Long, ByVal fDirection _
         As Integer, ByVal szDSN As String, _
         ByVal cbDSNMax As Integer, pcbDSN As
Integer, _
         ByVal szDescription As String, ByVal
cbDescriptionMax _
         As Integer, pcbDescription As Integer) As
Integer
```

```
Private Declare Function SQLAllocEnv Lib "ODBC32.DLL" _
        (env As Long) As Integer

Private Sub Form_Load()
'*********************
'Sample VB6 Program
' prompts before exit
'5/5/05 jfd
'*************************
'Declarations:
'*************************
Dim retCode As Integer
Dim DRVItem As String
Dim DSNLen As Integer
Dim DRVLen As Integer
Dim EnvHandle As Long
Dim DSNItem As String
'*********************
'Begin:
'*********************
If (SQLAllocEnv(EnvHandle) <> SQL_ERROR) Then
      Do

      DSNItem = Space$(1024)
      DRVItem = Space$(1024)

         retCode = SQLDataSources(EnvHandle,
SQL_FETCH_NEXT, DSNItem, Len(DSNItem), DSNLen,
DRVItem, Len(DRVItem), DRVLen)

         Combo1.AddItem Left$(DSNItem, DSNLen)

      Loop Until retCode <> SQL_SUCCESS
   End If
'*********************
'End
'*********************
End Sub
```

```
Private Sub Command1_Click()
'**************************
'Defines and opens a local
' SQL database
'   jfd
'   10/10/05
'**************************
'Declarations:
'**************************
Dim cn As ADODB.Connection
'**************************
'Begin
'**************************

        Set cn = New ADODB.Connection
        cn.Open "DSN=" & Combo1.Text
        cn.Close

'**************************
'End
'**************************
End Sub
```

If you are adventurous, you can also add some code to create the ODBC connection if it is not available when you call it. Keep in mind, though, that if you are going to create an ODBC connection, you may want to prompt the user for his or her username, password, and the server name. After all, if you knew this information ahead of time, you would be using connection strings and saving yourself the trouble of coding for ODBC.

## VB6

```
'**********************
'Declarations:
' Types
'**********************
Option Explicit
```

```
Private Const SQL_SUCCESS As Long = 0
Private Const SQL_ERROR As Long = -1
Private Const SQL_FETCH_NEXT As Long = 1

Private Declare Function SQLDataSources Lib
"ODBC32.DLL" (ByVal hEnv As Long, ByVal fDirection
As Integer, ByVal szDSN As String, ByVal cbDSNMax
As Integer, pcbDSN As Integer, ByVal szDescription
As String, ByVal cbDescriptionMax As Integer,
pcbDescription As Integer) As Integer

Private Declare Function SQLAllocEnv Lib "ODBC32.DLL"
(env As Long) As Integer

Private Declare Function SQLConfigDataSource Lib
"ODBCCP32.DLL" (ByVal hwndParent As Long, ByVal
fRequest As Long, ByVal lpszDriver As String, ByVal
lpszAttributes As String) As Long

Private Sub Command1_Click()
'**************************
'Defines and opens a local
' SQL database
'   jfd
'   10/10/05
'**************************
'Declarations:
'**************************
Dim Retrn As Long
Dim cn As ADODB.Connection
'**************************
'Begin
'**************************

      Set cn = New ADODB.Connection
      cn.Open "DSN=MyServer"
      cn.Close

'**************************
```

```
'End
'**************************
End Sub

Private Sub Form_Load()
'**********************
'Sample VB6 Program
' searches for ODBC DSN "MyServer"
' if it is not found, "MyServer"
' is created automatically
'   jfd
'   5/5/05
'**************************
'Declarations:
'**************************
Dim retCode As Integer
Dim drvItem As String
Dim dsnLen As Integer
Dim drvLen As Integer
Dim envHandle As Long
Dim dsnItem As String
Dim dsnExist As Boolean
Dim attrib As String
Dim rtrncode As Long
'**********************
'Begin:
'**********************
If (SQLAllocEnv(envHandle) <> SQL_ERROR) Then
      Do While retCode = SQL_SUCCESS

         dsnItem = Space$(1024)
         drvItem = Space$(1024)
         retCode = SQLDataSources(envHandle,
SQL_FETCH_NEXT, dsnItem, Len(dsnItem), dsnLen,
drvItem, Len(drvItem), drvLen)
```

```
            If dsnItem <> "MyServer" Then
               dsnExist = False
            Else
               dsnExist = True
               Exit Do
            End If

         Loop
         If dsnExist = False Then
            attrib = "DSN=MyServer" & vbNullChar &
"Server=(local)" & vbNullChar
            rtrncode = SQLConfigDataSource(0&, 1, "SQL
Server", attrib)
         End If
      End If
'**********************
'End
'**********************
End Sub
```

There are a couple of things going on in this example that you should be aware of. First, we are using multiple application programming interface (API) calls, one of which writes to the system registry. On a basic level, DSNs (datasource names) are nothing more than registry entries. Therefore, to create one on the fly, one simply needs to navigate the registry and add the correct information.

Luckily, there is an API call created specifically for this purpose. `SQLConfigDataSource` serves the triple purpose of creating, deleting, and modifying DSNs. The digit 1 in the following line tells the function that we are adding a new DSN:

```
rtrncode = SQLConfigDataSource(0&, 1, "SQL Server",
attrib)
```

A solution like this is useful if you know that the client needs to use a specific DSN that does not change. However, if it is a more dynamic environment, you should change the code a bit. That is, you can easily modify this solution to prompt the user for driver, name, and login information. This will allow your application to be as flexible as possible.

The final example in this scenario will tend to the delicate subject of closing a database.

## Closing a Database

The best way to deal with anything that can be opened — files, refrigerators, doors, and databases — is to close them when you are finished with them. In the case of databases, closing them frees up resources and tells your application that you are finished with the services required to maintain the data connections. Therefore, closing a database should be just as important to your application as opening it.

Applications that do not close databases, releasing their connections, can cause locks. These locks can prevent other instances of your application, or possibly anybody else's application, from connecting to the same database.

The examples that follow contain a bug related to the closing of a database. Take the time to carefully look at the sample code and try to find the bugs.

### VB6

```
'*********************
'Declarations:
'  Types
'*********************
Dim udlExist As Boolean

Private Sub Command1_Click()
'*************************
'Defines and opens a local
'  SQL database
'    jfd
'    10/10/05
'*************************
'Declarations:
'*************************
Dim cn As adodb.Connection
Dim rs As adodb.Recordset
'*************************
'Begin
'*************************
```

```
If (udlExist) Then
       Set cn = New adodb.Connection
       Set rs = New adodb.Recordset
       cn.Open "File Name=c:\test.udl"
       cn.Close
       rs.Open "Select * from employee", cn,
adOpenForwardOnly, adLockReadOnly

End If
'**************************
'End
'**************************
End Sub

Private Sub Form_Load()
'**********************
'Sample VB6 program
'Checks for the existence of and
' Opens a .udl file
'
'5/5/05 jfd
'**********************
'Begin:
'**********************
udlExist = False
If Dir("c:\test.udl", vbNormal) <> "" Then
    udlExist = True
Else
    udlExist = False
    MsgBox "The requested .udl file does not exist."
End If
'**********************
'End
'**********************

End Sub
```

### VB.NET

```
Imports System.Data.SqlClient

Private Sub Button1_Click(ByVal sender As
System.Object, ByVal e As System.EventArgs) Handles
Button1.Click
'****************************
'Sample VB .NET Program
'   jfd
'   10/10/05
'****************************
'Declarations:
'****************************
Dim cn As New
SqlConnection("server=(local);database=pubs;uid=sa;p
wd=;")
Dim cmd As SqlCommand
'****************************
'Begin
'****************************
cn.Open()
cmd = New SqlCommand("Select * from employee", cn)
cn.Close()
Dim dr As SqlDataReader = cmd.ExecuteReader()
'****************************
'End
'****************************
End Sub
```

### C#

```
private void button1_Click(object sender,
System.EventArgs e)
{
//****************************
//Declarations:
//****************************
```

```
SqlConnection cn = new SqlConnection("server=(local);
database=pubs;uid=sa;");

//*****************************
//Begin
//*****************************
    cn.Open();
    SqlCommand cmd = new SqlCommand( "Select * from
employee",cn);

    cn.Close();
    SqlDataReader dr = cmd.ExecuteReader();
//*****************************
//End
//*****************************
}
```

These code samples pass the compiler without error. However, on execution, the following errors are thrown:

### VB6

```
Run-time error '3709':

The connection cannot be used to perform this
operation. It is either closed or invalid in this
context.
```

### VB.NET and C#

```
An unhandled exception of type
'System.InvalidOperationException' occurred in
system.data.dll

Additional information: ExecuteReader requires an
open and available Connection. The connection's
current state is Closed.
```

The problem with these examples is that the code to close the database is executed before the code that attempts to retrieve data. This causes the database to throw an error.

To correct this problem, the code that closes the database should be moved to a separate region of the code. In fact, the best way to keep a problem like this from appearing at an inopportune time is to move the code to a place where you will be sure no further manipulations to the database will be required.

The corrected code is as follows:

**VB6**

```
'**********************
'Declarations:
'  Types
'**********************
Dim udlExist As Boolean

Private Sub Command1_Click()
'*************************
'Defines and opens a local
'  SQL database
'    jfd
'    10/10/05
'*************************
'Declarations:
'*************************
Dim cn As adodb.Connection
Dim rs As adodb.Recordset
'*************************
'Begin
'*************************
If (udlExist) Then
       Set cn = New adodb.Connection
       Set rs = New adodb.Recordset
       cn.Open "File Name=c:\test.udl"
       rs.Open "Select * from employee", cn,
adOpenForwardOnly, adLockReadOnly
       cn.Close
End If
```

```
'*************************
'End
'*************************
End Sub

Private Sub Form_Load()
'*********************
'Sample VB6 program
'Checks for the existence of and
' Opens a .udl file
'
'5/5/05 jfd
'*********************
'Begin:
'*********************
udlExist = False
If Dir("c:\test.udl", vbNormal) <> "" Then
    udlExist = True
Else
    udlExist = False
    MsgBox "The requested .udl file does not exist."
End If
'*********************
'End
'*********************

End Sub
```

**VB.NET**

```
Private Sub Button1_Click(ByVal sender As
System.Object, ByVal e As System.EventArgs) Handles
Button1.Click
'***************************
'Sample VB .NET Program
'   jfd
'   10/10/05
```

```
'****************************
'Declarations:
'****************************
Dim cn As New
SqlConnection("server=(local);database=pubs;uid=sa;
pwd=;")
Dim cmd As SqlCommand
'****************************
'Begin
'****************************
cn.Open()
cmd = New SqlCommand("Select * from employee", cn)

Dim dr As SqlDataReader = cmd.ExecuteReader()
cn.Close()
'****************************
'End
'****************************

End Sub
```

**C#**

```
private void button1_Click(object sender,
System.EventArgs e)
{
//****************************
//Declarations:
//****************************
SqlConnection cn = new
SqlConnection("server=(local);database=pubs;
uid=sa;");

//****************************
//Begin
//****************************
      cn.Open();
```

```
        SqlCommand cmd = new SqlCommand( "Select *
from employee",cn);
        SqlDataReader dr = cmd.ExecuteReader();
        cn.Close();
//******************************
//End
//******************************
}
```

This scenario covered many of the common bugs that can come from opening databases. Although we have tamed many of these bugs, there are many more yet to be found. In the next scenario we will cover the bugs that will come from reading data from a database.

# Chapter 16

# Real-World Scenarios: Reading a Database

Now that we have opened the database, it is time to read the data that is in it. Most likely, that is the real reason why you would be opening a database in the first place — to read from it or write to it. Especially with Visual Studio .NET's implementation of ADO.NET, there are many ways to read data from a database.

Entire volumes have been dedicated purely to the subject of Visual Basic .NET or C# and their interactions with databases. Although we do not have the space or the need to go into as much detail as some of these other tomes, we will cover some of the more prevalent facts. In doing so, we will uncover some fairly common bugs that you can avoid in your daily business.

The first bugs we will examine will be related to the use of a DataReader.

## Using a DataReader

In the last example of the previous scenario, we quickly looked at the DataReader. This scenario will focus on the DataReader in a bit more detail. Because the DataReader is unique to the .NET framework, there will be no Visual Basic 6 examples in this scenario.

Let us take a look at a simple example that throws an error when executed. We will examine two code samples that attempt to extract data using a DataReader from the pubs database, a sample database shipped with Microsoft Structure Query Language (SQL) Server. If you are not familiar with the pubs database in Microsoft SQL Server, the following table is a sample of the data from the employee table. This is the data we will be working with for these examples.

| emp_id | fname | lname | job_id | job_lvl | pub_id | hire_date |
|---|---|---|---|---|---|---|
| PMA42628M | Paolo | Accorti | 13 | 35 | 0877 | 1992-08-27 |
| PSA89086M | Pedro | Afonso | 14 | 89 | 1389 | 1990-12-24 |
| VPA30890F | Victoria | Ashworth | 6 | 140 | 0877 | 1990-09-13 |
| H-B39728F | Helen | Bennett | 12 | 35 | 0877 | 1989-09-21 |
| L-B31947F | Lesley | Brown | 7 | 120 | 0877 | 1991-02-13 |
| F-C16315M | Francisco | Chang | 4 | 227 | 9952 | 1990-11-03 |
| PTC11962M | Philip | Cramer | 2 | 215 | 9952 | 1989-11-11 |
| A-C71970F | Aria | Cruz | 10 | 87 | 1389 | 1991-10-26 |

Now let us take a look at some VB.NET and C# code. Again, take some time and try to identify the bug.

## VB.NET

```
Private Sub Button1_Click(ByVal sender As
System.Object, ByVal e As System.EventArgs) Handles
Button1.Click
'****************************
'Sample VB .NET Program
'   jfd
'   10/10/05
'****************************
'Declarations:
'****************************
Dim cn As New
SqlConnection("server=(local);database=pubs;uid=sa;p
wd=;")
Dim cmd As SqlCommand
Dim i As Integer
Dim empID(10) As Integer
'****************************
'Begin
```

```
'***************************
    cn.Open()
    cmd = New SqlCommand("Select * from employee", cn)
    Dim dr As SqlDataReader = cmd.ExecuteReader()
    i = 0
    While dr.Read()
          empID(i) = dr("emp_id")
          i = i + 1
  End While
  cn.Close()
'***************************
'End
'***************************

End Sub
```

**C#**

```
private void button1_Click(object sender,
System.EventArgs e)
{
//******************************
//A simple C# program
//  jfd
//  10/10/05
//******************************
//******************************
//Declarations:
//******************************
SqlConnection cn = new
SqlConnection("server=(local);database=pubs;
uid=sa;");
int i;
int[] empID = new int [10];
//******************************
//Begin
//******************************
```

```
cn.Open();
SqlCommand cmd = new SqlCommand( "Select * from
employee",cn);
SqlDataReader dr = cmd.ExecuteReader();
i = 0;
while(dr.Read())
{
    empID[i] = dr["emp_id"] ;
    i++;
}
cn.Close();
//*****************************
//End
//*****************************
}
```

Although both of these examples perform the same functions, and both contain the same bug, they are handled slightly differently by the compiler. The VB.NET sample above will compile correctly; however, when it is run it will throw the following error:

### VB.NET

```
An unhandled exception of type
'System.InvalidCastException' occurred in
microsoft.visualbasic.dll

Additional information: Cast from string "PMA42628M"
to type 'Integer' is not valid.
```

This error is fairly descriptive and to the point. Looking at the error — or at the previously supplied table of data from pubs— it is easy to see that the emp_id field is a string and not an integer. Therefore, because the code sample attempts to store this value in an integer array, an error is thrown warning us of the type conflict.

The corrected code is as follows:

### VB.NET

```
Private Sub Button1_Click(ByVal sender As
System.Object, ByVal e As System.EventArgs) Handles
Button1.Click
```

```
'****************************
'Sample VB .NET Program
'   jfd
'   10/10/05
'****************************
'Declarations:
'****************************
Dim cn As New
SqlConnection("server=(local);database=pubs;uid=sa;
pwd=;")
Dim cmd As SqlCommand
Dim i As Integer
Dim empID(10) As String
'****************************
'Begin
'****************************
    cn.Open()
    cmd = New SqlCommand("Select * from employee", cn)
    Dim dr As SqlDataReader = cmd.ExecuteReader()
    i = 0
    While dr.Read()
          empID(i) = dr("emp_id")
          i = i + 1
    End While
    cn.Close()
'****************************
'End
'****************************

End Sub
```

If you are adapting this code sample for your own use, take care not to hard code the size of your array. Because you cannot accurately predict how many rows a database might return, you should also dimension your arrays as open arrays. You can then re-dimension them using a count of the returned records as your Ubound value. For example:

## VB.NET

```
Private Sub Button1_Click(ByVal sender As
System.Object, ByVal e As System.EventArgs) Handles
Button1.Click
'****************************
'Sample VB .NET Program
'   jfd
'   10/10/05
'****************************
'Declarations:
'****************************
Dim cn As New
SqlConnection("server=(local);database=pubs;uid=sa;p
wd=;")
Dim cmd As SqlCommand
Dim i As Integer
Dim empID() As String
'****************************
'Begin
'****************************
cn.Open()
cmd = New SqlCommand("Select * from employee", cn)
Dim dr As SqlDataReader = cmd.ExecuteReader()
i = 0
'****************************
'This piece of code counts the
' number of records returned
'****************************
While dr.Read()
      i = i + 1
End While
'****************************
dr.Close()'close the datareader so it can be re-
executed

ReDim empID(i)'redim the empID array with the number
returned
```

```
'****************************
're-execute the reader and
' assign the values to the array
'****************************
dr = cmd.ExecuteReader()
i = 0
While dr.Read()
      empID(i) = dr("emp_id")
      i = i + 1
End While
dr.Close()
cn.Close()
'****************************
'End
'****************************
End Sub
```

Although this closes our VB.NET example, we must still examine the C# example. The C# example we supplied did not throw an error like the VB.NET example. In fact, the C# example does not compile. The compiler catches the type mismatch and prompts the developer as follows:

```
Cannot implicitly convert type 'object' to 'int'
```

Again, this code sample suffers from the same bug as the VB.NET example. We attempt to write a string value to an integer array. The corrected code for C# is as follows:

### C#

```
private void button1_Click(object sender,
System.EventArgs e)
{
//*******************************
//Declarations:
//*******************************
SqlConnection cn = new
SqlConnection("server=(local);database=pubs;
uid=sa;");
int i;
string[] empID = new string [10];
```

```
//*******************************
//Begin
//*******************************
cn.Open();
SqlCommand cmd = new SqlCommand( "Select * from
employee",cn); SqlDataReader dr =
cmd.ExecuteReader();
i = 0;
while(dr.Read())
{
      empID[i] = dr["emp_id"].ToString() ;
      i++;
}
cn.Close();
//*******************************
//End
//*******************************
}
```

Let us review one more set of code samples using DataReaders. These samples are slightly more complicated and contain a bit more code. However, the bug is one that you have seen before. Take the time now to go through these two new samples and try to locate the resident bugs.

Keep in mind that we will try to make these examples a bit more convoluted and difficult than they would normally have to be to get the same job done — just to try to trip you up. Not everyone writes clean, concise code. Therefore, you can never anticipate what condition the code you are debugging will be in.

## VB.NET

```
Private Sub Button1_Click(ByVal sender As
System.Object, ByVal e As System.EventArgs) Handles
Button1.Click
'****************************
'Sample VB .NET Program
'   jfd
'   10/10/05
'****************************
```

```
'Declarations:
'****************************
Dim cn As New
SqlConnection("server=(local);database=pubs;
uid=sa;pwd=;")
Dim cmd As SqlCommand
Dim i As Integer
Dim empID() As String
Dim emptyTable As Boolean
'****************************
'Begin
'****************************
cn.Open()
cmd = New SqlCommand("Select * from employee", cn)
Dim dr As SqlDataReader = cmd.ExecuteReader()
i = 0                        'set the counter to 0
'****************************
'This piece of code counts the
' number of records returned
'****************************
While dr.Read()
      i = i + 1
End While
'****************************
ReDim empID(i)     'redim the array to the size of
the records
'****************************
'if the table is empty, flag it
'****************************
If i = 0 Then
    emptyTable = True
Else
    emptyTable = False
End If
'****************************
'report the number of rows found
```

```
'***************************
    MsgBox("The first pass is complete, there are "
& i & " records in the employee table.")
'***************************
'if the table is not empty
' copy each record to the array
'***************************
If emptyTable <> True Then
    dr = cmd.ExecuteReader()
    i = 0
    While dr.Read()
         empID(i) = dr("emp_id")
         i = i + 1
    End While
End If
dr.Close()
cn.Close()
'***************************
'End
'***************************
End Sub
```

**C#**

```
private void button1_Click(object sender,
System.EventArgs e)
{
//****************************
//Declarations:
//****************************
SqlConnection cn = new
SqlConnection("server=(local);database=pubs;uid=sa;"
);
int i;
bool emptyTable;
//****************************
//Begin
```

```
//*****************************
    cn.Open();
    SqlCommand cmd = new SqlCommand( "Select * from
employee",cn);
    SqlDataReader dr = cmd.ExecuteReader();
    i = 0;
    emptyTable =false;
//*****************************
//Counts the number of records
// returned to the DataReader
//*****************************
    while(dr.Read())
    {
       i++;
    }
//*****************************
    string[] empID = new String [i]; //set the ubound
array
//*****************************
//if the table is empty, flag it
//*****************************
    if (i==0)
    {
       emptyTable = true;
    }
//*****************************
//report the number of rows found
//*****************************
    MessageBox.Show ("The first pass is complete,
there are " + i + " records in the employee
table.","Database Sample");
//*****************************
//if the table is not empty
// copy each record to the array
//*****************************
    if (emptyTable != true)
```

```
    {
        dr = cmd.ExecuteReader();
        i =0;
        while(dr.Read ())
        {
            empID[i] = dr["emp_id"].ToString();
            i++;
        }
    }

    cn.Close();
//*****************************
//End
//*****************************
}
```

Both of these examples compile correctly, and both will execute to a point. However, there is a bug embedded in each. This is a bug that we have already looked at in this scenario.

What makes this particular bug a bit harder to find now is that the code is a little more realistic. It is not clear, concise code — perfect for masking small bugs. This is the kind of code you need to look through very carefully.

When both examples are executed, the following error is thrown:

### VB.NET and C#

```
An unhandled exception of type
'System.InvalidOperationException' occurred in
system.data.dll

Additional information: There is already an open
DataReader associated with this Connection which must
be closed first.
```

> For now, do not focus on the `unhandled exception`. You can use the different error handlers discussed in this book to tame that. What you should pay attention to here is the `Additional information`.

The problem here is that the code uses the DataReader twice: once to count the number of records and again to copy each record to an array. Although the same DataReader can be used many times through an application, the flaw in the execution here is that the DataReader must be closed before it can be re-executed. The previous two code samples do not invoke `dr.Close()` before re-executing the reader.

Take a look now through the corrected code. We have also added some handlers in the code as well. Although the new code functions properly, there is still room for improvement. Take some time on your own to work with the corrected code and optimize it.

## VB.NET

```
Private Sub Button1_Click(ByVal sender As
System.Object, ByVal e As System.EventArgs) Handles
Button1.Click
'***************************
'Sample VB .NET Program
'   jfd
'   10/10/05
'***************************
'Declarations:
'***************************
Dim cn As New
SqlConnection("server=(local);database=pubs;uid=sa;
pwd=;")
Dim cmd As SqlCommand
Dim i As Integer
Dim empID() As String
Dim emptyTable As Boolean
'***************************
'Begin
'***************************
cn.Open()
cmd = New SqlCommand("Select * from employee", cn)
Dim dr As SqlDataReader
'***************************
'execute within a try...catch
```

```
'****************************
Try
    dr = cmd.ExecuteReader()
Catch operationException As
System.InvalidOperationException
    'perform more logic based on error
    MsgBox("There was an error in the operation!")
End Try
i = 0  'set the counter to 0
'****************************
'This piece of code counts the
' number of records returned
'****************************
While dr.Read()
    i = i + 1
End While
'****************************
ReDim empID(i) 'redim the array to the size of the
records
'****************************
'if the table is empty, flag it
'****************************
' dr.Close()  'close the datareader
If i = 0 Then
    emptyTable = True
Else
    emptyTable = False
End If
'****************************
'report the number of rows found
'****************************
MsgBox("The first pass is complete, there are " & i
& " records in the employee table.")
'****************************
'if the table is not empty
' copy each record to the array
```

```
'****************************
If emptyTable <> True Then
    Try
       dr = cmd.ExecuteReader()
    Catch opExcept As System.InvalidOperationException
       'perform more logic based on error
       MsgBox("There was an error in the operation!")
    End Try
    i = 0
    While dr.Read()
       empID(i) = dr("emp_id")
       i = i + 1
    End While
End If
dr.Close()
cn.Close()
'****************************
'End
'****************************
End Sub
```

**C#**

```
private void button1_Click(object sender,
System.EventArgs e)
{
//****************************
//Declarations:
//****************************
SqlConnection cn = new
SqlConnection("server=(local);database=pubs;
uid=sa;");
int i;
bool emptyTable;
SqlDataReader dr;
//****************************
//Begin
```

```
//*******************************
    cn.Open();
    i = 0;
    SqlCommand cmd = new SqlCommand( "Select * from
employee",cn);try
    {
       dr = cmd.ExecuteReader();
       while(dr.Read())
       {
          i++;
       }
       dr.Close();
    }
    catch (System.InvalidOperationException
opException)
    {
       MessageBox.Show( opException.ToString() );
    }
    emptyTable =false;
    string[] empID = new String [i]; //set the ubound
array
//*******************************
//if the table is empty, flag it
//*******************************
    if (i==0)
    {
       emptyTable = true;
    }
//*******************************
//report the number of rows found
//*******************************
    MessageBox.Show ("The first pass is complete,
there are " + i + " records in the employee
table.","Database Sample");
//*******************************
//if the table is not empty
```

```
// copy each record to the array
//*****************************
    i=0;
    if (emptyTable != true)
    {
       try
       {
          dr = cmd.ExecuteReader();
          while(dr.Read ())
          {
          empID[i] = dr["emp_id"].ToString();
          i++;
          }
       }
       catch(System.InvalidOperationException
opException)
       {
          MessageBox.Show(opException.ToString() );
       }
       i =0;
       }
       cn.Close();
//*****************************
//End
//*****************************
}
```

The DataReader is a very versatile tool when dealing with databases. It offers a quick way to open a database and retrieve information based on specific criteria. DataReaders are also a small part of a larger solution that can offer more exciting and new bugs to explore.

In our next scenario we will examine searching for and manipulating data from databases.

# Chapter 17

# Real-World Scenarios: Searching a Database

To this point in our examination of common debugging scenarios, we have devoted a large amount of energy to debugging and discussing code related to databases. Databases, being so prevalent in the current corporate climate, can be a catchall for bugs if you are not careful in executing your code.

In Chapter 16 we will be looking at the next step in database work. We started by opening the database, moved on to reading from it, and now we will search for and manipulate specific information. We will examine the bugs that can show up in code when one tries to execute queries and searches against databases.

As with many of the other scenarios we have covered, there will be some reoccurring themes when we look at the bugs. However, it is great practice to look for bugs again and again. The more practice you have looking for, identifying, and remediating specific bugs, the less likely you will be to repeat such errors.

In our first example, we will look at some bugs that can show up as we query information from a standard Microsoft Structure Query Language (SQL) table.

## Querying Tables

In this example we will be executing searches against one of the prepackaged Microsoft SQL databases `pubs`. The table we will use for all of these examples is the jobs table. This table contains prepopulated information and should be the same for most installations of SQL.

> If you are not familiar with T-SQL or the structure query language used by MSSQL, take a moment to look over this quick explanation.

Remember, this scenario is about debugging Visual Basic 6, Visual Basic .NET, or C# code. We are not going to plant hidden bugs in T-SQL code just to trip you up. However, one of the many methods that can be leveraged in searching databases is to execute a SQL query.

You may have noticed the use of these queries in the past scenarios. The good thing about using T-SQL queries in this book is that they read almost like plain English. For example, the following table of data was retrieved with the query `Select top 10 * from jobs`.

| job_id | job_desc | min_lvl | max_lvl |
|---|---|---|---|
| 1 | New hire – job not specified | 10 | 10 |
| 2 | Chief executive officer | 200 | 250 |
| 3 | Business operations manager | 175 | 225 |
| 4 | Chief financial officer | 175 | 250 |
| 5 | Publisher | 150 | 250 |
| 6 | Managing editor | 140 | 225 |
| 7 | Marketing manager | 120 | 200 |
| 8 | Public relations manager | 100 | 175 |
| 9 | Acquisitions manager | 75 | 175 |
| 10 | Productions manager | 75 | 165 |

In English this query tells the database that it wants to select the top 10 rows for every column from the jobs table. This should give you an idea as to what the queries may look like in these examples. Just keep in mind that if you are unfamiliar with T-SQL code, you can most likely work through it and still understand where the bugs may be in the applications.

> One more note: For this example, we will be using a .udl file for our VB6 examples and passing string credentials for our .NET examples. Again, this is just to get you used to looking at different methods for similar bugs.

In our first example, we will build several small applications that ask us to query all of the information from the jobs table based on the `job_id` field. The applications will have one text box, one button, and three labels. The user will type a job_id in the text box, press the button, and the remaining fields of the table will be populated into the labels. Take some time now to look over these samples and try to spot the bug.

> If the applications are a bit daunting, or if you want to work with the compiler, try executing the applications on your own.

### VB6

```
'**********************
'Declarations:
'  Types
'**********************
Dim openData As Boolean
Dim udlExist As Boolean

Private Sub Command1_Click()
'*************************
'Defines and opens a local
'  SQL database
'    jfd
'    10/10/05
'*************************
'Declarations:
'*************************
Dim cn As adodb.Connection
Dim rs As adodb.Recordset
Dim query As String
Dim job_desc As Integer
Dim min_lvl As Integer
Dim max_lvl As Integer
'*************************
'Begin
```

```
'**************************
openData = False
If (udlExist) Then
      Set cn = New adodb.Connection
      Set rs = New adodb.Recordset
      query = "Select * from jobs where job_id ='"
& jobIDtxt.Text & "'"
      cn.Open "File Name=c:\test.udl"
      rs.Open query, cn, adOpenForwardOnly,
adLockReadOnly
      openData = True
      '**************************
      'count the records returned
      ' if more than 0, assign to vars
      '**************************
      If rs.RecordCount <> 0 Then
         job_desc = rs.Fields("job_desc")
         min_lvl = rs.Fields("min_lvl")
         max_lvl = rs.Fields("max_lvl")
      Else
         openData = False
         MsgBox "No fields were returned by that
query"
         Exit Sub
      End If
      '**************************
      'display the results
      '**************************
      JobDescLbl.Caption = job_desc
      MinLvlLbl.Caption = min_lvl
      MaxLvlLbl.Caption = max_lvl
      Set rs = Nothing
      cn.Close
      openData = False
End If
'**************************
```

```
'End
'**************************
End Sub

Private Sub Form_Load()
'**********************
'Sample VB6 program
'Checks for the existence of and
' Opens a .udl file
'
'5/5/05 jfd
'**********************
'Begin:
'**********************
udlExist = False
If Dir("c:\test.udl", vbNormal) <> "" Then
    udlExist = True
Else
    udlExist = False
    MsgBox "The requested .udl file does not exist."
End If
'**********************
'End
'**********************

End Sub

Private Sub Form_Terminate()
'**************************
'Prompts user before closing app
'**************************
'Declarations:
'**************************

'**************************
'Begin
'**************************
```

```
Select Case MsgBox("Are you sure you want to exit?",
vbYesNoCancel)
Case vbYes
    If (openData) Then
       If (MsgBox("Do you want to save your data?",
vbYesNo)) = vbYes Then
          End
       End If
    Exit Sub
 End If
 End
Case vbNo
'do not close app
Case vbCancel
'do not close app
End Select

'**************************
'End
'**************************
End Sub
```

## VB.NET

```
Inherits System.Windows.Forms.Form
Dim openData As Boolean

Private Sub Button1_Click(ByVal sender As
System.Object, ByVal e As System.EventArgs) Handles
Button1.Click
'****************************
'Sample VB .NET Program
'   jfd
'   10/10/05
'****************************
'Declarations:
'****************************
```

```
Dim cn As New
SqlConnection("server=(local);database=pubs;uid=sa;
pwd=;")
Dim cmd As SqlCommand
Dim i As Integer
Dim query As String
Dim job_desc As Integer
Dim min_lvl As Integer
Dim max_lvl As Integer
'***************************
'Begin
'***************************
openData = False
cn.Open()
query = "Select * from jobs where job_id = '" &
jobIDtxt.Text & "'"
cmd = New SqlCommand(query, cn)
Dim dr As SqlDataReader
'***************************
'execute within a try...catch
'***************************
Try
    dr = cmd.ExecuteReader()
Catch operationException As
System.InvalidOperationException
    'perform more logic based on error
    MsgBox("There was an error in the operation!")
End Try
i = 0 'set the counter to 0
'***************************
'This piece of code counts the
' number of records returned
'***************************
While dr.Read()
    i = i + 1
End While
```

```
'****************************
dr.Close()  'close the datareader
If i > 0 Then
    openData = True
    Try
       dr = cmd.ExecuteReader()
    Catch opExcept As
System.InvalidOperationException
       MsgBox("There was an error in the operation!")
    End Try
    Do While dr.Read()
       job_desc = dr("job_desc")
       min_lvl = dr("min_lvl")
       max_lvl = dr("max_lvl")
    Loop
End If
jobDescLbl.Text = job_desc
minLvlLbl.Text = min_lvl
maxLvlLbl.Text = max_lvl
openData = False
dr.Close()
cn.Close()
'****************************
'End
'****************************
End Sub

Protected Overrides Sub OnClosing(ByVal e As
System.ComponentModel.CancelEventArgs)
'****************************
'Sample VB .NET Program
'   jfd
'   10/10/05
'****************************
'Declarations:
'****************************
```

```
'****************************
'Begin
'****************************
Select Case MsgBox("Are you sure you want to exit?",
vbYesNoCancel)
    Case vbYes
       If (openData) Then
          If (MsgBox("Should I save your data?",
vbYesNo)) = vbYes Then
             e.Cancel = False
          End If
       End If
    Case vbNo
       e.Cancel = True
    Case vbCancel
       e.Cancel = True
End Select

'****************************
'End
'****************************
End Sub
```

**C#**

```
private void button1_Click(object sender,
System.EventArgs e)
{
//*******************************
//Declarations:
//*******************************
SqlConnection cn = new
SqlConnection("server=(local);database=pubs;
uid=sa;");
int i;
bool emptyTable;
string query = "";
```

```
SqlDataReader dr;
SqlCommand cmd;
int job_desc = 0;
int min_lvl = 0;
int max_lvl = 0;
//******************************
//Begin
//******************************
cn.Open();
query = "Select * from jobs where job_id ='" +
jobIDTxt.Text + "'";
cmd = new SqlCommand(query,cn);
i = 0;
try
{
    dr = cmd.ExecuteReader();
    while(dr.Read())
    {
       i++;
    }
    dr.Close();
}
catch (System.Data.SqlClient.SqlException
opException)
{
    MessageBox.Show( opException.ToString() );
}
emptyTable =false;
//******************************
//if the table is empty, flag it
//******************************
if (i==0)
{
    emptyTable = true;
}
//******************************
```

```
//if the table is not empty
// copy each record to the array
//*****************************
if (emptyTable != true)
{
    try
    {
        dr = cmd.ExecuteReader();
        while(dr.Read ())
        {
            job_desc = dr.GetString(1) ;
            min_lvl = Convert.ToInt16
(dr["min_lvl"].ToString() ;
            max_lvl = Convert.ToInt16
(dr["max_lvl"].ToString() );

        }
        dr.Close();
    }
    catch(System.InvalidOperationException
opException)
    {
    }
    jobDescLbl.Text = job_desc;
    minLvlLbl.Text = min_lvl.ToString() ;
    maxLvlLbl.Text = max_lvl.ToString() ;
}
cn.Close();
//*****************************
//End
//*****************************

}
```

What we have just looked through is an example of the same application written in the three different languages. This application allows the user to specify a `job_id` and will return the `job_desc`, `min_lvl`, and `max_lvl`.

Looking at the Visual Basic 6 and the Visual Basic .NET examples, you can see that we have added some functionality to the form termination code. In an earlier scenario we changed this code to prompt users whether they wanted to close the application. Now, if the application is working with an open database at the time the users terminate, the application will ask them if they want to save their data.

> No logic has been added to save the data, but the application will prompt.

The Visual Basic 6 and Visual Basic .NET examples compile correctly. However, when the user clicks on the form's button, the following errors are thrown:

### VB6

```
Run-time error '13':

Type Mismatch
```

### VB.NET

```
An unhandled exception of type
'System.InvalidCastException' occurred in
microsoft.visualbasic.dll

Additional information: Cast from string "New Hire
- Job not specified" to type 'Integer' is not valid.
```

The same bug is throwing both of these errors; however, the Visual Basic .NET error is by far the most descriptive. Again, do not worry too much about the `unhandled exception`; the `additional information` gives us enough data for our example.

Sure enough, the variable we used to handle the value for `job_desc` was dimensioned as an integer rather than a string.

The C# code suffers from the same bug. To C#'s credit, as has happened in a couple of our examples, the compiler catches the error. The compiler in this case catches the error in two places rather than one. The first is when the DataReader passes the string value to the integer variable. The second is when the integer variable attempts to assign its value to the label's text property.

Visual Basic is still a much more forgiving application in this regard. VB will tend to autocast values into specific types on the fly. C# forces you to be a bit more vigilant with your code.

Let us go through the three samples and correct the bugs:

## VB6

```
'**********************
'Declarations:
' Types
'**********************
Dim openData As Boolean
Dim udlExist As Boolean

Private Sub Command1_Click()
'**************************
'Defines and opens a local
' SQL database
'   jfd
'   10/10/05
'**************************
'Declarations:
'**************************
Dim cn As adodb.Connection
Dim rs As adodb.Recordset
Dim query As String
Dim job_desc As String
Dim min_lvl As Integer
Dim max_lvl As Integer
'**************************
'Begin
'**************************
openData = False
If (udlExist) Then
```

```
      Set cn = New adodb.Connection
      Set rs = New adodb.Recordset
      query = "Select * from jobs where job_id ='"
& jobIDtxt.Text & "'"
      cn.Open "File Name=c:\test.udl"
      rs.Open query, cn, adOpenForwardOnly,
adLockReadOnly
      openData = True
      '*************************
      'count the records returned
      ' if more than 0, assign to vars
      '*************************
      If rs.RecordCount <> 0 Then
         job_desc = rs.Fields("job_desc")
         min_lvl = rs.Fields("min_lvl")
         max_lvl = rs.Fields("max_lvl")
      Else
         openData = False
         MsgBox "No fields were returned by that
query"
         Exit Sub
      End If
      '*************************
      'display the results
      '*************************
      JobDescLbl.Caption = job_desc
      MinLvlLbl.Caption = min_lvl
      MaxLvlLbl.Caption = max_lvl
      Set rs = Nothing
      cn.Close
      openData = False
End If
'*************************
'End
'*************************
End Sub
```

```
Private Sub Form_Load()
'*********************
'Sample VB6 program
'Checks for the existence of and
' Opens a .udl file
'
'5/5/05 jfd
'*********************
'Begin:
'*********************
udlExist = False
If Dir("c:\test.udl", vbNormal) <> "" Then
    udlExist = True
Else
    udlExist = False
    MsgBox "The requested .udl file does not exist."
End If
'*********************
'End
'*********************

End Sub

Private Sub Form_Terminate()
'*************************
'Prompts user before closing app
'*************************
'Declarations:
'*************************

'*************************
'Begin
'*************************

Select Case MsgBox("Are you sure you want to exit?",
vbYesNoCancel)
Case vbYes
```

```
    If (openData) Then
       If (MsgBox("Do you want to save your data?",
vbYesNo)) = vbYes Then
          End
       End If
       Exit Sub
    End If
    End
Case vbNo
'do not close app
Case vbCancel
'do not close app
End Select

'**************************
'End
'**************************
End Sub
```

## VB.NET

```
Inherits System.Windows.Forms.Form
Dim openData As Boolean

Private Sub Button1_Click(ByVal sender As
System.Object, ByVal e As System.EventArgs) Handles
Button1.Click
'****************************
'Sample VB .NET Program
'   jfd
'   10/10/05
'****************************
'Declarations:
'****************************
Dim cn As New
SqlConnection("server=(local);database=pubs;uid=sa;
pwd=;")
```

```
Dim cmd As SqlCommand
Dim i As Integer
Dim query As String
Dim job_desc As String
Dim min_lvl As Integer
Dim max_lvl As Integer
'***************************
'Begin
'***************************
openData = False
cn.Open()
query = "Select * from jobs where job_id = '" &
jobIDtxt.Text & "'"
cmd = New SqlCommand(query, cn)
Dim dr As SqlDataReader
'***************************
'execute within a try...catch
'***************************
Try
    dr = cmd.ExecuteReader()
Catch operationException As
System.InvalidOperationException
    'perform more logic based on error
    MsgBox("There was an error in the operation!")
End Try
i = 0  'set the counter to 0
'***************************
'This piece of code counts the
' number of records returned
'***************************
While dr.Read()
    i = i + 1
End While
'***************************
dr.Close()  'close the datareader
```

```
If i > 0 Then
    openData = True
    Try
       dr = cmd.ExecuteReader()
    Catch opExcept As System.InvalidOperationException
       MsgBox("There was an error in the operation!")
    End Try
    Do While dr.Read()
       job_desc = dr("job_desc")
       min_lvl = dr("min_lvl")
       max_lvl = dr("max_lvl")
    Loop
End If
jobDescLbl.Text = job_desc
minLvlLbl.Text = min_lvl
maxLvlLbl.Text = max_lvl
openData = False
dr.Close()
cn.Close()
'***************************
'End
'***************************
End Sub

Protected Overrides Sub OnClosing(ByVal e As
System.ComponentModel.CancelEventArgs)
'***************************
'Sample VB .NET Program
'   jfd
'   10/10/05
'***************************
'Declarations:
'***************************
'***************************
'Begin
'***************************
```

```
Select Case MsgBox("Are you sure you want to exit?",
vbYesNoCancel)
    Case vbYes
        If (openData) Then
            If (MsgBox("Should I save your data?",
vbYesNo)) = vbYes Then
                e.Cancel = False
            End If
        End If
    Case vbNo
        e.Cancel = True
    Case vbCancel
        e.Cancel = True
End Select
'*****************************
'End
'*****************************
End Sub
```

### C#

```
private void button1_Click(object sender,
System.EventArgs e)
{
//*****************************
//Declarations:
//*****************************
SqlConnection cn = new
SqlConnection("server=(local);database=pubs;
uid=sa;");
int i;
bool emptyTable;
string query = "";
SqlDataReader dr;
SqlCommand cmd;
string job_desc = "";
```

```
int min_lvl = 0;
int max_lvl = 0;
//******************************
//Begin
//******************************
cn.Open();
query = "Select * from jobs where job_id ='" +
jobIDTxt.Text + "'";
cmd = new SqlCommand(query,cn);
i = 0;
try
{
    dr = cmd.ExecuteReader();
    while(dr.Read())
    {
       i++;
    }
    dr.Close();
}
catch (System.Data.SqlClient.SqlException
opException)
{
    MessageBox.Show( opException.ToString() );
}
emptyTable =false;
//******************************
//if the table is empty, flag it
//******************************
if (i==0)
{
    emptyTable = true;
}
//******************************
//if the table is not empty
// copy each record to the array
//******************************
```

```
if (emptyTable != true)
{
    try
    {
        dr = cmd.ExecuteReader();
        while(dr.Read ())
        {
            job_desc = dr.GetString(1) ;
            min_lvl = Convert.ToInt16
(dr["min_lvl"].ToString() ;
            max_lvl = Convert.ToInt16
(dr["max_lvl"].ToString() );

        }
        dr.Close();
    }
    catch(System.InvalidOperationException
opException)
    {
    }
    jobDescLbl.Text = job_desc;
    minLvlLbl.Text = min_lvl.ToString() ;
    maxLvlLbl.Text = max_lvl.ToString() ;
}

cn.Close();
//******************************
//End
//******************************

}
```

Given the relative size of these applications, the changes have been noted in bold font. After changing the variable type of job_desc, the applications perform as expected.

In our next example, we will take a look at some of the bugs that can come up when searching through databases using stored procedures rather than string queries.

## Using Stored Procedures

Stored procedures are queries that reside within a Microsoft SQL server. Stored procedures are useful for a couple of difference reasons. The first is that they allow for different applications and users to call the same query many times over without having to input it by hand every time.

The second and more relevant reason is that the bulk of the processing for a query is performed on the server. Therefore, if you are executing queries with large amounts of manipulated data, it is more advantageous to let the server take the hit on the processing and let the application wait for the results.

However, stored procedures are treated a bit differently from string queries. The three samples in the example will all contain a common bug related to the execution of a stored procedure. The sample stored procedure we will be calling from our code is as follows:

```
CREATE PROCEDURE GetAuthorInfo
        @au_id varchar (11),
        @au_lname varchar(40),
        @au_fname varchar(20)

as

select * from authors where au_id = @au_id and
au_lname= @au_lname and au_fname = @au_fname

 return
GO
```

Basically, this stored procedure accepts three parameters: au_id, au_lname, and au_fname. It then passes these parameters to a query, much like the string queries we have been using. These parameters correspond to fields in the following table:

| au_id | au_lname | au_fname | Phone | Address | City | State |
|---|---|---|---|---|---|---|
| 172-32-1176 | White | Johnson | 408 496-7223 | 10932 Bigge Rd. | Menlo Park | CA |
| 213-46-8915 | Green | Marjorie | 415 986-7020 | 309 63rd St. #411 | Oakland | CA |
| 238-95-7766 | Carson | Cheryl | 415 548-7723 | 589 Darwin Ln. | Berkeley | CA |
| 267-41-2394 | O'Leary | Michael | 408 286-2428 | 22 Cleveland Ave. #14 | San Jose | CA |
| 274-80-9391 | Straight | Dean | 415 834-2919 | 5420 College Ave. | Oakland | CA |
| 341-22-1782 | Smith | Meander | 913 843-0462 | 10 Mississippi Dr. | Lawrence | KS |
| 409-56-7008 | Bennet | Abraham | 415 658-9932 | 6223 Bateman St. | Berkeley | CA |
| 427-17-2319 | Dull | Ann | 415 836-7128 | 3410 Blonde St. | Palo Alto | CA |
| 472-27-2349 | Gringlesby | Burt | 707 938-6445 | P.O. Box 792 | Covelo | CA |

Therefore, using this stored procedure, if we supply the parameters as follows:

```
Au_id = 172-32-1176
Au_lname = White
Au_fname = Johnson
```

we should receive the following data in return:

```
172-32-1176 White Johnson 408 496-7223 10932 Bigge
Rd. Menlo Park CA
```

Let us slightly modify the applications we had for the last example. We will add two more text boxes to accept the added input variables. Additionally, we will modify the code to call a stored procedure rather than use a string query.

Look through the following samples and see if you can locate the bugs:

## VB6

```
'**********************
'Declarations:
' Types
'**********************
Dim openData As Boolean
Dim udlExist As Boolean

Private Sub Command1_Click()
'**************************
'Defines and opens a local
' SQL database
'   jfd
'   10/10/05
'**************************
'Declarations:
'**************************
Dim cn As ADODB.Connection
Dim cmd As ADODB.Command
Dim rs As ADODB.Recordset
Dim au_id As ADODB.Parameter
Dim au_lname As ADODB.Parameter
```

```
Dim au_fname As ADODB.Parameter
Dim address As ADODB.Parameter
Dim city As ADODB.Parameter
Dim state As ADODB.Parameter
'***************************
'Begin
'***************************
openData = False
If (udlExist) Then
       Set cn = New ADODB.Connection
       Set cmd = New ADODB.Command
       cn.Open "File Name=c:\test.udl"
       cmd.ActiveConnection = cn
       cmd.CommandType = adCmdStoredProc
       cmd.CommandText = "GetAuthorInfo"
       '***************************
       'assign values to the parameters
       '***************************
       Set au_id = cmd.CreateParameter("@au_id",
adVariant, adParamInput, 11, auIDtxt.Text)
       Set au_lname = cmd.CreateParameter("@au_lname",
adVarChar, adParamInput, 40, auLnameTxt.Text)
       Set au_fname = cmd.CreateParameter("@au_fname",
adVarChar, adParamInput, 20, auFnameTxt.Text)
       '***************************
       'assign the parameters to
       ' the stored procedure
       '***************************
       cmd.Parameters.Append au_id
       cmd.Parameters.Append au_lname
       cmd.Parameters.Append au_fname
       Set rs = cmd.Execute
       '***************************
       'assign the return values
       ' to the labels
```

```
        '**************************
        addressLbl.Caption = rs.Fields("address")
        cityLbl.Caption = rs.Fields("city")
        stateLbl.Caption = rs.Fields("state")

        openData = True
        '**************************
        'count the records returned
        ' if more than 0, assign to vars
        '**************************
        cn.Close
        openData = False
End If
'**************************
'End
'**************************
End Sub

Private Sub Form_Load()
'**********************
'Sample VB6 program
'Checks for the existence of and
' Opens a .udl file
'
'5/5/05 jfd
'**********************
'Begin:
'**********************
udlExist = False
If Dir("c:\test.udl", vbNormal) <> "" Then
    udlExist = True
Else
    udlExist = False
    MsgBox "The requested .udl file does not exist."
End If
```

```
'**********************
'End
'**********************

End Sub

Private Sub Form_Terminate()
'*************************
'Prompts user before closing app
'*************************
'Declarations:
'*************************

'*************************
'Begin
'*************************

Select Case MsgBox("Are you sure you want to exit?",
vbYesNoCancel)
Case vbYes
    If (openData) Then
       If (MsgBox("Do you want to save your data?",
vbYesNo)) = vbYes Then
          End
       End If
       Exit Sub
    End If
    End
Case vbNo
'do not close app
Case vbCancel
'do not close app
End Select

'*************************
'End
'*************************
End Sub
```

## VB.NET

```
Private Sub Button1_Click(ByVal sender As
System.Object, ByVal e As System.EventArgs) Handles
Button1.Click
'*****************************
'Sample VB .NET Program
'   jfd
'   10/10/05
'*****************************
'Declarations:
'*****************************
Dim cn As New
SqlConnection("server=(local);database=pubs;uid=sa;
pwd=;")
Dim cmd As SqlCommand
Dim i As Integer
Dim dr As SqlDataReader
'*****************************
'Begin
'*****************************
openData = False
cn.Open()
cmd = New SqlCommand("GetAuthorInfo", cn)
cmd.CommandType = CommandType.StoredProcedure
'*****************************
'execute within a try...catch
'*****************************
Try
    cmd.Parameters.Add("@au_id", SqlDbType.Variant,
11)
    cmd.Parameters("@au_id").Value = auIDTxt.Text
    cmd.Parameters.Add("@au_lname", SqlDbType.VarChar,
40)
    cmd.Parameters("@au_lname").Value =
auLnameTxt.Text
    cmd.Parameters.Add("@au_fname", SqlDbType.VarChar,
20)
```

```
    cmd.Parameters("@au_fname").Value =
auFnameTxt.Text
    dr = cmd.ExecuteReader()
Catch operationException As
System.InvalidOperationException
    'perform more logic based on error
    MsgBox("There was an error in the operation!")
Catch sqlExc As SqlClient.SqlException
    MsgBox(sqlExc.ToString)
End Try
i = 0  'set the counter to 0
'***************************
'This piece of code counts the
' number of records returned
'***************************
While dr.Read()
    i = i + 1
End While
'***************************
dr.Close()  'close the datareader
If i > 0 Then
    openData = True
    Try
        dr = cmd.ExecuteReader()
    Catch opExcept As
System.InvalidOperationException
        MsgBox("There was an error in the operation!")
    End Try
    Do While dr.Read()
        addressLbl.Text = dr("address")
        cityLbl.Text = dr("city")
        stateLbl.Text = dr("state")
    Loop
End If
openData = False
dr.Close()
```

```
cn.Close()
'****************************
'End
'****************************
End Sub

Protected Overrides Sub OnClosing(ByVal e As
System.ComponentModel.CancelEventArgs)
'****************************
'Sample VB .NET Program
'   jfd
'   10/10/05
'****************************
'Declarations:
'****************************
'****************************
'Begin
'****************************
Select Case MsgBox("Are you sure you want to exit?",
vbYesNoCancel)
       Case vbYes
          If (openData) Then
             If (MsgBox("Should I save your data?",
vbYesNo)) = vbYes Then
                e.Cancel = False
             End If
          End If
          Case vbNo
             e.Cancel = True
          Case vbCancel
             e.Cancel = True
End Select

'****************************
'End
'****************************
End Sub
```

**C#**

```
private void button1_Click(object sender,
System.EventArgs e)
{
//******************************
//Declarations:
//******************************
SqlConnection cn = new
SqlConnection("server=(local);database=pubs;
uid=sa;");
int i;
bool emptyTable;
SqlDataReader dr;
SqlCommand cmd;
//******************************
//Begin
//******************************
cn.Open();
cmd = new SqlCommand("GetAuthorInfo",cn);
cmd.CommandType = CommandType.StoredProcedure ;
i = 0;
try
{
    //******************************
    //assign the text values to
    // SQL parameters
    //******************************
    cmd.Parameters.Add ("@au_id",
SqlDbType.Variant,11);
    cmd.Parameters["@au_id"].Value = auIDTxt.Text;
    cmd.Parameters.Add ("@au_lname",
SqlDbType.VarChar,40);
    cmd.Parameters["@au_lname"].Value =
auLnameTxt.Text;
    cmd.Parameters.Add ("@au_fname",
SqlDbType.VarChar,20);
```

```
    cmd.Parameters["@au_fname"].Value =
auFnameTxt.Text;
    //*******************************
    dr = cmd.ExecuteReader();
    while(dr.Read())
    {
       i++;
    }
    dr.Close();
}
catch (System.Data.SqlClient.SqlException
opException)
{
    MessageBox.Show( opException.ToString() );
}
emptyTable =false;
//*****************************
//if the table is empty, flag it
//*****************************
if (i==0)
{
    emptyTable = true;
}
//*****************************
//if the table is not empty
// copy each record to the array
//*****************************
if (emptyTable != true)
{
    try
    {
       dr = cmd.ExecuteReader();
       while(dr.Read ())
       {
          //*******************************
          // assign the Stored Procedure
```

```
            // return values to labels
            //******************************
            addressLbl.Text = dr["address"].ToString() ;
            cityLbl.Text = dr["city"].ToString() ;
            stateLbl.Text = dr["state"].ToString() ;
        }
        dr.Close();
    }
    catch(System.InvalidOperationException
opException)
    {
    }
}

cn.Close();
//******************************
//End
//******************************
}
```

These three examples demonstrate a very simplistic application in three languages. This application accepts three field inputs by way of form text boxes. These three input values are then passed to a stored procedure when code behind a "For Button" is executed. The stored procedure uses the values to retrieve a row from the `author` table of a SQL database.

The retrieved row is passed back to the application as a DataReader (in Visual Basic .NET and C#) or as a recordset (in Visual Basic 6). The application then displays the retrieved row on the form.

All three of these samples compile correctly. However, when the user clicks on the button to execute the stored procedure, the following errors are thrown:

### VB6

```
Run-time error '-2147217900(80040e14)':

Implicit conversion from data type sql_variant to
varchar is not allowed. Use the CONVERT function to
run this query.
```

## VB.NET

```
System.Data.SqlClient.SqlException: Implicit
conversion from data type sql_variant to varchar is
not allowed. Use the CONVERT function to run this
query.
 at System.Data.SqlClient.SqlCommand.ExecuteReader
(CommandBehavior cmdBehavior, RunBehavior runBehavior,
Boolean returnStream)
 at System.Data.SqlClient.SqlCommand.ExecuteReader()
 at BookExampleFile.Form1.Button1_Click(Object
sender, EventArgs e) in F:\BookExampleFile\
Form1.vb:line 156An unhandled exception of type
'System.NullReferenceException' occurred in
BookExampleFile.exe

Additional information: Object reference not set to
an instance of an object.
```

Looking back through the code, and comparing it to the sample SQL data, we can see that the parameter for au_id is passed as a variant. This parameter should be a VarChar like the other two parameters in the stored procedure.

For a verification of this, take a look once again at the code for the stored procedure `GetAuthorInfo`:

```
CREATE PROCEDURE GetAuthorInfo
       @au_id varchar (11),
       @au_lname varchar(40),
       @au_fname varchar(20)

as

select * from authors where au_id = @au_id and
au_lname= @au_lname and au_fname = @au_fname

 return
GO
```

Lines 2 through 4 define the input variables for the stored procedure. Here we can see that `@au_id`, `@au_lname`, and `@au_fname` are all defined as `varchar`. Therefore, when our code attempts to pass these parameters to the stored procedure, it must also pass them as a `varchar`.

The correct code is as follows:

> The corrected lines have been bolded to make them easier to find; however, you should still see them in context.

**VB6**

```
'**********************
'Declarations:
' Types
'**********************
Dim openData As Boolean
Dim udlExist As Boolean

Private Sub Command1_Click()
'**************************
'Defines and opens a local
' SQL database
'   jfd
'   10/10/05
'**************************
'Declarations:
'**************************
Dim cn As ADODB.Connection
Dim cmd As ADODB.Command
Dim rs As ADODB.Recordset
Dim au_id As ADODB.Parameter
Dim au_lname As ADODB.Parameter
Dim au_fname As ADODB.Parameter
Dim address As ADODB.Parameter
Dim city As ADODB.Parameter
Dim state As ADODB.Parameter
'**************************
'Begin
'**************************
openData = False
```

```
If (udlExist) Then
      Set cn = New ADODB.Connection
      Set cmd = New ADODB.Command
      cn.Open "File Name=c:\test.udl"
      cmd.ActiveConnection = cn
      cmd.CommandType = adCmdStoredProc
      cmd.CommandText = "GetAuthorInfo"
      '**************************
      'assign values to the parameters
      '**************************
      Set au_id = cmd.CreateParameter("@au_id",
adVarChar, adParamInput, 11, auIDtxt.Text)
      Set au_lname =
cmd.CreateParameter("@au_lname", adVarChar,
adParamInput, 40, auLnameTxt.Text)
      Set au_fname =
cmd.CreateParameter("@au_fname", adVarChar,
adParamInput, 20, auFnameTxt.Text)
      '**************************
      'assign the parameters to
      ' the stored procedure
      '**************************
      cmd.Parameters.Append au_id
      cmd.Parameters.Append au_lname
      cmd.Parameters.Append au_fname
      Set rs = cmd.Execute
      '**************************
      'assign the return values
      ' to the labels
      '**************************
      addressLbl.Caption = rs.Fields("address")
      cityLbl.Caption = rs.Fields("city")
      stateLbl.Caption = rs.Fields("state")

      openData = True
      '**************************
      'count the records returned
```

```
        ' if more than 0, assign to vars
        '**************************
        cn.Close
        openData = False
End If
'**************************
'End
'**************************
End Sub

Private Sub Form_Load()
'*********************
'Sample VB6 program
'Checks for the existence of and
' Opens a .udl file
'
'5/5/05 jfd
'*********************
'Begin:
'*********************
udlExist = False
If Dir("c:\test.udl", vbNormal) <> "" Then
    udlExist = True
Else
    udlExist = False
    MsgBox "The requested .udl file does not exist."
End If
'*********************
'End
'*********************

End Sub

Private Sub Form_Terminate()
'*************************
'Prompts user before closing app
'*************************
```

```
'Declarations:
'**************************

'**************************
'Begin
'**************************

Select Case MsgBox("Are you sure you want to exit?",
vbYesNoCancel)
Case vbYes
    If (openData) Then
       If (MsgBox("Do you want to save your data?",
vbYesNo)) = vbYes Then
          End
       End If
       Exit Sub
    End If
    End
Case vbNo
'do not close app
Case vbCancel
'do not close app
End Select

'**************************
'End
'**************************
End Sub
```

**VB.NET**

```
Private Sub Button1_Click(ByVal sender As
System.Object, ByVal e As System.EventArgs) Handles
Button1.Click
'****************************
'Sample VB .NET Program
'   jfd
'   10/10/05
```

```
'****************************
'Declarations:
'****************************
Dim cn As New
SqlConnection("server=(local);database=pubs;uid=sa;
pwd=;")
Dim cmd As SqlCommand
Dim i As Integer
Dim dr As SqlDataReader
'****************************
'Begin
'****************************
openData = False
cn.Open()
cmd = New SqlCommand("GetAuthorInfo", cn)
cmd.CommandType = CommandType.StoredProcedure
'****************************
'execute within a try...catch
'****************************
Try
    cmd.Parameters.Add("@au_id", SqlDbType.VarChar,
11)
    cmd.Parameters("@au_id").Value = auIDTxt.Text
    cmd.Parameters.Add("@au_lname",
SqlDbType.VarChar, 40)
    cmd.Parameters("@au_lname").Value =
auLnameTxt.Text
    cmd.Parameters.Add("@au_fname",
SqlDbType.VarChar, 20)
    cmd.Parameters("@au_fname").Value =
auFnameTxt.Text
    dr = cmd.ExecuteReader()
Catch operationException As
System.InvalidOperationException
    'perform more logic based on error
    MsgBox("There was an error in the operation!")
Catch sqlExc As SqlClient.SqlException
```

```
    MsgBox(sqlExc.ToString)
End Try
i = 0  'set the counter to 0
'***************************
'This piece of code counts the
' number of records returned
'***************************
While dr.Read()
    i = i + 1
End While
'***************************
dr.Close()  'close the datareader
If i > 0 Then
    openData = True
    Try
       dr = cmd.ExecuteReader()
    Catch opExcept As
System.InvalidOperationException
       MsgBox("There was an error in the operation!")
    End Try
    Do While dr.Read()
       addressLbl.Text = dr("address")
       cityLbl.Text = dr("city")
       stateLbl.Text = dr("state")
    Loop
End If
openData = False
dr.Close()
cn.Close()
'***************************
'End
'***************************
End Sub

Protected Overrides Sub OnClosing(ByVal e As
System.ComponentModel.CancelEventArgs)
```

```
'****************************
'Sample VB .NET Program
'   jfd
'   10/10/05
'****************************
'Declarations:
'****************************
'****************************
'Begin
'****************************
Select Case MsgBox("Are you sure you want to exit?",
vbYesNoCancel)
    Case vbYes
       If (openData) Then
          If (MsgBox("Should I save your data?",
vbYesNo)) = vbYes Then
             e.Cancel = False
          End If
       End If
    Case vbNo
       e.Cancel = True
    Case vbCancel
       e.Cancel = True
End Select

'****************************
'End
'****************************
End Sub
```

**C#**

```
private void button1_Click(object sender,
System.EventArgs e)
{
//****************************
//Declarations:
```

```
//******************************
SqlConnection cn = new
SqlConnection("server=(local);database=pubs;
uid=sa;");
int i;
bool emptyTable;
SqlDataReader dr;
SqlCommand cmd;
//******************************
//Begin
//******************************
cn.Open();
cmd = new SqlCommand("GetAuthorInfo",cn);
cmd.CommandType = CommandType.StoredProcedure ;
i = 0;
try
{
    //******************************
    //assign the text values to
    // SQL parameters
    //******************************
    cmd.Parameters.Add ("@au_id",
SqlDbType.VarChar,11);
    cmd.Parameters["@au_id"].Value = auIDTxt.Text;
    cmd.Parameters.Add ("@au_lname",
SqlDbType.VarChar,40);
    cmd.Parameters["@au_lname"].Value =
auLnameTxt.Text;
    cmd.Parameters.Add ("@au_fname",
SqlDbType.VarChar,20);
    cmd.Parameters["@au_fname"].Value =
auFnameTxt.Text;
    //******************************
    dr = cmd.ExecuteReader();
    while(dr.Read())
    {
       i++;
```

```
    }
    dr.Close();
}
catch (System.Data.SqlClient.SqlException
opException)
{
    MessageBox.Show( opException.ToString() );
}
emptyTable =false;
//*****************************
//if the table is empty, flag it
//*****************************
if (i==0)
{
    emptyTable = true;
}
//*****************************
//if the table is not empty
// copy each record to the array
//*****************************
if (emptyTable != true)
{
    try
    {
       dr = cmd.ExecuteReader();
       while(dr.Read ())
       {
          //*******************************
          // assign the Stored Procedure
          // return values to labels
          //*******************************
          addressLbl.Text = dr["address"].ToString() ;
          cityLbl.Text = dr["city"].ToString() ;
          stateLbl.Text = dr["state"].ToString() ;
       }
       dr.Close();
```

```
    }
    catch(System.InvalidOperationException
opException)
    {
    }
}

cn.Close();
//*****************************
//End
//*****************************
}
```

Let us look at one final example of where a bug may show up when you are working with a stored procedure.

Building on the previously corrected code, take a look at the following snippets from the three applications. They seem to compile correctly and can run correctly at times.

## VB6

```
'*********************
'Declarations:
'  Types
'*********************
Dim openData As Boolean
Dim udlExist As Boolean

Private Sub Command1_Click()
'*************************
'Defines and opens a local
'  SQL database
'    jfd
'    10/10/05
'*************************
'Declarations:
'*************************
Dim cn As ADODB.Connection
Dim cmd As ADODB.Command
```

```
Dim rs As ADODB.Recordset
Dim au_id As ADODB.Parameter
Dim au_lname As ADODB.Parameter
Dim au_fname As ADODB.Parameter
Dim address As ADODB.Parameter
Dim city As ADODB.Parameter
Dim state As ADODB.Parameter
'**************************
'Begin
'**************************
openData = False
If (udlExist) Then
      Set cn = New ADODB.Connection
      Set cmd = New ADODB.Command
      cn.Open "File Name=c:\test.udl"
      cmd.ActiveConnection = cn
      cmd.CommandType = adCmdStoredProc
      cmd.CommandText = "GetAuthorInfo"
      '**************************
      'assign values to the parameters
      '**************************
      Set au_id = cmd.CreateParameter("@au_id",
adVarChar, adParamInput, 11, auIDtxt.Text)
      Set au_lname = cmd.CreateParameter
("@au_lname", adVarChar, adParamInput, 40,
auLnameTxt.Text)
      Set au_fname = cmd.CreateParameter
("@au_fname", adVarChar, adParamInput, 20,
auFnameTxt.Text)
      '**************************
      'assign the parameters to
      ' the stored procedure
      '**************************
      cmd.Parameters.Append au_id
      cmd.Parameters.Append au_lname
      cmd.Parameters.Append au_fname
```

```
        Set rs = cmd.Execute
        '*************************
        'assign the return values
        ' to the labels
        '*************************
        addressLbl.Caption = rs.Fields("address")
        cityLbl.Caption = rs.Fields("city")
        stateLbl.Caption = rs.Fields("state")

        openData = True
        '*************************
        'count the records returned
        ' if more than 0, assign to vars
        '*************************
        cn.Close
        openData = False
End If
'*************************
'End
'*************************
End Sub

Private Sub Form_Load()
'*********************
'Sample VB6 program
'Checks for the existence of and
' Opens a .udl file
'
'5/5/05 jfd
'*********************
'Begin:
'*********************
udlExist = False
If Dir("c:\test.udl", vbNormal) <> "" Then
    udlExist = True
Else
```

```
    udlExist = False
    MsgBox "The requested .udl file does not exist."
End If
'*********************
'End
'*********************

End Sub
```

## VB.NET

```
Private Sub Button1_Click(ByVal sender As
System.Object, ByVal e As System.EventArgs) Handles
Button1.Click
'***************************
'Sample VB .NET Program
'   jfd
'   10/10/05
'***************************
'Declarations:
'***************************
Dim cn As New
SqlConnection("server=(local);database=pubs;uid=sa;p
wd=;")
Dim cmd As SqlCommand
Dim i As Integer
Dim dr As SqlDataReader
'***************************
'Begin
'***************************
openData = False
cn.Open()
cmd = New SqlCommand("GetAuthorInfo", cn)
cmd.CommandType = CommandType.StoredProcedure
'***************************
'execute within a try...catch
'***************************
```

```
Try
    cmd.Parameters.Add("@au_id", SqlDbType.VarChar,
11)
    cmd.Parameters("@au_id").Value = auIDTxt.Text
    cmd.Parameters.Add("@au_lname", SqlDbType.VarChar,
40)
    cmd.Parameters("@au_lname").Value =
auLnameTxt.Text
    cmd.Parameters.Add("@au_fname", SqlDbType.VarChar,
20)
    cmd.Parameters("@au_fname").Value =
auFnameTxt.Text
    dr = cmd.ExecuteReader()
Catch operationException As
System.InvalidOperationException
    'perform more logic based on error
    MsgBox("There was an error in the operation!")
Catch sqlExc As SqlClient.SqlException
    MsgBox(sqlExc.ToString)
End Try
i = 0 'set the counter to 0
'***************************
'This piece of code counts the
' number of records returned
'***************************
While dr.Read()
    i = i + 1
End While
'***************************
dr.Close() 'close the datareader
If i > 0 Then
    openData = True
    Try
        dr = cmd.ExecuteReader()
        Catch opExcept As
System.InvalidOperationException
        MsgBox("There was an error in the operation!")
```

```
        End Try
        Do While dr.Read()
            addressLbl.Text = dr("address")
            cityLbl.Text = dr("city")
            stateLbl.Text = dr("state")
        Loop
    End If
    openData = False
    dr.Close()
    cn.Close()
    '****************************
    'End
    '****************************
    End Sub
```

**C#**

```
private void button1_Click(object sender,
System.EventArgs e)
{
//*****************************
//Declarations:
//*****************************
SqlConnection cn = new SqlConnection("server=(local);
database=pubs;uid=sa;");
int i;
bool emptyTable;
SqlDataReader dr;
SqlCommand cmd;
//*****************************
//Begin
//*****************************
cn.Open();
cmd = new SqlCommand("GetAuthorInfo",cn);
cmd.CommandType = CommandType.StoredProcedure ;
i = 0;
```

```
try
{
    //******************************
    //assign the text values to
    // SQL parameters
    //******************************
    cmd.Parameters.Add ("@au_id",
SqlDbType.VarChar,11);
    cmd.Parameters["@au_id"].Value = auIDTxt.Text;
    cmd.Parameters.Add ("@au_lname",
SqlDbType.VarChar,40);
    cmd.Parameters["@au_lname"].Value =
auLnameTxt.Text;
    cmd.Parameters.Add ("@au_fname",
SqlDbType.VarChar,20);
    cmd.Parameters["@au_fname"].Value =
auFnameTxt.Text;
    //*******************************
dr = cmd.ExecuteReader();
    while(dr.Read())
    {
       i++;
    }
    dr.Close();
}
catch (System.Data.SqlClient.SqlException
opException)
{
    MessageBox.Show( opException.ToString() );
}
emptyTable =false;
//******************************
//if the table is empty, flag it
//******************************
if (i==0)
{
    emptyTable = true;
```

```
}
//*****************************
//if the table is not empty
// copy each record to the array
//*****************************
if (emptyTable != true)
{
    try
    {
        dr = cmd.ExecuteReader();
        while(dr.Read ())
        {
            //********************************
            // assign the Stored Procedure
            // return values to labels
            //********************************
            addressLbl.Text = dr["address"].ToString() ;
            cityLbl.Text = dr["city"].ToString() ;
            stateLbl.Text = dr["state"].ToString() ;
        }
        dr.Close();
    }
    catch(System.InvalidOperationException
opException)
    {
    }
}

cn.Close();
//*****************************
//End
//*****************************
}
```

Although this code is technically correct, and is known to work, when the user executes the stored procedure code, the following errors are thrown:

### VB6

```
Run-time error '-2147217900 (80040e14)':
Could not find stored procedure 'GetAuthorInfo'.
```

### VB.NET and C#

```
System.Data.SqlClient.SqlException: Could not find
stored procedure 'GetAuthorInfo'.
 at System.Data.SqlClient.SqlCommand.ExecuteReader
(CommandBehavior cmdBehavior, RunBehavior
runBehavior, Boolean returnStream)
 at System.Data.SqlClient.SqlCommand.ExecuteReader()
 at BookExampleFile.Form1.Button1_Click(Object
sender, EventArgs e) in F:\BookExampleFile\
Form1.vb:line 156
```

Reading these errors, it should come as no surprise where our bug is. The code does not check for the existence of the stored procedure before executing it. Logic dictates that if it is not resident within our code, then it can be moved or deleted. Therefore, we must modify this code again to check for the existence of our stored procedure before we attempt to execute it.

The following corrected examples will show this code in one of two ways. In Visual Basic 6 and in Visual Basic .NET we will create a separate function to return true or false, depending on if the stored procedure works. In C# we will build the code directly into the On_Click event of the button. This should give you a good perspective on the different ways you may see this in your daily programming.

The way we are going to search for the existence of the stored procedure is to pull the name field from the `sysobjects` table of the pubs database. By setting the `type` to `P` in the query, we will pull just the names of all stored procedures in the pubs database. We can then compare that list within our application to locate the stored procedure.

Take some time now to look through the completed, corrected examples.

### VB6

```
'**********************
'Declarations:
' Types
```

```
'*********************
Dim openData As Boolean
Dim udlExist As Boolean

Private Sub Command1_Click()
'*************************
'Defines and opens a local
' SQL database
'   jfd
'   10/10/05
'*************************
'Declarations:
'*************************
Dim cn As ADODB.Connection
Dim cmd As ADODB.Command
Dim rs As ADODB.Recordset
Dim au_id As ADODB.Parameter
Dim au_lname As ADODB.Parameter
Dim au_fname As ADODB.Parameter
Dim address As ADODB.Parameter
Dim city As ADODB.Parameter
Dim state As ADODB.Parameter
'*************************
'Begin
'*************************
openData = False
If (udlExist) Then
    If StoredProcExist("GetAuthorInfo") = True Then
       Set cn = New ADODB.Connection
       Set cmd = New ADODB.Command
       cn.Open "File Name=c:\test.udl"
       cmd.ActiveConnection = cn
       cmd.CommandType = adCmdStoredProc
       cmd.CommandText = "GetAuthorInfo"
       '*************************
       'assign values to the parameters
```

```
        '*************************
        Set au_id = cmd.CreateParameter("@au_id",
adVarChar, adParamInput, 11, auIDtxt.Text)
        Set au_lname = cmd.CreateParameter
("@au_lname", adVarChar, adParamInput, 40,
auLnameTxt.Text)
        Set au_fname = cmd.CreateParameter
("@au_fname", adVarChar, adParamInput, 20,
auFnameTxt.Text)
        '*************************
        'assign the parameters to
        ' the stored procedure
        '*************************
        cmd.Parameters.Append au_id
        cmd.Parameters.Append au_lname
        cmd.Parameters.Append au_fname
        Set rs = cmd.Execute
        '*************************
        'assign the return values
        ' to the labels
        '*************************
        addressLbl.Caption = rs.Fields("address")
        cityLbl.Caption = rs.Fields("city")
        stateLbl.Caption = rs.Fields("state")

        openData = True
        '*************************
        'count the records returned
        ' if more than 0, assign to vars
        '*************************
        cn.Close
        openData = False
    End If
End If
'*************************
'End
'*************************
```

```
End Sub
Private Function StoredProcExist(procName As String)
As Boolean
'*********************
'Function to test for
' existence of Stored Procedures
' Returns: Boolean
'
'   jfd
'   10/10/05
'*********************
'Declarations:
'*********************
Dim query As String
Dim rs As ADODB.Recordset
Dim cn As ADODB.Connection
StoredProcExist = False
'*********************
'Begin:
'*********************
If (udlExist) Then
       Set cn = New ADODB.Connection
       Set rs = New ADODB.Recordset
       cn.Open "File Name=c:\test.udl"
       query = "Select name from sysobjects where
type = 'P'"
       rs.Open query, cn, adOpenForwardOnly,
adLockReadOnly
       openData = True
       '*************************
       'if records are returned
       ' perform search
       '*************************
       If rs.RecordCount <> 0 Then
          Do While rs.EOF <> True
             '*********************
             'if the stored procedure is
```

```
            ' located, return true and
            ' close connections
            '*************************
            If procName = rs.Fields("name") Then
               rs.Close
               cn.Close
               openData = False
               StoredProcExist = True
               Exit Function
            End If
            rs.MoveNext 'in VB6 the record must be
moved
         Loop
      End If
   End If
'**********************
'End:
'**********************
End Function
Private Sub Form_Load()
'**********************
'Sample VB6 program
'Checks for the existence of and
' Opens a .udl file
'
'5/5/05 jfd
'**********************
'Begin:
'**********************
udlExist = False
If Dir("c:\test.udl", vbNormal) <> "" Then
    udlExist = True
Else
    udlExist = False
    MsgBox "The requested .udl file does not exist."
End If
```

```
'*********************
'End
'*********************

End Sub

Private Sub Form_Terminate()
'*************************
'Prompts user before closing app
'*************************
'Declarations:
'*************************

'*************************
'Begin
'*************************

Select Case MsgBox("Are you sure you want to exit?",
vbYesNoCancel)
Case vbYes
    If (openData) Then
       If (MsgBox("Do you want to save your data?",
vbYesNo)) = vbYes Then
          End
       End If
       Exit Sub
    End If
    End
Case vbNo
'do not close app
Case vbCancel
'do not close app
End Select

'*************************
'End
'*************************
End Sub
```

**VB.NET**

```
Private Sub Button1_Click(ByVal sender As
System.Object, ByVal e As System.EventArgs) Handles
Button1.Click
      '****************************
      'Sample VB .NET Program
      ' jfd
      ' 10/10/05
      '****************************
      'Declarations:
      '****************************
      Dim cn As New
SqlConnection("server=(local);database=pubs;uid=sa;p
wd=;")
      Dim cmd As SqlCommand
      Dim i As Integer
      Dim dr As SqlDataReader
      '****************************
      'Begin
      '****************************
      If StoredProcExist("GetAuthorInfo") = True
Then
         openData = False
         cn.Open()
         cmd = New SqlCommand("GetAuthorInfo", cn)
         cmd.CommandType =
CommandType.StoredProcedure
         '****************************
         'execute within a try...catch
         '****************************
         Try
            cmd.Parameters.Add("@au_id",
SqlDbType.VarChar, 11)
            cmd.Parameters("@au_id").Value =
auIDTxt.Text
            cmd.Parameters.Add("@au_lname",
SqlDbType.VarChar, 40)
```

```
            cmd.Parameters("@au_lname").Value =
auLnameTxt.Text
            cmd.Parameters.Add("@au_fname",
SqlDbType.VarChar, 20)
            cmd.Parameters("@au_fname").Value =
auFnameTxt.Text
            dr = cmd.ExecuteReader()
            Catch operationException As
System.InvalidOperationException
               'perform more logic based on error
               MsgBox("There was an error in the
operation!")
            Catch sqlExc As SqlClient.SqlException
               Debug.Write(sqlExc.ToString)
            End Try
            i = 0 'set the counter to 0
            '***************************
            'This piece of code counts the
            ' number of records returned
            '***************************
            While dr.Read()
            i = i + 1
            End While
            '***************************
            dr.Close() 'close the datareader
            If i > 0 Then
               openData = True
               Try
                  dr = cmd.ExecuteReader()
               Catch opExcept As
System.InvalidOperationException
                  MsgBox("There was an error in the
operation!")
               End Try
               Do While dr.Read()
                  addressLbl.Text = dr("address")
                  cityLbl.Text = dr("city")
```

```
                    stateLbl.Text = dr("state")
                Loop
            End If
            openData = False
            dr.Close()
            cn.Close()
        End If
        '****************************
        'End
        '****************************
    End Sub
    Private Function StoredProcExist(ByVal procName
As String) As Boolean
        '**********************
        'Function to test for
        ' existence of Stored Procedures
        ' Returns: Boolean
        '
        ' jfd
        ' 10/10/05
        '**********************
        'Declarations:
        '**********************
        Dim cn As New
SqlConnection("server=(local);database=pubs;uid=sa;
pwd=;")
        Dim cmd As SqlCommand

        '****************************
        'Begin
        '****************************
        StoredProcExist = False
        openData = False
        cn.Open()
        cmd = New SqlCommand("Select name from
sysobjects where type = 'P'", cn)
        Dim dr As SqlDataReader = cmd.ExecuteReader()
```

```
        While dr.Read()
            openData = True
            If procName = dr("name") Then
                StoredProcExist = True
                cn.Close()
                dr.Close()
                openData = False
                Exit Function
            End If
        End While
        cn.Close()
        '*****************************
        'End
        '*****************************

    End Function

    Protected Overrides Sub OnClosing(ByVal e As
System.ComponentModel.CancelEventArgs)
        '*****************************
        'Sample VB .NET Program
        ' jfd
        ' 10/10/05
        '*****************************
        'Declarations:
        '*****************************

        '*****************************
        'Begin
        '*****************************
        Select Case MsgBox("Are you sure you want to
exit?", vbYesNoCancel)
        Case vbYes
            If (openData) Then
                If (MsgBox("Should I save your data?",
vbYesNo)) = vbYes Then
                    e.Cancel = False
```

```
            End If
         End If
      Case vbNo
         e.Cancel = True
      Case vbCancel
         e.Cancel = True
      End Select

      '*****************************
      'End
      '*****************************
   End Sub
```

**C#**

```
private void button1_Click(object sender,
System.EventArgs e)
{
    //******************************
    //Declarations:
    //******************************
SqlConnection cn = new
SqlConnection("server=(local);database=pubs;
uid=sa;");
    int i;
    bool procExist;
    bool emptyTable;
    SqlDataReader dr;
    SqlCommand cmd;
    //******************************
    //Begin
    //******************************
    cn.Open();
    procExist = false;
    cmd = new SqlCommand ("Select name from sysobjects
where type='P'", cn);
    //******************************
```

```
    //execute a reader just to
    // search for the desired
    // stored procedure
    //****************************
    dr = cmd.ExecuteReader();
    while(dr.Read())
    {
       if(dr["name"].ToString() == "GetAuthorInfo")
       {
          procExist = true;
       }
    }
    dr.Close();
    //****************************
    //datareader has been closed so
    // that it can be reused later
    //****************************
    if (procExist)
    {
       cmd = new SqlCommand("GetAuthorInfo",cn);
       cmd.CommandType = CommandType.StoredProcedure ;
       i = 0;
       try
       {
          cmd.Parameters.Add ("@au_id",
SqlDbType.Variant,11);
          cmd.Parameters["@au_id"].Value =
auIDTxt.Text;
          cmd.Parameters.Add ("@au_lname",
SqlDbType.VarChar,40);
          cmd.Parameters["@au_lname"].Value =
auLnameTxt.Text;
          cmd.Parameters.Add ("@au_fname",
SqlDbType.VarChar,20);
          cmd.Parameters["@au_fname"].Value =
auFnameTxt.Text;
          dr = cmd.ExecuteReader();
```

```
            while(dr.Read())
            {
               i++;
            }
            dr.Close();
         }
         catch (System.Data.SqlClient.SqlException
opException)
         {
            MessageBox.Show( opException.ToString() );
         }
         emptyTable =false;
         //******************************
         //if the table is empty, flag it
         //******************************
         if (i==0)
         {
            emptyTable = true;
         }
         //******************************
         //if the table is not empty
         // copy each record to the array
         //******************************
         if (emptyTable != true)
         {
            try
            {
               dr = cmd.ExecuteReader();
               while(dr.Read ())
               {
                  addressLbl.Text =
dr["address"].ToString(); cityLbl.Text =
dr["city"].ToString();
                  stateLbl.Text =
dr["state"].ToString();
               }
```

```
                dr.Close();
            }
            catch(System.InvalidOperationException
opException)
            {
            }
        }
    }
    cn.Close();
    //********************************
    //End
    //********************************
    }
```

Take a further look through these examples. Modify them and add code to handle errors and perform more functions. Keep in mind that code is a living style of document that should be constantly changing and adapting. The key to creating and executing consistent error-free code is to be watchful of some of the bugs and pitfalls we have discussed in this section.

This brings our discussion of some common bugs to a conclusion. I sincerely hope that you can build upon some of the basic lessons examined in this book and work them into your daily coding.

# Index

## D

# E

## F



## G



## H



## I

## J



## L



## M



## N



## O

## P



## Q



## R



## S

## T

## U



## V

## W



## X